MOVE TO FIRE

MOVE TO FIRE

A family's tragedy,

a lone attorney,

and a teenager's victory

over a corrupt gunmaker

Michael W. Harkins

Back cover photo of Brandon Maxfield and Richard Ruggieri Photo courtesy of Law Center to Prevent Gun Violence and Greg Habiby, copyright © Greg Habiby Images.

Cover design by Writesite & Story and Pictures, © 2015

For media and sales inquiries, contact info@movetofire.com

To all those who go where and when others won't

CONTENTS

FOREWORD

Move to Fire is an only-in-America story. The people in it are all of us: parents, kids, business people, lawyers, good people, and bad people. There are guns, an accidental shooting, and a lawsuit. It's an American trifecta. It's our best, our worst, and exposes how little we may actually know about things for which we voice our opinions, sometimes voiced at the top of our lungs.

In this country where debate occurs when no debate should exist — climate change, immunizations — and bumpersticker rhetoric trumps critical thinking — guns don't kill people, people kill people — moderate, informed debaters are often drowned out by the loudest proponents of competing, extreme positions. Opinions about guns are a complex mix of personal and family history, programming, and, for many, anchored, visceral feelings about guns and responsibility, and it is those deep-seated feelings that make constructive dialog about guns difficult.

The more any opinion develops from and is fed by personal belief, the less likely facts and data will matter, *even* when an opinion holder knows objectively that the opinion is ill-informed or, simply, wrong.

This is especially true of opinions about guns.

Move to Fire is a journalistic narrative about people, events and crossed-paths, and about the tremendous commitment required to take on an apparently unwinnable cause. It corrects misconceptions about what happened to a little boy in 1994, why it happened, and recounts how the unwavering work of one man resulted in a measure of justice for a family, and a society, unjustly wounded by a dangerous status quo.

But underlying it all is something so crucially relevant yet widely unknown that without it there would be no Move to Fire story.

America's consumer products are regulated by the Consumer Product Safety Commission (CPSC), "an independent federal regulatory agency created in 1972 by Congress in the Consumer Product Safety Act. In that law, Congress directed the Commission to protect the public against unreasonable risks of injuries and deaths associated with consumer products."

But not if that consumer product is a gun. That's not widely known, even though that exemption has been in place since the CPSC's formation.

Industries cannot self-regulate in a free market democracy. It's rarely in industry's own best interests to do anything against itself, and history is replete with examples of companies that rationalized or delayed action on a problem rather than do the 'right' thing. The Ford Pinto's dangerous, defective gas tank issue and subsequent revelations that the company knew of the problem, and put the car in the marketplace anyway, stands as only one classic example of why keeping society safe requires objective oversight.

For every product or service, industry-standard safeguards are in place to protect users, and to protect non-users, those people, communities, and environments that could still be affected by an industry's or business' regulatory avoidance or deception.

When a defect becomes known to a manufacturer,

whether the defect is inadvertent or deliberate, and regardless of 'why' the defect came to exist, it's the manufacturer's legal and ethical responsibility to fix it. If for some reason the manufacturer will not undertake action or is slow to do so, the federal government, through the Consumer Product Safety Act, can require the manufacturer to act, including forcing the manufacturer to implement a product recall.

Unless the product is a gun.

On occasion when there have been guns with some kind of defect, some manufacturers have sent safety warnings or recall notices to gun dealers.

But not always.

That's something else not widely known, that hundreds of gun models examined by the Bureau of Alcohol, Tobacco, Firearms and Explosives, law enforcement laboratories, independent laboratories, or the guns' manufacturers, have been found to be defective in some manner.

More surprising, certainly, is that the defect in many of those models was that the gun could fire on its own, known as an "unintentional discharge."

Allow me to reiterate: there have been and are defective guns that can fire without the trigger being touched, but they cannot be recalled or taken off the market except by the manufacturer.

And no government entity can force a gun manufacturer to recall a defective gun. Even a civil judgment against a gun manufacturer for a defective gun model cannot force that manufacturer to recall or remove all those models.

Attorney Richard Ruggieri puts it this way: "When a child is injured by a blender, or lawnmower, or practically anything else, the full weight of the U.S. government is brought to bear to make sure that it doesn't happen to anyone else. But if it's a gun, the only force brought to bear is that which can be mustered by an already overwhelmed child and his parents, whose primary concern has to be compensation to pay his medical bills, and even if he files a lawsuit against the manufacturer and wins, there's nothing to stop the manufacturer from continuing to sell the defective product and wait for the next injury."

So, the worst extension of all this is that an unethical gun manufacturer could choose to create and sell a gun it knew to be defective, and, still, no entity could stop that from happening.

That happened.

Rules, parameters, limitations, and restrictions are placed upon industry not to hinder progress or stifle growth, but to keep users and innocent bystanders, and society, safe. Products and services are made available to anyone who can pay for them. This includes the veteran user and first-time buyer, the easy adapter and the barely capable, the most intelligent and the illiterate. If you are going to sell to everyone, you must make every effort to keep everyone who uses your product, and anyone close by, safe when the product is used in the manner intended.

Conforming to regulatory oversight, anticipating how a product might be used incorrectly and divining solutions to keep users as safe as possible, even if in using it the user makes a mistake, are the costs of doing business. Industry knows this.

We know accidents happen. We know people make mistakes. Sometimes the results of a mistake are inconsequential, sometimes horrific. Some mistakes are unavoidable, some are foreseeable.

As we get older, we continue to make simple mistakes — reach for something, look away for a moment, and knock over our glass — but the complexities of our adult lives expose us to more potentially catastrophic mistakes — run a red light, hurt someone. Some people admit their mistake, stand up and say, "Sorry, that was my fault, I'll make it right." Others might be part of a string of incidents that involve them in a mistake. And there are those who go to great lengths to avoid any responsibility for their mistake and its consequences.

We feel horrible just knowing about some innocent mistakes that turn tragic, even as we wonder how something like it could happen (an infant forgotten in a car on a hot day). The complexities of a tragedy can obscure a tragedy's root cause, and discovering the root cause, or multiple failures leading to the root cause, rarely takes less than a long, diligent investigation. Remarkably, a tragedy's catalyst can often be traced to something simple. An aircraft once crashed because its pilots became so focused on a burnt-out control panel light they didn't realize the plane was steadily losing altitude. Many of the greatest engineering minds in this country were shocked when a sixteen-inch piece of foam eventually caused the destruction of a multi-billion dollar Space Shuttle and the deaths of its crew.

Occasionally, a defect-caused tragedy occurs because someone chose not to fix a defect, even though it was known to exist.

If something happens, something that should have worked one way instead works another way, even though we followed the instructions, we expect that things can be exchanged, adjustments made, or our money can be returned.

We've been conditioned to expect this on the smallest and largest levels. It's part of our upbringing, a simple lesson taught early, to do what's fair: "You broke it, you have to pay for it."

The premise of fair remains constant in our lives, yet as we age our objectivity is obscured by emotions or opinions. We may reduce to a sentence or two our observation about an incident. While an observation may be valid on its own, like, *don't point the gun at something you don't intend to shoot,* applying it to every situation of a similar nature, like accidental shootings, ignores everything about what *caused* something to happen.

Every day, somewhere, there is an unintentional discharge of a weapon. We're made aware of some, and often our opinion about the incident is based on a few inches of newsprint, a forty-second piece on TV or YouTube, or a short paragraph on the screen of our smartphone. The tragic incidents touch our hearts — a child accidentally shot by the father's handgun in the truck — make us shake our heads in wonder — a Navy SEAL inadvertently kills himself while playing Russian roulette with a gun he thought was unloaded — or leave us what-in-the-world stunned — the police officer who shoots his thumb off in a gun store after being handed a pistol he's thinking of buying.

Each of those examples happened.

Move to Fire is about people, circumstances, and events that for a short time received wide media exposure, enabling many to know a little about what had occurred. To this day, conclusions reached and opinions about what happened have been formed mostly without the benefit of the how and why of it all. Move to Fire adds that sorely needed how and why, not just in the hope of revelation, but in the hope that newly informed, important conversations occur about guns in America, and so that the story of an amazing family and their attorney secures its very deserved place in history.

* * *

I relied upon personal interviews; deposition and trial transcripts; case evidence, filings and motions documents; publicly accessible commercial, law enforcement, and government data and records; and published media interviews, articles, and news reports, to create Move to Fire. Everything in the text is verifiable. There is no intended slant right or left politically, but I certainly take full credit for striving to accurately convey the emotions, thoughts, and perspectives of people directly involved with the events.

I have also decided, for various reasons, not to use the real names of several people. I don't believe they'll feel slighted.

CHAPTER 1

APRIL 6, 1994

Brandon Maxfield stood in front of Jerry Morris, facing him, four feet away and staring at the gun in Morris' hand. For a brief moment he could see inside the gun's barrel, then everything disappeared in a blinding flash.

Moving at one-thousand feet per second, the bullet shattered seven-year old Brandon's jaw, destroyed the C2-C3 vertebrae at the top of his spine and rocketed out the back of his neck. The .380 caliber bullet ricocheted several times in its micro-second flight before burrowing into the kitchen wall above the stove. Unencumbered, it could have traveled the length of several football fields in the same time it took to careen around the living room and kitchen.

Bullets can take wild, unpredictable paths inside a body, bouncing off bones and tumbling through organs that alter the bullet's speed and trajectory. The bullet that tore through Brandon, though, was barely affected in its path. No human anatomy can withstand the damage wrought by a metal projectile the size of a pebble traveling faster than the speed of sound, especially the young, developing anatomy of a child.

Moments before the accident, Brandon, his five-year old brother Rocky, and their twelve-year old uncle John had been transfixed by the gun in Jerry's right hand.

At just over six feet tall, Jerry Morris, barely twenty years old, towered over the other boys. Brandon's mother, Sue, had lived with Morris' family for a time when she first moved to the rural, Northern California town of Willits almost ten years before. Now that Sue and Clint Stansberry, her husband and Brandon's stepfather, finally had a place of their own, a single-wide trailer home, they let Morris move into a small camper on the property after Sue learned the young man had been homeless for several months.

Morris was reserved around people he didn't know. He had a subtle, physical defect and a mild learning disability, but he had graduated high school and worked for the California Conservation Corps. After completing fire fighter training and basic first aid programs, he'd taken an introductory computer course at a local community college. He was a quiet, big guy. The family liked him, as did Brandon, but he wasn't working now and hadn't had a job for months. For the last year he helped out around the remote, wooded property, occasionally watching the kids for Sue and Clint.

Their single-wide trailer home, with an addition that Clint had built as an extra bedroom, was on the flat section of the almost two acres they purchased two years earlier. The property was in the beautiful but rugged hills seven miles outside of town, an elevated area where land was affordable and working people could find space to live as they pleased, in structures that ranged from one-room shacks, to single- and double-wide trailer homes, to large houses.

John McCullough, Sue's twelve-year-old brother, had

stepped slightly behind Brandon's left shoulder, and was staring at the gun when it went off.

What just happened?, he thought, trying to make sense of the loud bang and the intense ringing in his ears.

Although Brandon liked Jerry, he was closer to his young uncle, and John liked his nephew. John had lived off and on with his sister Sue for years. Unlike Jerry, John stood no more than five feet tall. He was a slightly built twelve-year old with a tiny voice, and energy that kept him and Brandon at play for hours in the woods around the property. His life with Sue and Clint gave him a sense of family and an adolescence absent from his early years. He and Sue both experienced what could be best described as an unsettled upbringing, a lack of family cohesion and stability that resulted from their mother's early, multiple and abusive marriages.

Although they had different fathers, Sue and John stayed close, and it was Sue, twelve years older, who tended to keep watch over him, becoming both a big sister and mother. He and Brandon looked and acted like brothers, both with fine, blond hair and slightly round faces.

When the gun went off, John was only inches off the line of fire. After tearing through Brandon, the bullet passed just between John and Brandon's five-year old stepbrother, Rocky, who was sitting on the couch watching the big boys.

John's thoughts didn't come together until he saw blood run from the back of Brandon's neck, but even as he realized Brandon had been shot, he couldn't reconcile that Brandon was seriously injured, because the little boy was still standing in front of him.

A second seemed to pass before Brandon collapsed, blood flowing from the bullet's exit wound and filling his throat and mouth. John reached out and grabbed him under the arms, dropping with him to the floor.

Brandon could still see, but he couldn't hear anything thing except a loud buzzing sound. John's face appeared over him, and his mouth moved, but Brandon couldn't hear what his uncle was saying. He knew something had happened, but all he could hear, all he could think about, was the buzzing in his head, and he wondered what it was.

Brandon had twisted as he fell, corkscrewed to the floor, his head now at Jerry's feet. John leaned over close to Brandon's face, somehow managing to function even as his young mind reeled at what was happening.

"Brandon, can you breathe?" John asked.

Brandon looked up at him, barely moved his head in a way that John believed was 'no'.

"Do you want me to breathe for you?"

The buzzing in Brandon's head wouldn't go away, and then the world as he could see it, with John's face above him, John's mouth moving without sound, turned gray, the buzzing began to subside, and the world went dark.

As John looked into his nephew's face, Brandon's eyelids partially closed, showing only an eerie sliver of pinkish white as Brandon lost consciousness.

"Oh my god. Brandon! Brandon!"

Jerry looked down at the boys, his senses rocked by the scene at his feet. He threw the gun to the side, flung it out of his hand. "Holy shit, holy shit..." he said. He dropped down and moved John aside, put his hand under the back of Brandon's neck and began mouth-to-mouth resuscitation, his hand quickly covered in Brandon's blood, his cheeks smeared with the blood from Brandon's mouth.

John jumped up and grabbed the phone, dialed 911

and said "there's been an accident, my nephew's been shot, he's been shot and we need help!" He gave the address and hung up quickly.

Morris stopped his mouth-to-mouth repetitions long enough to check Brandon's pulse. It was several seconds before he could find it and so weak he wasn't sure that it was really there. Brandon's eyes fluttered and Morris felt the pulse stop. He started mouth-to-mouth again as the phone rang. John answered, confirming with the 911 operator that he had just called and that they needed an ambulance. He hung up, put the phone on the floor next to Morris, then found Rocky, who had jumped up when the gun fired and run across the small room, took him outside and told him to "stay outside, you stay right here," before he ran up the gravel driveway to wait for the paramedics.

For the next seven minutes, until the first Mendocino County sheriffs' deputies arrived, Brandon Maxfield's only chance for life over death lay in the hands and with every breath of the young man who shot him.

There was nothing extraordinary about the day. There were errands to run and brush to be cleared and burnt. It was cool but not cold, and the sky was gray. The weather might be described as overcast or as a low sky in other parts of the country, but it was actually morning fog, not unusual early morning weather for many Northern California towns less than an hour's drive from the coast.

Clint had gone to work, his uncle picking him up and driving to a site only three miles up the road. At thirty-three years old, Clint was still a physical kind of guy, a big man used to hard work but, ten years before as a welder, he had blown out a disc in his back while moving a heavy tank. Through a retraining program he learned auto body repair and painting, but he preferred working for his uncle's landscaping company, where he could still get the satisfaction of physical, outside work, while avoiding the kind of stress and situations that could aggravate his injury. The accident had laid him up for months, and a settlement from the employer's insurance company in 1990 enabled Clint and Sue, who had been together since Brandon was three months old, to move from their tiny rented house right on the main street of Willits and buy the trailer home on the secluded land where they lived now.

His uncle had two crews working in the same area that day, clearing and burning brush, one of the last chances to do a burn just before the waning cool days of spring transitioned into the long, hot and dry days of summer. It was the same kind of work that Clint had given to Jerry and John, the perfect task for young men. It required work, yet carried with it the responsibility of watching over and maintaining the burning brush. It was hard and fun, in its own way, something the boys didn't really mind doing, gathering up the dead, excess brush, tree limbs and other natural refuse around the property and burning it.

There was a utility bill that had to be paid today, and it had come with a forty-eight hour cut-off notice. Sue was going to go to the local utility office to pay it, pick up some friends and then come back and work with John and Jerry cleaning up the property. She'd be back in less than an hour. She would take the baby of the family, Trish, with her and leave Rocky and Brandon, home because of a school holiday, with the boys.

Like most of their friends and many of the area's population, Sue and Clint made enough to get by, but not much else. It was an area of no manufacturing to speak of, and many jobs were working class; if someone didn't have a manual labor job or their own small business, they held a low-paying service job. Sue was a hostess at Perko's restaurant, one of the largest family-type restaurants in town, where her mother also worked.

Service work didn't bother Sue. It was all she had ever known. On her own since she was thirteen, she'd had her own apartment at sixteen and had Brandon at eighteen.

Her early years had not been easy, and those years had shaped her into a small firecracker of a woman on the outside, with a buried but uncompromising longing for the love and stability of family that she had never experienced herself. Barely five feet tall, not an excess pound on her, she cherished Brandon, her firstborn, as one of the first souls who loved her unconditionally. Now with Clint and his children in her life, she began to see a future for herself and her family that could be different from her own upbringing.

She and Clint had jobs, their own piece of heaven in the hills, her kids were healthy, and Brandon had grown into a cute, energetic, smart little boy with a slightly quiet way about him. He was everything she could hope for in a son, and, the forty-eight hour utility cutoff notice notwithstanding, life was good.

Sue was ready to go. "Brandon, you stay here with Uncle John and Jerry. I've got to run some errands, I'll be right back." She turned to the big boys and said, "I've got to pay the utility bill, then I'm going to mom's before I go get Toni and Gene."

"I want to come with you," Brandon said, standing at her side.

"No, honey, I've got to take Trish to see your Grandma Kandace, then I'm going to go get Toni and Gene, so there won't be room. I'll be right back. I put Free Willy in the VCR for you, okay?"

He wasn't happy about it, but he wasn't a kid who threw fits or argued with his mom. He turned away and sat down in the middle of the floor to watch the movie as John and Jerry came inside. Sue scooped up Trish, kissed Brandon and Rocky goodbye and left. As she drove up the gravel driveway, John asked Brandon if he wanted to come outside while John and Jerry worked, but Brandon was happily watching the movie with Rocky, who climbed onto the couch.

Brandon was an easy kid, as happy to be outside running through the woods with his little brother as he was watching WWF Wrestling on TV or playing Nintendo. His aggravation with his mom – at his sister, really, since from Brandon's point of view she seemed to be getting more than a fair share of the attention lately – had passed within minutes, and now he was just a content kid, watching a movie, knowing that his mom would be back in a little while.

Outside, Jerry and John both stopped working as they heard a woman scream.

The layout of the property was such that the closest house to the Stansberry's was a few hundred feet away, behind and slightly above them. Both places shared a common entrance off the road for about thirty yards, then split, fifty yards down to the Stansberry's and fifty or more yards up and around to the neighbors. A dense patch of trees and bushes on the steep slope behind the Stansberry's trailer home blocked any sight of the neighbors, but sounds traveled easily.

The woman screamed again.

Jerry walked up the slope into the trees, John following but staying behind him. The woman, genuine fear in her voice, yelled again, and the boys couldn't understand everything she said, but they were sure she was screaming, "Please, stop it, put down that axe!"

Jerry shouted, "Is everything okay up there?"

A man's voice shouted back, "Mind your own fucking business!"

After a moment of silence, as Jerry and John turned to go back down the slope, they heard the woman again, but her scream was drowned out by the loud, piercing whine of a revving chainsaw.

Although Brandon could hear some noise outside, it wasn't enough to distract him or Rocky from the TV, until John and Jerry came inside the house. Even to a seven-year old, it was obvious that the big kids seemed scared. He stayed on the floor, and he kept watching the TV, but Brandon also turned to watch John pick up the phone.

John dialed 911.

"Yeah, there's this woman at this house and some guy is chasing her with an axe and a chainsaw, and he's trying to kill her or something."

He gave his name and address, hung up the phone and went outside with Jerry. Less then ten minutes later, they watched as two county sheriff patrol cars turned off the road and headed up the neighbor's driveway. They listened for any more noise, hoping to hear what was going on, but were too scared to venture up the slope.

Above, the deputies had found a couple, a man and woman, staying at the house. The owners were away and the man and woman were renting it for the week. The woman appeared to have some bruises on her legs, but declined to say what had happened or give the deputies any reason to do anything but warn the couple to keep it down. Within minutes of arriving the deputies were on their way back down the hill.

Jerry and John watched them drive away, wondering what had happened.

The man's voice rolled down the slope again.

"I told you this was none of your fucking business, asshole!"

Jerry and John stood silent, and scared, looking up at the unseen house.

The sharp, quick pop of several small caliber gunshots suddenly echoed from above. Startled, and now in full fear, John and Jerry ran. Both of them knew the sound of gunshots, and John was certain he'd just heard a .22 caliber gun.

The presence of guns for hunting, sport, or protection, was certainly not unusual in an isolated, rural area, and this community was no different. Both John and Jerry had seen and heard guns owned by fathers and friends as they grew up, and both had fired a rifle or handgun, under the watchful eye of an adult, at least once.

Now John feared that the angry man above could come right down that hill with that gun looking for him and Jerry.

This time when the big boys charged into the house, Brandon knew there was something serious happening. He watched John go right to the phone.

John dialed his mother's phone number. It had been less than thirty minutes since Sue had driven away and John hoped she was there by now. She wasn't, so John told Kandace, as best he could, in an excited, scared voice, that he'd heard a gun and he was afraid.

Kandace lived in town, a fifteen-minute drive from Sue and Clint. Mother and daughter were strikingly similar in looks, build and demeanor. Barely in her forties, Kandace had already been married several times and coped with her own and her husband's ongoing abuse demons. One of those demons had been an alcohol-fueled incident with a gun when Sue, barely into adolescence, saw her dad shove a loaded gun into Kandace's mouth during an argument. It was a stark, frightening incident, a permanent scar on her memory that became the foundation of her strong dislike of guns.

Through all the dysfunction, and while occasionally staying away from her mother when she felt it was best, returning to support her whenever she came out of a bad situation, Sue remained close to Kandace, emotionally and geographically. It was Sue who helped her mother get through difficult times, Sue who had the better judgment.

Sue had paid the utility bill, picked up her friends Toni and Gene, and had just pulled up to Kandace's, when her mother said, "John called and said there's some kind of trouble and someone's got a gun."

Sue went right to the phone and called the house. "What's going on, John?"

John's words, with a voice usually full of high-pitched energy anyway, tumbled out, jumbling together as he tried to tell Sue what was happening. "...and the sheriffs left....and he's shooting...if he comes down here to kill us...I'll use the gun...I'll shoot him first..."

"The gun? You unload that gun and put it up, do you understand me? I'm coming home right now!"

Sue slammed down the phone. "There's some kind of fight going on, those goddamn neighbors or something. Mom, can you watch the baby? Damn it, why would he get the gun out? Damn it."

Toni and Gene followed her out the door. Toni and Sue had known each other since Sue struck out on her own at sixteen, when she worked at MacDonald's and took on babysitting jobs. One of those jobs was for Toni, and later when Toni's husband Gene had to go out of town for several months, Sue accepted Toni's offer to move in as a roommate and to help take care of the kids. Over the years their friendship had grown into a combination mother-daughter, best friends relationship.

Toni knew Sue could be a hellfire cat when she was upset, but she also knew as a young mom striving to bring up a family, there was nothing more important to Sue, and nothing she looked forward to more, than experiencing what she had missed, the family picnics, camping trips, things that families do together.

It was obvious in the way she treated her kids, especially Brandon.

Brandon was a small infant, and Sue had been one of those young moms whose compact body didn't change much during pregnancy; she showed, but if she had her back to you, you wouldn't know she was pregnant even in her ninth month. Three days after Brandon was born, she bundled him up and, with Toni driving, took a drive west, through the high hills, to an overlook near Fort Bragg, a town close to the Northern California coast. The elevation was several thousand feet, high enough and still early enough in the spring, that a fresh layer of fluffy snow blanketed the hills.

She got out of the car, holding Brandon like a little doll, rolled up in several soft baby blankets, and carried him to the edge of the overlook.

She held him close and whispered, "Welcome to the top of the world, baby." She wanted him to see what she felt. She knew he couldn't really see it, but she believed he could feel it. She was blessed to have this baby, this child who loved her unconditionally, just as she loved him. She truly felt on top of the world, and the magical look of the snowy hills around them seemed so right, as if God had created this special moment just for her and Brandon.

John hung up the phone, walked past Jerry and entered Sue and Clint's bedroom, a forbidden zone for any of the kids. The single-wide was small, and in order to have a semblance of privacy and adult confidentiality, that bedroom was sacrosanct. Crossing the line into Sue and Clint's room, without permission, was a serious family breach. Brandon wasn't sure exactly what was going on, but something important was happening.

The gun was in that room. John knew this in the way that kids know more about adults' lives than adults realize or admit. He hadn't seen it when Sue and Clint brought it home two years before, but a few months later, Clint let John and Brandon watch as he showed Sue how to fire the gun.

Clint had set a few dirt-filled cans on top of a log in a corner of the property, away from the trailer home. He squeezed off a few shots from the small handgun and showed Sue how to pull back on the slide, "so you know how to get a bullet in and out of the chamber."

He handed her the gun and she pulled with everything her petite body could muster, but she couldn't get the slide to move. Clint then stood behind her, using his arms to help her aim and shoot.

She fired it once, said "that's plenty for me," and never touched it again.

John wanted to shoot. Clint took the clip out, waved John to come over and as he held the gun out to the boy he said, "keep this pointed at the ground, away from yourself and anyone else, and don't touch the trigger."

At seven inches long, an inch thick and only thirty-six ounces, it was small enough for Sue to hold easily and, although he was a slight kid, John had no trouble getting his hand around the gun's grip. It was lighter in his hand than a schoolbook.

Clint stood beside him and said, "Here's the deal. If you can pull the slide back, I'll let you shoot the gun."

John made several attempts, but he could neither grip the rear of the slide firmly enough nor did he have the strength to pull the slide back at all. Clint took the gun, slid the magazine of bullets back into its handle and fired off two more shots. As he put the gun away, he told the boys, "Don't you ever touch this gun, don't you ever let your sister or brother touch it, don't ever get it out. If someone does get it out, get away from it and stay away from it." He put the gun's safety in the 'safe' position, put the gun back into its thin, small, blue box and carried it into the house.

The boys didn't see where Clint put it that day, but they saw him walk into the bedroom. He had placed the box in the top drawer of the dresser, where Sue kept her jewelry and odds and ends. Sue and Clint believed it to be the best place in the house for the gun: the drawer was way too high for the reach of the smaller kids, it was in their bedroom and in Sue's private drawer. Somewhere along the last couple of years, though, John figured it out.

He knew he wasn't supposed to touch it, but he and Jerry were in charge, and the crazy guy above them had a gun. There was a lot that could happen before the sheriffs could get back here. How could you protect yourself from someone with a gun, unless you had one too?

John pulled open the drawer, reached inside and lifted the top off the gun's box. Inside was the small, chrome plated Bryco Model 38, a .380 caliber, semi-automatic handgun manufactured by Bryco Arms, in Costa Mesa, California. Next to the gun was a dark-gray magazine.

The bottom of that magazine was bright, brushed aluminum.

With each move – entering the bedroom, opening the dresser drawer, opening the box with the gun in it – John was breaking all the major rules of the home. Any one of the infractions alone was enough for serious punishment, but John could only think of the crazy people up above, and the gunshots. Sue had said over the phone to *"unload the gun"*, so he removed the magazine from the box and used his thumb to push out the bullets, five of them, one by one, letting them drop into the box, then he picked up the gun.

At least they had the gun, even if Sue had made him unload it. At least they had it and they could load it again if they needed to.

Although small, the Bryco Model 38 had the classic shape of a semi-automatic, straight lines and right angles, similar to the Colt .45 semi-automatic, seen in multitudes of war movies and TV shows. Without actually knowing how the gun worked, millions of people, mostly male, knew to pull back the spring-powered slide then release it, and it would instantly slide forward with a distinct, loud metal-to-metal 'click'.

That action clears the way for a cartridge, or 'round', to be pushed up from the magazine inside the gun's hollow grip and moved forward into the firing chamber. Pull the trigger and the forceful release of gasses caused by the mini-explosion of a bullet being rocketed out of its shell casing pushes the slide back automatically, ejects the now empty shell casing, and allows the next round to be pushed up and into the firing chamber.

Pulling back the slide also opens and exposes the inside of the chamber, as a way to visually confirm that there is or isn't a cartridge in it. Pulling the slide back automatically ejects any round inside, unless there is a malfunction of some kind. Just as important, if there is a loaded magazine clip in the grip of the pistol, a cartridge will be pushed into the chamber to take the place of the one ejected.

When there is no magazine or it is is empty, pulling back the slide and ejecting a round from the firing chamber will leave it empty; an unloaded gun.

John had only his own notion of how the Bryco 38 worked, from having seen the .45 semi-automatic in movies and from having watched Clint fire the Bryco. He also knew he still couldn't pull the slide back. Holding the now empty magazine in one hand and the gun in the other, he turned to go back into living room.

Jerry was standing right behind him. John turned, saw Jerry, held out the gun and Jerry took it. Neither boy said anything. Jerry walked out of the room, John following and holding the empty magazine. In the two years since he'd come to stay with the family, Jerry had never seen the gun before. A basic shotgun firearms course was part of his firefighter training with the California Department of Forestry (CDF) and, years before, a friend had shown him how to shoot a 9-millimeter semi-automatic, but he'd neither held nor fired the Bryco.

Clint thought about getting a gun soon after they bought the trailer home, but he put it off for two years. In town, their small rental house had been right on the main drag, and people came to see them all the time, often without calling. It had been fun for a while, a young couple with lots of friends, right there in town off the street that everyone used to get from one end of town to the other, but their new place out on this rural ridgeline had a wonderful, reassuring sense of privacy; its downside was the remoteness.

The rugged, encircling forests and hills of Mendocino County were home for a wide range of wildlife, including bobcat, mountain lion and, even in the areas around Willits, bear. Soon after they moved onto the property, a neighbor less than three miles away saw a good-size bear near his house, and throughout the years pictures and stories about bears in the area were in the local newspaper. Clint wasn't interested in hunting, but he was going to protect his family and his property. A small handgun of some kind seemed to be a good choice.

Sue was against it. The memory of her father's abusive behavior with a gun heightened her fears, reasonable or not, about having a gun of any kind in the house. But she understood Clint's concerns about being isolated and needing to be safe, and of wanting the security of a gun. Still, there was also the problem of money. Rifles and handguns could be expensive and of all the things on which they could spend money, a gun wasn't on the 'gotta have it' list.

It was Sue who, ironically, knew where to find guns they could afford.

Willits Pawn was right on the main drag, not far from where Sue and Clint had lived in town. Sue knew the owners because she babysat their young children over the years and shared a rental with their oldest daughter when Sue was eighteen. She remembered that the shop sold handguns, rifles and shotguns, having seen them when she bought her first small TV almost eight years before from Walter, the pawnshop's owner.

Willits Pawn, like many pawnshops across the country, carried a mix of pawned and new items, including guns. Working class people at the lower wage-earning end of the pay scale, like Clint and Sue, had become a niche market for smaller, inexpensive handguns, offered as an affordable gun for self-defense. These new, small guns, including the Bryco Model 38, were priced much lower than used guns that were manufactured by more recognizable and respected names.

Low prices and easy concealment also made guns like the Bryco increasingly appealing to criminals. A good handgun, new, could cost anywhere from five-hundred to well over one-thousand dollars. The inexpensive, smaller handguns could be had for less than one-hundred dollars. Many compared favorably in firepower with the larger handguns, but their accuracy, reliability and overall quality ranged from barely adequate to poor and dangerous. As a group, the small handguns had acquired several nicknames, with *Saturday night special* becoming the de facto term used by the media and law enforcement.

None of these issues were on Clint or Sue's minds as they scanned the shop's display cases. Clint told Walter he was looking for a gun for protection, simple as that, and he was looking for something he could afford. Walter pulled out a new, shiny, Bryco Model 38, a small pistol that used the same bullet size as a nine-millimeter semi-automatic.

"Will it stop a bear?" Clint asked.

Walter assured him it would. It also came with two ammunition magazines, ammunition, and a great price: eighty-nine dollars.

Sue filled out the necessary paperwork to buy the gun. Two weeks later, after the state-mandated waiting period, she wrote a check and picked up the gun.

Jerry now had that gun in his right hand as he entered the living room. He was the adult here, the older, responsible person, and although he was also scared by the craziness happening at the neighbor's house, he wasn't sure having this gun was a good idea. He was nervous about the neighbor and at least as nervous about the gun in his hand.

It was only a few steps from the bedroom to the living room. Brandon stood up as soon as he saw Jerry with the gun. As Jerry stepped to the middle of the room and John, still holding the magazine he had emptied in the dresser drawer, stepped behind Brandon, Jerry turned his wrist, palm toward the floor, so he could see the side of the gun. Though he'd never seen this particular gun before, he knew he had to pull the slide back so he could check the gun's chamber. He could see the empty magazine in John's hand but knew there could still be a bullet in the gun.

The slide on the Bryco Model 38 wouldn't move with the safety on, so Jerry moved the safety to the 'fire' position and began to pull back the slide. His line of fire shifted when he turned his wrist, which is why Brandon could see right into the barrel just before he was shot.

John had run back down from the top of the driveway, adrenaline coursing through him. Several minutes had passed since his call to 911. Each moment seemed like an eternity. John looked inside the house; Jerry was still performing mouth-to-mouth on Brandon. John waited another minute, pacing, not sure what else to do, and looked up as the same two patrol cars that had responded to the earlier call pulled off the road and drove up the neighbor's driveway. He sprinted up after them, yelling "No, no, down here!" then turned and ran back to the house.

Deputies Darrell Forrester and Randall Johnson entered the house quickly but cautiously, aware that this was a call about a shooting. Forrester kneeled down and took over mouth-to-mouth, as Johnson asked Jerry, "Where's the gun?"

"I don't know."

He asked John, but John couldn't remember what had happened to it either.

Detective Lt. Charles Boone arrived, entered the home and immediately began to work on Brandon with Forrester. Deputy Johnson began searching for the gun.

The boys could only watch now. It had taken almost seven minutes for the deputies to arrive and Jerry had performed mouth-to-mouth the entire time. The front of his shirt was covered with blood. For seven minutes he had kept Brandon alive.

It would be another seven minutes – fourteen minutes since the shooting – before paramedics would arrive.

Paramedic Vivian Robertson had been with Northern Pacific Ambulance for just over four years, and she'd been dispatched to shootings before, but she'd never been dispatched to a shooting involving a little boy. She momentarily allowed herself to think of her own small children as she drove out of town, speeding away from Willits' small hospital where the ambulance crews spent their shifts.

Mark Robertson prepped the back of the ambulance and configured his trauma bag to treat a child with a serious bullet wound. As the EMT II, he was in charge, and any decisions and plans of action in getting a victim from the accident scene to the hospital were his responsibility. As they sped down highway 101, he looked at the gray skies and knew he wouldn't be able to call-in the region's medical evacuation helicopter. A serious gunshot wound, especially to a child, would normally warrant calling for a flight, but the low, gray skies made it too risky, at least right now.

Additional deputies and a California Department of Forestry fire truck crew (CDF), stationed only a few miles away, had also been dispatched and were already lined up along the driveway when the ambulance arrived. The Robertsons grabbed their equipment and entered the house. Vivian noticed a bloody handprint on the glass of the door.

Vivian carried an oxygen tank and heart monitor as she kneeled next to the motionless little boy with the tiny hole in his jaw. *He's the same age as my son,* she thought, as she bent down and felt for a pulse. It was faint and hard to find.

Deputies moved aside as Mark opened his trauma bag. There was a lot of blood around this skinny, little boy's mouth, and the boy could not breathe on his own.

"I'm going to intubate," Mark said.

Intubation is a critical procedure in emergency trauma treatment, difficult to accomplish even under the controlled conditions of an emergency room, daunting and formidable in the field. A victim who has an injury to his airway that prevents the flow of air into or out of the lungs will most certainly die without the insertion of a thin oxygen line through the trachea. Paramedics train constantly to hone this technique. Under ideal conditions, drugs are used to relax the anatomical structures that make intubation a major challenge. In a field situation, there may be no time to use these drugs, or the drugs may not be available.

Mark had several challenges as he readied the device that inserts a tracheal tube into Brandon's mouth, down the throat, through the vocal cords and into the trachea. In a healthy seven-year old, insertion into the trachea is challenging due to the very tiny size of the throat, and the shortness of the trachea, no more than six or seven centimeters. Compounding the difficulty was the tremendous quantity of blood still filling Brandon's mouth and throat. In essence, Mark was working almost blind.

Sue had wanted nothing more than to go straight home, but the fuel gauge needle was on empty.

"Shit, I've got to stop." Sue pulled in to a gas station near the edge of town.

She heard the siren before she saw the ambulance. Her heart began to pound. She saw the ambulance coming her way, and hoped, prayed, that it would stop or turn before it reached her. But it came at her, past the station and down the highway.

She had a bad, bad feeling as she pushed some money at the attendant and drove after the ambulance.

As more deputies arrived, John told them Sue was on her way home, but Clint was working a few miles up the road, outside, unreachable by phone. A deputy and the CDF crew's captain left to go get Clint.

Sue pulled up less than a minute later.

Oh God, oh God, she thought, as she rounded the last curve of the road and saw the emergency vehicles lined up along her driveway.

She stopped the car and ran to the house, but Deputy Johnson stepped in front of her, wrapping his arms around her and backing her away.

"No, Sue, no, you can't go inside, they're working on your boy."

"Why, what happened? Is he going to be all right?"

"I don't know. He was shot. It's bad."

The world spun around, a blur of tears and hurt, a psychic cord between herself and her son shredded. As Toni and Gene stepped up to hold her, John ran to her and told her that Jerry shot Brandon.

"He didn't mean it," John said. "The gun was empty!"

Vivian suctioned Brandon's mouth and throat as Mark began the intubation.

A tense few seconds passed. Procedure dictated that Mark would have only two opportunities to intubate before he would have to stop, load the boy and go. The ride to the hospital would take almost fifteen minutes. Without intubation this skinny little boy would die, probably right here on the floor.

"I'm in," he said, even as he thought, *I can't believe I just did that.*

At the same time, Vivian thought, *that's miraculous.*

Within the next two minutes, a cervical collar immobilized Brandon's neck and head. He was secured to a backboard and loaded into the ambulance.

Sue was hyperventilating, trying to move, trying to talk through tears. "I've got to see him!" she screamed at the deputy. Another deputy carried Rocky toward her, but handed the frightened child to Toni.

Behind the deputy, the paramedics and firefighters guided the stretcher out of the house. Sue could only assume that Brandon was on the stretcher, because she couldn't see him. His tiny body took up little space on the backboard, and the paramedics and firefighters blocked any view of him as they loaded the stretcher into the ambulance.

Sue clung to Deputy Johnson as the ambulance moved up the driveway. "Is my boy going to live?"

"We don't know, they're working on his heart."

She screamed through her tears.

Johnson held onto her. "We sent someone to go find Clint, but you need to head to the hospital, right now."

Toni took Sue by the shoulders, turned her toward the

car, said, "Give Gene your keys," and yelled for John to get Rocky and get in the car.

Jerry stayed behind to watch the house, to be interviewed, and to wait for Clint.

"Please, please let him live," Sue begged, as Gene pulled out of the driveway, repeating it all the way to the hospital "Please, please, let him live."

Vivian maneuvered the ambulance down the winding, hillside roads toward the highway, giving the hospital an update over the radio while Mark and two CDF firefighters worked on Brandon. The priorities had been followed on the scene: assess and clear the airway, get the victim breathing, assess and facilitate blood circulation. Successful trauma scene treatment was commonly referred to as load-and-go, and now that Brandon was in the ambulance on his way to the hospital, Mark began a more thorough check of the injuries. Blood from the bullet's exit wound still seeped into the cervical collar around Brandon's neck.

As they arrived at the emergency room, small breaks appeared in the morning fog. It was going to clear up. Mark called for an emergency medical flight. A medical helicopter flight service out of Santa Rosa, California, almost one hundred miles south of Willits, would arrive in forty minutes.

Willits Howard Memorial hospital was small, with twenty-eight beds. It had top-of-the-line equipment and good doctors, but as Brandon arrived it was clear that this major trauma was better suited for a larger hospital. It would be a challenge to keep Brandon alive and stable until the helicopter arrived, at least forty-five minutes. It would take five to ten minutes to load Brandon for the forty-five minute flight to Santa Rosa Memorial, the closest large hospital with advanced trauma capabilities.

As they wheeled Brandon into the emergency room, Mark thought that the little boy's chances for survival were very, very slim.

Twenty-four hours before the shooting, and six-hundred miles south, in Anaheim, California, a fax was transmitted from Brown & Wilcox, a commercial insurance underwriter, to an agent at an insurance brokerage, regarding Bryco Arms, the manufacturer of the Bryco Model 38.

Bryco had just come off of a good year, with \$7,000,000 in sales from 1993-1994, and \$14,000,000 sales projections for the next year. The small, privately owned company held the top spot of the small handgun industry. Sales for the Bryco Model 38 were more than \$2,500,000 dollars. But the company had been negotiating the cost of liability insurance. The current policy had officially lapsed on April 1st. The new policy would be almost \$250,000, an almost \$40,000 increase.

Bryco Arms and other small handgun manufacturers were seeing increasing premiums across the board. Market forces, changes in gun laws, especially in California, growing anti-gun sentiment, bad press and a slow but steady rise in litigation against gun makers had insurance companies re-evaluating their clients. The makers of small guns were serious liability risks, and the insurance companies that continued to insure handgun manufacturers had increased premiums and narrowed coverage. As Bryco Arms' policy neared expiration and the company shopped around for a new policy, three major insurance companies declined to quote coverage for the company.

Bryco Arms negotiated with its insurance agent until the liability coverage expired on April 1, 1994. An offer was made to extend coverage until April 8th, for an additional $8,000, but, as the broker noted on an April 5th fax to the commercial underwriter, "...it is my feeling the insured will not be renewing with us. He feels the cost is too high..."

And so, two days before seven-year old Brandon Maxfield had been wheeled into his small town's emergency room, closer to death than life, unable to breathe on his own, his spine shattered just below the base of his skull, the manufacturer of the Bryco Model 38 had chosen to 'go bare' — Bryco Arms was now without insurance to compensate anyone injured by a defective Bryco handgun.

Clint stopped hacking at a patch of brush as his uncle Marvin, a deputy sheriff, and a CDF firefighter walked toward him.

"Clint, there's been an accident."

Marvin followed in his car as Clint rode back to the house with the deputy. The deputy gave Clint a quick rundown on what had happened, including that Brandon was "in really, really bad shape, but the paramedics are already there."

Questions filled Clint's head: Why did they have the gun out; how did they know where the gun was; and just what the hell happened? As they pulled into his driveway, Clint's emotions swung between concern for his son and anger at the fighting neighbors. That the ambulance had already left for the hospital only added to his increasingly edgy emotions.

Jerry stood nearby as the deputies told Clint that Sue had already left for the hospital, and that Brandon was still alive, barely, when he was loaded into the ambulance. As Jerry tried to tell Clint how things had happened, Clint found himself getting angrier about the neighbors, especially as the deputies confirmed Jerry's story about the first call to 911. Deputies were still going through the house and would question Jerry in a few minutes. They needed to talk to Clint, but that could wait, so, with Clint's uncle at the wheel, he headed for the hospital.

Earlier, as deputy Forrester and detective Boone had worked to save Brandon in the living room, deputy Johnson had searched the house and found the gun, several bullets, and the empty magazine all in the open gun box, unexpectedly sitting on top of Sue and Clint's dresser. His first responsibility was to secure the weapon, so he picked it up, walked outside and placed it in his patrol car. He quickly grabbed a camera, locked the car and went back into the house. The gun remained locked in the car until detective Alvin Tripp arrived a few minutes later.

Howard Memorial's ER physician quickly examined the tiny boy on the emergency room table, as the medical team checked and recorded Brandon's vital signs and prepared him for X-rays.

"Brandon, can you hear me? Open your eyes, Brandon. Come on, Brandon."

Brandon opened his eyes slightly but made no sounds and didn't move. He wasn't thrashing, wasn't moaning, and his eyes closed moments after they opened. The small wound on the right side of his tiny but swollen face was not bleeding, and his heartbeat was now rapid but steady, even though his blood pressure was low. The ER team suctioned his chest and throat several times, and cleared blood from both nostrils. The cervical collar would not be removed until after Brandon's transfer to another facility, so the doctor could not directly examine the exit wound on Brandon's neck.

"Brandon, move your toes for me. Can you move your toes? Can you move your fingers for me?"

Brandon's reflexes were normal but he had no voluntary movements. A Foley catheter, a long, thin tube with a round, inflatable end, was inserted into Brandon's penis and up into his bladder. The insertion was done without anesthetic, not unusual for an urgent, trauma situation, and even though it was a very painful procedure, Brandon had no reaction.

He was put on an IV drip of epinephrine, the same substance produced naturally by an adrenaline rush, strong medication used to keep a gravely injured person alive by increasing the heart rate, respiration rate, and blood pressure.

Through it all, and as they moved him from the ER and into the X-ray lab, Brandon remained unconscious and still.

As Jerry paced outside, deputy Johnson photographed the rooms. In the bedroom, he photographed the dresser, then picked up the top of the gun's box to take a picture of the gun's serial number, printed on a small tag. On the top of the box were the words BRYCO ARMS, IRVINE, CALIFORNIA, printed in large, black letters, and below those, slightly smaller but still prominent, were the words EXTRA MAGAZINE INCLUDED.

Some of the furniture in the living room had been moved, and an end table was pushed against a wall. As he photographed the living room, Johnson found and photographed a single, empty shell casing on the floor, just in front of the sofa. Neither he nor any other deputy had noticed it until now.

Outside, detective Alvin Tripp arrived and introduced himself to Jerry. Tripp, a heavy set man with a paced, methodical personality, had been with the county sheriff's department for almost twenty-five years, a detective for the last ten. He talked to Jerry in a calm, almost folksy way, said that he understood how emotional Jerry might feel right now, but there were questions that needed answers. Jerry wasn't under arrest; this was just part of the investigative process. John and Rocky would also be interviewed.

Johnson was still taking pictures as detective Tripp and Jerry walked inside. He gave Tripp a quick overview about the shooting, showed him the different areas he had photographed and told him about the shell casing on the floor. In the bedroom he showed detective Tripp the gun's box on top of the dresser, with the magazine and the loose bullets in it.

Tripp turned on a small tape recorder, stood beside Jerry, whose hands trembled slightly, stated the date, time and address, then began the interview.

TRIPP: Tell me what happened here today.

JERRY: Uh, we've been, uh, burning brush, most of the day. The neighbors had a fight. And we had called the police, um, so they could deal with them up there.

TRIPP: Were they fighting and screaming and everything up the hill?

JERRY: Uh-huh. The guy was chasing her around with an axe.

TRIPP: Okay. What happened then?

JERRY: Um, John came in, and I came in after him. He got the gun, uh, the clip was sitting next to the gun. Not even in the gun. He took the rounds out of the clip. I held the gun and looked at it because I, it's been a long time since I've seen it.

TRIPP: Uh-huh.

JERRY: I just held it there, and, it went off somehow.

And I didn't even know there was a round in the chamber. Because the clip was not even in the, uh, gun. It was out of the gun, with, uh, three rounds in it, and the gun went off.

TRIPP: You said John went and got the gun?

JERRY: Uh, he got it out of the drawer, because, I guess, uh, Sue said take the rounds out or something. I don't know what all…

The shooting had happened less than an hour ago, but Jerry was already having trouble piecing together an accurate sequence of events. He wasn't trying to deceive the detective. He was still trying to cope with the reality of his situation, for which there might be frightful consequences, and he kept thinking about Brandon, wondering if he was still alive:

TRIPP: Was the barrel pointing toward him, or pointing toward John, or towards the kitchen, towards where Brandon was standing?

JERRY: Yeah . . . uh, I didn't see Brandon behind me. I was facing straight towards the window.

TRIPP: Do you remember which hand the gun was in when you were holding it?

JERRY: The right hand.

TRIPP: Did you have your finger around it, like you would hold a gun, in your hand, or…?

JERRY: Not, not with my finger in, uh, in the trigger, no. Kinda, kinda holding it, and somehow the finger slipped or something and there was a round in the chamber, that nobody knew because the clip was sitting next to it. Not even in the gun.

TRIPP: John was there, to my right…

JERRY: Um-hm.

TRIPP: He had the magazine with bullets in it. And he took the bullets out of it, right?

JERRY: Yeah. And he put it into the, uh, gun box.

Tripp was doing his best to clarify the sequence of events and where each boy had been when the accident happened, not just because it was a necessary component of the investigation but because at this stage there was no additional information, no other eye witness or other clear indications as to whether this had truly been an accidental shooting. He didn't feel there had been any horseplay, or a Russian roulette kind of incident, and he hadn't seen or heard anything that led him to believe that the little boy had been shot intentionally. Based on years of work with the innocent and the guilty, the criminals and the victims, Tripp thought this tall young man might have simply been reckless.

And Tripp had already made up his own mind about irresponsible parents who didn't keep a loaded gun under lock and key.

He was, indeed, attempting to get an accurate picture of how the accident had happened, and he was in no rush to get everything right. He wasn't put off by Jerry's inaccuracies or the young man's nervousness. As a cop, Tripp found that it was very normal for someone in this situation to make mistakes, or not remember certain things very well immediately after an accident. No, it wasn't Jerry's anxiousness about where everyone was when the gun went off that Tripp was slowly working towards, it was the 'how' that he was working up to now.

Jerry had said several times that "it just went off," and he had insisted at one point that he "didn't even have my finger on the trigger." For Tripp, all possibilities remained open until his investigation and interviews were completed, even though he was already leaning toward the shooting as accidental. And, if all possibilities were still open, that had to include that the gun had malfunctioned, which wouldn't be unheard of but which was, really, pretty rare in situations like this; the human factor, such as a finger inadvertently touching a trigger, was almost always the root cause.

He continued to work with Jerry on the layout of the room, and off-handedly slipped in a question that had nothing to do with the diagram:

TRIPP: Think you touched the trigger by accident, do you think?

JERRY: I might have. By accident, not realizing it.

It was the first admission by Jerry that he might have pulled the trigger during the brief moment he had his other hand on the slide.

Tripp continued with a few questions about how long it took the paramedics to arrive, then shifted the interview again.

TRIPP: It's pretty isolated back here, isn't it?

JERRY: Oh yeah, it is.

TRIPP: Does Clint always keep guns like this laying around?

JERRY: He don't keep 'em laying around. He usually has them put up, put up, and, uh, without rounds. And that's all the rounds that we had, and we've been having quite a bit of incidents, uh, a dog attacking chickens.

TRIPP: Yeah.

JERRY: ...at nighttime. And wolves and stuff.

TRIPP: Well, where does Clint normally keep his guns?

JERRY: He usually keeps it in this drawer.

TRIPP: In the drawer, Clint's room?

JERRY: Yeah, and the kids usually aren't allowed in there, unless their mother's around.

TRIPP: Any more guns in there...

JERRY: No.

TRIPP: ...that could be loaded?

JERRY: No. There's no more guns at all.

TRIPP: Okay, just the one handgun?

JERRY: Yeah. That's the only one, uh, for protecting them around here.

TRIPP: Okay. Brandon is your little brother, then?

JERRY: He's my nephew.

More pictures were taken inside, including the entrance hole in the kitchen wall, which detective Tripp then cut around to find the bullet sitting on small cross brace between two wall studs. He and deputy Forrester picked up the gun's box, with the magazine and loose bullets, bagged them and carried them outside to deputy Johnson's car.

Johnson unlocked his car and brought out the Bryco to show Tripp, who had yet to see the gun. The moment detective Tripp picked it up he realized there was a magazine in it. The bottom, underside of the grip that appeared to be empty – a "black hole" is how Tripp later described it in his official report – was actually the bottom of a black magazine. The gun was still loaded and neither Johnson, when he picked it up and locked it in his patrol car, nor Tripp, at first glance, noticed the magazine, a professional mistake given that standard procedure is to always check and unload a gun before isolating it, usually by placing it into an evidence bag.

Johnson slid the magazine out of the gun, moved the safety switch from 'safe' to 'fire', pulled back the slide and ejected the last round from the chamber.

Now, the Bryco was finally empty.

What had just happened to the two professional, career police officers mirrored what had happened to John and Jerry less than an hour ago. The officers' mistake had resulted in no more than a moment of quiet, professional embarrassment, and was quickly rectified. Jerry and John's fateful mistake had started the same way.

What Jerry saw when he entered the bedroom, his perception of what he saw when he walked up behind John had set up the domino effect that eventually resulted in the shooting. John had already lifted off the top of the box and put it aside before Jerry walked in, removing the 'extra magazine included' information from sight.

Tripp stored the gun, the box, and other evidence in the patrol car. The detective and the deputies packed up and drove away, leaving Jerry alone in the house.

Jerry began to clean up, working to get as much blood as possible out of the carpet.

Sue, the Holders, John and Rocky were already at the hospital as Clint bolted from his uncle's car and ran to the ER entrance.

Brandon had been here for over twenty minutes, and although Sue had been only ten minutes behind, she still hadn't seen her son. She was a mess, her puffy, red eyes brimming with tears, and she could barely stand. Clint wanted, demanded to see his son, but was initially refused; this was not the time, he was told. Everything that could be done was being done, it was better that he stay out. But he couldn't get any real information, and the doctor who could best give him information was working on Brandon right now.

Howard Memorial was a one-floor hospital, and the distance from the back of an ambulance at the ER entrance to inside the emergency room was no more than fifteen feet. Four patients could be treated simultaneously, but the actual ER working space was smaller than a single treatment area in many larger, metropolitan hospitals. There simply wasn't a lot of room.

Clint would not be denied, whether it was the right thing to do or not. The waiting room was directly across the hall from the ER, and he easily pushed past several nurses and stood in the doorway of the trauma area. He could see Brandon, motionless on a gurney, several doctors and nurses moving around him.

A nurse said, "He's still unconscious and there isn't anything you can do to help right now."

Brandon had been X-rayed and was being prepared for the medical flight to a trauma center in Santa Rosa. Sue and Clint were told to "leave now" because the helicopter would arrive soon and it would be in Santa Rosa long before the family could get there.

Sue didn't want to leave without seeing Brandon, but she was also too distraught to put up a fight. Before they left, they called and had friends take John, Rocky and Trish to stay with Kandace, and they left with Toni and Gene for the long, torturous drive.

Sue went into a near trance-like state, reciting the mantra she'd first started as she left the house: "please let him live…"

Redwood Empire Air Care Helicopter, known by its acronym REACH, had just recently expanded its hospital affiliations and sponsors to include Howard Memorial, refining and standardizing the procedures for safe, fast and efficient transfers of patients from Willits to other Northern California medical centers. The small company, started a decade before by a visionary, Santa Rosa emergency room doctor, was a pioneer and a leader in the still young medical flight industry. The company's only helicopter was a well-equipped flying emergency room, operating at high, professional flight and operation standards, and providing specialized training for its crews, with an intense commitment to pediatric critical care.

On the east side of Willits, five minutes from the hospital, an ambulance was waiting at a CDF helipad as the REACH helicopter touched down. Two REACH crew members, a flight nurse and flight paramedic, transferred bags, monitors and equipment into the ambulance for the quick ride to Howard Memorial. Inside the ER, the hospital's ventilator, which Brandon still needed to stay alive, and each monitor connected to Brandon were all quickly switched over to the REACH crew's portable, battery powered equipment, as the flight nurse received a full report on Brandon's current condition.

Minutes later, Brandon's ambulance arrived back at the helipad and he was transferred and secured inside the helicopter. The portable technology that helped to keep him alive - cardiac monitor, blood pressure monitor, ventilator — combined with the skills and experience of the REACH crew, ensured that Brandon received the same level of care in this helicopter that he would receive in any emergency room. The lack of an on-board doctor was offset by a direct radio link to an emergency room physician, who could also monitor Brandon for the entire flight.

The crew had been advised of Brandon's condition before the flight had left its base in Santa Rosa, and had received continual updates. Now as the helicopter lifted off and turned south, Brandon's fight for life continued under the care of two highly specialized medical professionals, in a six-foot long, noisy, bumpy space, moving through the sky at one hundred-fifty miles an hour.

The pilot set a course that paralleled highway 101 and, at some point, overtook Sue and Clint in their car below. Both vehicles were moving the family away from their previous, normal lives, and toward an unknown future. Brandon was flying away from a normal childhood, leaving behind games of hide and seek in the woods, adventures on his bike and baseball games in the summer. Whether he lived or died, he would never take another step, never wave hello or goodbye, and never hug anyone again.

Ripples from the accident moved through the entire community, and the effects would touch, alter, and impact hundreds of lives. From its small but explosive beginning, the accident's economic and financial impact on people, schools, the health care and legal systems wouldn't be fully realized for years, but the effect on the local emergency services and medical system was already substantial, quickly hitting the tens of thousands of dollars in hard costs for the sheriff, paramedics and CDF responses, the ambulance and emergency room treatment, physicians and staff.

This ripple was now moving south at an altitude of two-thousand feet. Every passing minute the REACH chopper was in the air was a minute of calculated risk, and this flight would add $5,000 to the growing costs of Brandon's accident.

As in so many other aspects of their lives, the family was no different than many blue collar and low income working families, in that they had no health insurance to speak of, nothing that would address anything as catastrophic as Brandon's sudden medical and health care needs. At a point in the very near future, they would be forced to deal with the paperwork, documents and liens associated with all of this, but right now their toll was psychological, emotional devastation.

The drive to Santa Rosa Memorial hospital took almost ninety minutes. When they arrived, Sue and Clint were told the flight had been re-directed to Oakland's

Children's Hospital, another ninety-minute drive to the southeast.

They had left Willits an hour and a half ago, not knowing the condition of their boy, but because the helicopter had not stopped in Santa Rosa, no one there had any information about Brandon. Clint and Sue wouldn't know Brandon's condition for another at least another ninety minutes.

Children's Hospital is a premier pediatric care facility, an environment designed to treat, rehabilitate and comfort infants, babies and children. The halls and treatment areas are more colorful than most hospital interiors, with brightly colored walls and murals full of joyful, cartoon animals and magical scenes. Its two, twelve-story buildings, on either side of Martin Luther King, Jr. Drive, on the northeast side of Oakland, are busy all day with a steady stream of doctors, patients, families, visitors and staff. Many of the hospital's patients come from Oakland and its surrounding East and South Bay communities, but the hospital is a destination for sick and injured children from all over the Bay Area and Northern California.

Landing a helicopter in an urban environment, even an environment with a special area for just such a purpose, can never be considered routine, lest the people who work in that environment become complacent. It is, however, routine for Children's Hospital that a helicopter arrives on a regular basis with the smallest of patients, whose injuries may be compounded by their young age, even as their ability to survive is enhanced by the energy and vibrancy of youth.

Many veteran trauma center workers believe in the special, fighting spirit of children, and have seen firsthand that "kids want to live; at their age, they don't know anything about dying."

REACH had alerted Children's Hospital and, at five minutes out, hospital security cleared the helipad area and a trauma team with a specialized gurney waited just outside the building. The REACH helicopter settled onto the pad, the pilot shut down the engine and as the rotors slowed he made eye contact with the waiting trauma staff, giving them the approval to approach. The helicopter's side door opened and Brandon was transferred and secured to the hospital gurney, fifty-two minutes after leaving Willits.

Once inside the trauma area, a space ten times larger than the ER in Willits, the REACH crew transferred care and responsibility of Brandon to the Children's Hospital trauma team. No family member was present, but evaluation and treatment permissions had already been forwarded. Brandon was kept on the ventilator, his intake of oxygen measured, intravenous medicines continued, and he was quickly given CT scans, which provided a detailed series of internal images much clearer and more revealing than X-rays.

The scan of Brandon's head showed no damage other than his broken jaw, but the spinal scan clearly showed the damage to his second and third vertebrae, the first verification of Brandon's paralysis.

The family arrived an hour later. The drive had been an emotional roller coaster, with sporadic conversation and long silences. Toni Holder thought there might be a ray of hope. "Brandon must be doing better, or else why would they go ahead on to Oakland?"

She and her husband Gene lagged behind as Sue and Clint raced into the ER. Toni told Gene, "I'm afraid to go in. I'm afraid to see him."

Sue and Clint were led to a waiting area, and a minute later an ER doctor introduced himself to Clint and told him, gently but directly, "your son may not live, and, if he does live, he will be paralyzed."

It would be another hour before they would be allowed to see Brandon in the ICU.

At roughly the same time the REACH flight touched down in Oakland, Kandace's husband brought Rocky and John into the county sheriff's sub-station in Willits. Detective Tripp turned on his recorder and began his interview of the boys. He eased into the session, making a little small talk with them before he began. Most of his questions were for John, and the boy's answers corroborated many of the details from Jerry's interview just an hour before. Tripp had the same feeling about John that he'd had with Jerry, that neither boy was trying to hide anything.

TRIPP: You know, you took the gun out. If Jerry hadn't gotten the gun...

JOHN: None of this would have happened.

TRIPP: None of this would have happened.

JOHN: Cause all I did is I took a magazine and I took out the...

TRIPP: Was the magazine in the gun, or outside the gun?

JOHN: No. No. It was laying next to it in the case.

TRIPP: Laying next to it. Okay.

JOHN: So, I was just being safe and taking out the bullets and Jerry had grabbed the gun.

TRIPP: Okay.

JOHN: And, and then he just pulled it back and all of a sudden it went BOOM! Like that. And I just, he was saying, "Holy shit!" and I go, "What's wrong?" and I looked at Brandon when he fell on to my arms. And then I looked down and I could see the blood.

TRIPP: Okay.

Brandon was in the ICU when Sue finally saw him. The sight overwhelmed her, and she held on to Clint tightly.

A doctor had explained Brandon's injuries and described what would be done to keep him alive, but neither Sue, who had only the most tenuous ability to function, nor Clint, were prepared for what they saw.

A million tubes and wires seemed to snake around Brandon's bed. His small body was enveloped by everything around it, lost under a white sheet, an oxygen tube in his nose, several I.V. bags around the bed, tubes hanging down and needles at the end of every tube stuck into Brandon's thin arms. A ventilator and cardiac monitor glowed, beeped and hissed on either side of his bed.

The most jarring sight, though, were the large bandages taped over Brandon's eyes. With so much of Brandon covered up, and the bandages obliterating so much of his face, the eyes and the tussled blond hair that made this particular little boy Brandon Maxfield were erased, disconnecting Sue from her son. In her heart, she knew the little body surrounded by twinkling lights and plastic tubing was her little boy, but this sight just seemed to be surreal and cruel, like a punishment for letting her son come so close to death.

A spinal specialist had been consulted immediately, and after studying the CT scans, had decided against any spinal surgery because there was nothing surgery could do for Brandon's immediate condition. Another specialist evaluated Brandon's fractured jaw, which would have to be repaired soon but was unnecessarily risky to perform right now. The bandages had been taped over his eyes because while comatose his eyelids would not always remain closed, so a lubricant had been applied to his eyes and then covered to prevent them from drying out.

Clint, big, headstrong and accustomed making things work, put his arms around Sue as she clung to him. For the first time in his life he had no idea how to function. He was at the mercy of something totally out of his control, and at the center of a life-changing storm that destroyed what had been, for him, and for his wife and family, an idyllic, working-man's existence: a small house in the country, married, with good kids, in a small town.

Toni and Gene stayed for several hours, saddened by Brandon's critical condition but thankful he was still alive. They talked about everything that needed to be done, about helping Kandace watch the kids, getting clothes and watching the house, then left for the long drive back to Willits.

Sue and Clint slept in the ICU that night. In the morning the hospital set them up in a hospital-maintained family apartment less than a block away. Being in a residence so close to the hospital provided the important physical and emotional nearness families needed during long term care situations. For the first few days, even though the apartment was less than a minute's walk from the hospital, Sue only left the ICU to shower and change until, late on the third day, she fell into a deep, exhausted sleep at the apartment.

On day four Brandon was still in a coma, no longer at the precipice of death but not safe from it. When Sue wasn't sitting beside Brandon or getting updates from the doctors and ICU nurses, her thoughts turned bitter and she lashed out at God. *How could you let this happen? This is horrible.* In her most private moments, with nowhere to scream, nowhere to unleash her pain, she turned on Him, and let her spirit screech and wail.

Growing up too fast, and independent too soon, Sue's lack of a cohesive family environment never stopped her from believing in God and prayer. She still believed, but she saw everything that had happened as an un-God like thing to do to Brandon. There might not have been an 'every Sunday' kind of upbringing in her past, but she had created and fostered a personal religion, picking up a bit of spirituality here and there, and getting some early guidance from Ruby, her grandmother.

She hadn't had a chance to talk to her grandma Ruby yet, but she knew that the woman would be crushed to hear about Brandon's accident. Ruby loved Brandon in that way grandmothers do when they treat one grandson as though he was the only grandkid in the family.

What weighed on Sue the most, though, was her mounting guilt. She hated guns, but she let one come into her house. She hated guns, but she was the one who paid for it. She had let it come in and then shunned it, ignored it — out of sight, out of mind – but it had been there all along. She let it come in to her house and she felt, in her sad, sad heart, that she bore the largest share of responsibility for what happened.

As Sue fumed at God and herself, Clint worried about the family, the house and his job. He was old school, the patriarch, the provider. He'd managed to move forward, move up, bought a home. He was working steady, and he might not have been financially rich, but he had a plot of land and a pretty good life for himself and his family. Life had been a struggle, but they had a good time. They could party with their friends, and they could take the family camping. Life couldn't always be great, but it was pretty good, all things considered.

Now what? His son was barely alive, paralyzed for life, and still so close to not being alive that a machine was breathing for him. For every thought about Brandon and Brandon's future, Clint thought about the entire family, and all the mouths to feed, and to take care of, and how would he be able to do that? How was this all going to work?

How am I going to pay for all of this? What if I lose the house? What the hell is going to happen to us?

He was a provider who suddenly couldn't provide enough, and that terrified him. He sat in a chair next to Brandon's bed, leaned back, closed his eyes and tried not to think of the future.

Later, as Clint stepped out of the ICU, he heard, "Mr. Stansberry?"

The man approaching him in the corridor was Clint's age, not quite as tall, wearing a well-tailored, dark blue suit. He introduced himself as Michael Smith, an investigator with the law firm of A & B. As he handed his business card to Clint, he apologized for intruding during this terrible time and asked, "Has anyone offered you legal assistance?"

"What do you mean?"

"We learned of your son's accident, and many people aren't aware, especially so soon after an unfortunate accident like this, when there is so much going on, that in an accidental shooting sometimes a problem with the gun can be a factor. We wondered if anyone had talked to you about the accident, or about the gun?"

"No, we haven't talked to anyone about anything like that. How do you know about the shooting?"

"We have people who read the papers and take note of stories like yours because, as I said, you'd be surprised how many people won't realize that the accident may not entirely be their fault. I know you probably have things to do, but if we can just take a minute here, I'll be happy to answer any questions, and maybe I could just get some information from you, and I'll have one of the senior attorneys get in touch with you soon. If I may ask, how is your son doing?"

Smith and Clint spoke for a few minutes. Smith took some notes and before he left expressed his sincere hopes for Brandon's recovery.

Smith hadn't lied about anything he said to Clint, and he hadn't misrepresented himself or his firm, either. Smith had performed a smooth, textbook approach to this particular situation, even though what he was doing was against the law. The A & B firm was a large plaintiffs firm, and probably did have someone who "read the papers" with an eye toward stories like Brandon's. But, if you were a plaintiff's attorney who only used the newspaper to find and hopefully capitalize on situations like Brandon's, you would almost certainly be at the back of the line at best and, more likely, way too late. Successful plaintiffs firms with a go-get-the-lawsuit philosophy had a well-established network of individuals known in the legal profession as runners and cappers who, for a moderate 'finders fee,' would pass along information that could be of particular interest to a firm such as the one for which Mr. Smith worked.

From the moment a tragedy occurred, the number of people involved with and aware of victims like Brandon could grow significantly in a very short period of time. Taxi and truck drivers, lab workers, various admin workers, security guards, orderlies, even maintenance and laundry workers could all have enough information in the first few hours to the first few days after an accident, that a quick call to someone like Mr. Smith could be financially well worth their while.

Clint didn't say anything to Sue about the meeting as he came into Brandon's room. In the big scheme of things right now, Brandon was all he cared about. While Sue and Clint carried on their vigil at Brandon's bedside, Mr. Smith was on his way back to his firm, where he would give the family's information to one of the firm's partners. Mr. Smith would assemble a file of information, and an attorney would evaluate the accident to determine if there was exposure to liability by the gun maker, or anyone else involved in the accident.

Toward the end of Brandon's first week, doctors reduced the medications that had, in part, been used to keep Brandon in a drug-induced coma, and removed the bandages from his eyes. Even though he was still surrounded by monitors and IV tubes, and the ventilator's oxygen tube was still inserted through his nose, Sue was grateful to see her son's face, to be able to connect visually with her boy. Through the entire week, Sue had talked to him, saying, "We're right here, baby, we're right here with you," telling him everyone was praying for him, everyone was thinking about him.

A few days into the second week, a morning when she was alone in Brandon's room, Sue reached out and held Brandon's small hand. She leaned close to him and said, "Brandon, I promise you, I promise that if you live, if you'll just wake-up, I promise to be your arms and legs for the rest of your life."

Forty-five minutes later Sue was looking right at him when he opened his eyes for the first time since being shot.

His mom and his room were the first images of any kind that he'd had since the accident. There had been nothing else that he could remember, no bright light at the end of a long tunnel, no voices, no out-of-body experience, nothing before he opened his eyes.

The tube down his throat prevented him from speaking. Sue held her surging emotions in check as she moved close to his face.

His eyes were droopy. He couldn't move his head, couldn't really look around, but it didn't matter, because his eyes were fixed on his mother.

"Brandon, you can't talk because there's something in your throat, but it's okay. Can you blink your eyes for me?"

A moment passed, a moment where Sue's heart pounded hard, before he finally blinked. Sue smiled, and it took everything she had to keep the tears from flooding out of her eyes.

"I'll ask you some questions, and you just blink for me, okay? Blink once for yes, and two times for no. Do you know who I am?"

He blinked once.

"Does anything hurt you right now? Are you in pain?"

He blinked twice.

She leaned over and kissed his forehead, and rested her face softly on his head, feeling his fine, blond hair on her cheek. Clint walked in and kneeled down beside her, gently placed his hand on Brandon's shoulder and said, "Hi, son."

His mom and dad were there in front of him, he was in a bed that wasn't his bed, in a room that wasn't his room. Something had happened, and he couldn't ask what, and he couldn't see much of anything. And he was tired.

He didn't remember anything. He hadn't been dreaming. There had been nothing, nothing but dark gray, and now there was this place, and this room and his mom and dad.

He wondered if he was dead, or if he wasn't anywhere. Maybe this was actually the dream.

Chapter 2

LIFE MOVES ON

Brandon's refusal to die fueled hope for his recovery, but every moment in the ICU, every beep and alarm of the machines provided a continual reminder that Brandon was still as close to death as he was to life.

Sue and Clint had quickly realized that the hospital's doctors and nurses spoke with a directness that occasionally bordered on blunt, and they accepted that this was about the need for honest dialog in a place where no degree of false hope could be tolerated. Clear communication, no matter how grave the content, was the standard for everyone working to keep Brandon alive.

Yet, the flow and exchange of information became laborious, emotionally and physically draining when communicating with Brandon himself. He had already undergone three major surgeries in the weeks before he truly became aware of his surroundings, including the insertion of a plate to hold his jaw together, and a tracheotomy to facilitate the ventilator needed to breathe for him. The trach, jaw plate, and a feeding tube made it physically impossible for him to speak, while drugs and medications altered and clouded his perceptions. When he was finally able to communicate, after more than three weeks in the ICU, it was in the most rudimentary fashion, with a most rudimentary tool.

Outside Brandon's room, a nurse brought Sue a letter board, a one-foot by two-foot rectangle board with letters and numbers arranged on it in several rows. She gave Sue a brief explanation of how it could be used to help Brandon communicate, and a few minutes later Sue sat next to Brandon's bed, holding the board in front of him.

"I'm going to move my finger past these rows of letters, and when I get to a row with a letter in it that you need to spell a word, you blink for me, okay honey? Then I'll move to a letter and we'll start spelling the words together. It'll be like a game, and I'll try and guess your word before you can finish spelling it. Ready?"

Brandon blinked, and Sue smiled at him, grateful for what was about to be the closest thing to a conversation since the day of the accident. She moved her finger down along the board's edge, but Brandon didn't blink until her finger touched the last row. Over the next few minutes Sue realized that if Brandon had been even a year younger, he probably wouldn't have been able to know how to spell enough words to have this conversation.

After Sue guessed his first word, 'what', she knew within the next few letters that his first question was, "what happened?"

She had known that this time would come, but hadn't committed to an answer, continuing to avoid thinking about any details from three weeks ago. But, as Brandon looked at her, it was time.

"You got shot, Brandon, in your face. It was an accident. You were hurt pretty bad…"

His eyes moved back to the board, and Sue was

momentarily grateful at not having to say more. The next word he guided her to was 'where'.

"Where? Where are we?"

He blinked.

"We're in a hospital, far away from our house, where lots of people are taking care of you."

Over the next few minutes he guided her to the simplest of words, but their emotional weight almost crushed Sue. By the time she got to the last word she did her best not to break down completely, but her eyes did fill with tears. She knew she had to answer and hated having to do it. Her finger lingered on the board at the end of *Am I going to be okay?*, and she composed herself before she looked at him.

"You're really hurt, baby, and you can't, you can't walk. Your legs won't work right, because of where you were shot. It was an accident Brandon, and it's going to take you a long time to get better, but your legs, and your arms, they won't move like they used to. I'm sorry, honey."

He looked at her for a long time, his face puffy, a plastic tube running into an opening in his neck, his eyes locked on his mom. Sue pointed to the board and he followed her finger as she moved it from letter to letter, spelling out 'I love you'.

He looked at her, blinked once, and moved his eyes back to the board. Sue ran her finger down the rows of letters, until he blinked his reply, 'me too,' then he closed his eyes and slept.

Brandon was transferred from the ICU to the rehabilitation ward just before the end of the month. Imminent danger had ebbed but complications could occur in an instant. Life was in upheaval. With the move to rehab came different doctors and staff. Dr. Robert Haining, the hospital's top juvenile rehab doctor, would work with Brandon and the family through more operations and treatments, restoring some stability to Brandon's life, a life now filled with a quadriplegic's special physiological, neurological, biological, and psychological situations.

Financially, Sue and Clint had given over their lives to the State of California's Medi-Cal program and California's Department of Health Care Services, which provides health coverage for people with low income and limited ability to pay for health coverage. For uninsured families and victims of trauma who lacked the coverage necessary to pay for the high cost of life-saving medical technology, expensive medications and long hospital stays, Medi-Cal picked up the tab, but not for free. Even patients with otherwise wide ranging insurance policies could find their coverage exhausted in serious trauma cases, depleted by the daily hospital costs, treatment by specialists, the cost of constant tests and monitoring, and all the associated costs of recovery and long-term rehabilitation. For a quadriplegic, the rehabilitation, equipment, and treatment costs continue for life.

Brandon's hospital bill had reached the $100,000 mark before he was out of the ICU.

Occasionally the worry about money would slip into Sue's thoughts, but it was so overwhelming to grasp, and her life so thoroughly focused on Brandon, that Sue could quickly bury them with a quick read of Brandon's chart, a chat with a nurse, a meeting with a doctor, or a letterboard conversation with Brandon.

"Hi mom."

They were his first words since the accident, the first words Sue had heard from her oldest son since she left to run errands six weeks ago. Along with the letterboard, Sue and Brandon had been able to add 'clicking' to the way they communicated. Brandon could make click sounds with his tongue, indicating things in the same way he had blinked to talk. It had added only an incremental improvement to their conversations, and was still tiring and frustrating.

There was a lot of work ahead, but finally having the tube removed from his throat was a big change.

"Hi honey. Makes me really happy to hear your voice. Really happy."

"Where's dad?"

She explained that Clint was at the house, then picked up the phone and dialed home. She held the phone next to Brandon's face and realized this was one of the things, the simplest of things, that Brandon would never be able to do for himself the rest of his life.

The phone rang at the house. Clint stopped widening the doorway to Brandon's small bedroom, one of a hundred tasks that needed to be completed before Brandon could come home. No one could tell them when that would happen, but Clint wasn't going to put it off. Plus, when he worked, stayed busy, he could have a few seconds in which he stopped thinking about the accident, and those moments stopped his anger at everything and everyone – Sue's brother John, Jerry, himself, and the world.

He picked up the phone. "Hello."

"Hi dad. It's me"

"Hey, son! Man, I am so happy to hear you say hi."

"What are you doing?"

"Fixing up your room for when you come home. It's gonna be different, bigger. How you feeling?"

"My throat hurts, but I'm okay."

Clint, an imposing, take-no-shit kind of guy, held the

phone away from his ear for a moment, humbled by the innocence of his small son. *My throat hurts, but I'm okay.*

"I love you son."

"I love you too, dad."

"I'll see you tomorrow, Okay? We all miss you. Tell your mom I want to talk to her."

"Hi," Sue said.

"I just heard from Toni there's a story in the paper that says the district attorney isn't going to charge us with anything. Not going to charge Jerry, either."

On her end, Sue turned away from Brandon so he couldn't see her face. She hadn't thought about it for the last couple of weeks, but there had been no contact from the police about what, if anything, would happen to any of them because of the accident. For a moment her head pounded as she felt herself swing between relief and anger.

"They didn't call to tell us? We have to find out because it's in the paper? What the hell!"

"I know. Damn it, I know."

"Where is Jerry right now?"

Clint still had trouble even mentioning Jerry's name. "I don't know. He's not here."

They said goodbye and Sue told Brandon she'd be back in a few minutes.

Down the elevator, outside, and a block away from the hospital entrance, Sue finally stopped walking, lit a cigarette, leaned her head against the building wall and sobbed.

A managing partner at the A&B law firm had reviewed Mr. Smith's information and created a file for the case. The first document in the folder was a note written to the other firm partners: "This is a humongous case."

The firm sent Clint and Sue a retainer letter. Clint had talked to Sue about his encounter with Mr. Smith at the hospital, and in part because there would be no cost to them, and in part because Sue didn't really care about anything other than Brandon and her family, she agreed to let the firm do "whatever."

The firm also wrote to the Mendocino Sheriff's department requesting the case files and inquiring about the Bryco gun. The department responded that no tests had been performed on the gun and that it could be picked up by the registered owner any time.

In their small, hospital provided apartment, when Smith called to talk about retrieving the gun, Sue exploded. "I don't want that damn gun! I don't want to see it, I don't give a goddamn about that thing. I never want to see it or any other gun for the rest of my life."

Clint was a little surprised at his own calm response. "I know, but the lawyers need it. I can't get it, they won't give it to me. You just have to go get it and you can give it right to that Smith guy."

It would be another four months before Sue, accompanied by Smith, made one of the most emotional, disturbing journeys of her life as she walked into the Mendocino Sheriff's headquarters, signed several releases, and was handed a weighty envelope, the contents of which had altered her future, the future of her family, and permanently changed every aspect of her little boy's existence.

She closed her eyes as she picked up the bag and held it out to Smith, who took it from her, and then he and Sue walked outside.

Smith would take the Bryco Model 38 back to the firm's San Francisco office, where it would remain in the firm's evidence safe for another six months.

Four months after the shooting Brandon was doing well enough to make some day trips to the zoo and nearby parks. The trips were important for everyone's emotional well being, but they were also a no-holds barred preview of the family's massive lifestyle changes. And as was typical of his attitude towards everyone and everything, it seemed to everyone that Brandon made the quickest adjustment. He was as engaged and joyful as any seven year-old boy at the zoo. He smiled and laughed, asked — rather than demanded or whined — "Can we see the monkeys?" and "Let's go look at the snakes!"

He was able to come home for the Thanksgiving holidays, had to be readmitted – another glimpse into the rest of his life — and was finally discharged in time for Christmas, facing a lifetime of challenges, medical care, and an environment transformed by his family to accommodate his needs at home and school.

That Christmas was an emotional rollercoaster for everyone, including Brandon. There were laughs and tears, mood swings from the joy of Brandon at home, alive, to the crushing sadness of his first paralyzed Christmas. The family spread Brandon's gifts around the small living room so he could see them. Sue's brother John and several close friends played Brandon's video games for him, sitting on either side of his wheelchair, taking turns 'being' Brandon, as Brandon himself watched and yelled encouragement.

Missing from the holidays was Jerry. In the almost eight months between Brandon's accident and his Christmas return, other incidents unrelated to the shooting finally caused an irreparable rift between Jerry and the family, and he moved out. It would be a decade before the family saw him again.

When Smith went with Sue to get the Bryco Model 38,

he also picked up several documents, including a memo confirming that the sheriff's department had not performed any tests on the gun. In February of '95, while the A & B firm researched Brandon's accident and prepared a potential lawsuit, Smith delivered the Bryco Model 38 to a firearms expert about an hour south of San Francisco. In mid-March the expert reported that in initial tests the gun would not accidentally discharge.

Two weeks later, just two days short of a year since the accident, the A&B firm filed a complaint against Bryco Arms, Jennings Firearms, Willits Pawn, and Jerry Morris, suing them for products liability and general negligence. This was a routine step, taken out of an abundance of caution to ensure that the client's potential rights would not be barred by the statute of limitations. Except for Brandon's parents, the defendants named in the complaint included all known links in the chain of possession of the gun. As theories of liability were developed and other defendants discovered, the complaint could be refined and amended.

By January, 1996, there were still doubts about the case. The A&B firm was one of the largest and most respected plaintiffs firms on the West Coast, and its size allowed it to attract and retain hundreds of potentially major cases. Brandon's case had significant damages potential, but it was also fraught with major liability hurdles.

The preliminary gun tests hadn't indicated a defect, and an overview of the case seemed to point to the simple conclusion that Jerry had accidentally shot Brandon. Research revealed that Bryco Arms had been sued many times before without success.

Two weeks later a second test on the gun found that it

would not "slamfire." A memo directed attorneys to "pull [the] case, we're getting out!"

A slamfire occurs when the firearm discharges as the user releases the slide and allows it to close, but the user hasn't pulled the trigger. Faulty design or manufacturing, poor quality parts, the wrong or faulty ammunition, wear and tear, and poor maintenance can cause or contribute to a slamfire. Absent a slamfire, it seemed almost certain that the accidental discharge had happened because the Bryco Model 38's trigger had been pulled.

There are multiple designs that actually fire a bullet from a gun, but all require the same general process: the trigger is pulled; a spring drives a firing pin into a primer loaded at the rear of a cartridge; the primer ignites the gunpowder; and a contained explosion fires the bullet out of the gun. In a semi-automatic pistol like the Bryco, as the bullet leaves the barrel a slide on the top of the barrel is forced rearward, uncovering an ejection port, where the empty shell casing is flipped out. As the slide returns to its starting position it pushes a new cartridge from the magazine inside the gun's handgrip into the firing chamber and resets the trigger, and the gun is ready to fire again.

The entire process happens in a fraction of a second.

As the summer of '96 came to an end and Clint finished his remodel of the trailer home to make the old living room area Brandon's bedroom, the A&B firm sent Sue and Clint a letter withdrawing from the case. Internally, a memo went to Smith directing him to return the Bryco Model 38 to the client. The precautionary complaint was voluntarily dismissed 'without prejudice,' a legal term designating that while no action was being taken against any defendants, the possibility of a later lawsuit was preserved.

Life moved on. Brandon would be the center of the family, and everyone did whatever was needed to give Brandon a life that would facilitate his going to and succeeding in school, and to helping him be as vibrant and socialized as any other boy his age.

Neither Clint nor Sue sought any kind of counseling in the accident's aftermath. Brandon became everyone's therapeutic outlet, their efforts on his behalf their only version of therapy. While many professionals would encourage counseling after such a trauma, Sue explained on more than one occasion that she was afraid if she talked about the accident, "I would start crying and not be able to stop."

Brandon's educational needs would be met through the school district's special needs department. He would have an aide with him every school day until he graduated from high school, and Juanita Joy, the district's special needs supervisor, would oversee every facet of his educational program. Like his family, Brandon also never received any specific counseling regarding his emotional well being after the accident, but the school district and community provided an enormous level of support, beyond any expectations.

Brandon was for the most part an upbeat, engaged, happy kid. He was popular and did well in school, but during the two years immediately after the accident he did, privately, have periods of depression, an overall sadness as opposed to a 'why me' lament.

Clint and Sue became his at-home caregivers, something Sue fought for, figuratively and literally.

Brandon would require lifelong care and assistance, and even a seemingly small miscue, mistake, or device malfunction could have grave consequences. Every hygienic and bodily function, nutritional need, and the daily use of medical devices required the presence of a professional caregiver. Sue and Clint, especially Sue, were adamant that they would take care of Brandon.

Quadriplegia can impact normal respiratory function and require the continuous use of a ventilator for breathing. The lack of functional, normal respiration also makes quadriplegics very susceptible to respiratory infections, which can advance to serious and life-threatening status quickly. Brandon had adequate lung function so he only used a ventilator when he slept. California's Medi-Cal representatives understood Sue's passion for her son's needs, but were just as adamant as Sue in what was acceptable: Sue would have to show that she could operate and maintain the ventilator, and meet the same requirements as any other caregiver before the state would accept Sue and Clint as Brandon's caregivers.

Sue mastered the ventilator's operation and upkeep, and started taking classes to become a certified nurse's assistant, eventually working part-time in assisted living facilities after Clint became Brandon's full-time caregiver.

In 1999, they came for Clint in the middle of the night, knocking hard on the door, startling everyone inside.

When Clint threw open the door he was confronted by four deputies.

"Clint Stansberry, you've violated your probation."

"I'm not on probation."

"Seems that you are. You've got to come with us. If it's a mix up or whatever you have to sort that out with your probation officer, but we can't do anything for you here..."

"Alright, but I don't have a probation officer, because I'm not on probation."

Many years before, Clint had an altercation with a distant relative that resulted in a misdemeanor charge, but he was not, and had never been, on probation for anything.

He spent the night at the station and when the morning shift came on someone discovered that, indeed, a mistake had been made. Clint was released without an explanation or any details of why the mistake had been made. He asked a deputy, "I want to make sure this isn't part of some record, so can we fix that now?

"No, we don't do that."

"You don't do what?"

"Fix your record."

"But I don't have a record and I want to make sure I don't get one because someone here made a mistake."

"It's not something I can do. You'll have to talk to someone in the probation department. Call them."

It made no sense to Clint, but by now he knew better than to try and discuss things with people who had no motivation or ability to change things. Over the next two weeks he made several phone calls to the sheriff's department, but no one would commit to ensuring his one-night detention would be cleared from any kind of record. Frustrated but determined, he went to the library, made a list of attorneys, and spent several early mornings searching for a lawyer who might be able to make some headway with the sheriff's department.

One local attorney returned his call, listened to Clint's situation and said she wasn't right for the problem, but "there is an attorney in Marin County you should call. His name is Richard Ruggieri. He's not afraid to sue the police…"

CHAPTER 3

THE LAWYER

By the time Clint called in late 1999, attorney Richard Ruggieri had several reputations, as a defense and a plaintiff's attorney. The reputations were warranted, though Ruggieri didn't necessarily welcome them.

Twenty years earlier, in his first job as an attorney only a few months out of law school, he began to get a reputation while working on and defending asbestos litigation. Within his first three years, he became the golden boy at his new firm when he had two pending lawsuits dismissed on summary judgment, motions that stopped major litigation against his firm's clients before the cases could come to trial.

He was also the attorney who volunteered to attend the deathbed depositions of asbestos litigation plaintiffs in his early career because, "it reminded me that there were real humans involved, that people were suffering."

He has a smooth, unsettling ability to establish a respectful, easy-going rapport with judges, witnesses and juries, even as he relentlessly peels away layers of inconsistency and deception, whether in motions, depositions or in trial. His ability to know when to be humorous, colloquial, self-deprecating or hard-assed, at just the right time, are traits that can't be taught in law school or wholly gained by experience. Many attorneys possess some of these traits, but few have all. Good litigation attorneys are either blessed with them or not, like a good shortstop's reflexes or a mathematician's ease with numbers.

He's just under six-foot-two, with a neatly trimmed beard that he's had for thirty years. He is described as "wickedly funny" by his wife, Edith, but when he works, his face is the mask of his profession, serious but not quite stern, and his eyebrows and forehead work in tandem to display unmistakable expressions of curiosity, disbelief, skepticism or anger. His eyes lock on you in conversation, or as you testify, in a way that makes you understand he is truly listening to every word, and if there's something amiss with what you are saying, he'll be seeking clarification.

Growing up in the hot, agricultural community of Modesto, California, an hour east of San Francisco, Ruggieri had no early aspirations to be an attorney, and through high school had no particular aspirations at all. Although his father, Frank, was an attorney and a county supervisor, Ruggieri didn't feel the need to follow his father's lead, and his father neither encouraged nor discouraged him. What he did instill in his son was "the now obsolete notion that being an attorney was an honorable profession, first and foremost an officer of the court and a fiduciary, sworn to place clients' interests above my own and to be scrupulously honest."

A self-described "gearhead," Ruggieri's main interests through high school and college were cars and construction, explored in high school shop classes, off-school employment in an auto repair shop, and with a residential electrician. "I always had a curiosity and appreciation for mechanical things. We were never exposed to handguns growing up, but I did shoot shotguns and a .22 rifle at cans and bottles, though I don't think I ever hit one."

He completed two majors and graduated magna cum laude from Cal State University at Stanislaus, but didn't even make the decision to go to law school until his senior year, taking the LSAT (Law School Aptitude Test) almost on a whim. Scoring unexpectedly high, he applied to multiple law schools and was accepted by most, "but I chose to attend UC Berkeley's prestigious Boalt Hall School of Law (now Berkeley Law), largely because it started later than the others." He moved to Berkeley, selling his vintage 1956 Ford Thunderbird to pay for his first year costs. "I worked flat-out my first year, because I was surrounded by graduates of big name universities, and was afraid that I was at serious risk of flunking out." While most of his classmates sought summer jobs with law firms, Ruggieri, doubtful of his prospects and needing to finance the next school year, took a job driving a beer truck in Oakland.

By the end of that summer, though, first year grades came out and Ruggieri found that he was near the top of his class. "After that I relaxed quite a bit and started thinking I might graduate."

Many law school students have a pre-conceived notion of why they are there and what they will eventually accomplish as lawyers, usually something along the lines of making things right and fighting for those who have been somehow wronged. Those early notions are dispelled when students discover how the legal process actually works. "When you first go to law school, everyone starts out wanting to right wrongs," says Ruggieri. "But law school changes your perception, from 'did someone get screwed' to 'did someone break the law.'"

"Law school taught me a new and disciplined way of thinking. And, perhaps consistent with my mechanical talents, I found that I was good at distilling a mountain of facts to those few with legal significance. But, at no time during the three years of law school did I have any idea of what being a lawyer meant on a day to day basis."

The legal profession is increasingly specialized, and many law school graduates have a preference for a particular area when they graduate, "but when I graduated and passed the Bar exam, I still knew nothing about being an attorney, I was flat broke, and needed a job. I took the first legal job that I was offered."

In that same year, 1979, what would soon become the largest mass tort litigation in history was still in its infancy. Ruggieri was a junior attorney, earning $1,000 month, in an Oakland law firm that needed help handling approximately seventy-five asbestos injury cases. Three years later, the firm would have over 3,000 cases. The firm had an insurance-defense practice: plaintiffs firms filed lawsuits on behalf of persons claiming asbestos related injuries; the asbestos companies they sued turned the lawsuits over to their insurance companies; and the insurance companies hired insurance-defense law firms, like the one where Ruggieri worked, to fight the lawsuits on behalf of their insureds, the asbestos companies.

"It was not the type of law practice that drives anyone to attend law school," but this random first employment opportunity quickly provided Ruggieri with the most relevant and important legal lessons he ever received.

"They said there would be some other stuff, but 99% of the work was asbestos litigation. I asked 'what's that?', they said, 'you'll find out.' I didn't know anything about the physical problems associated with asbestos."

There is a well-known understanding amongst seasoned attorneys: first year associates (which is what non-partner attorneys are called in a law firm) don't know anything.

It's an interesting phenomenon, as true as it is well known. People spend tens of thousands of dollars to get a law degree and, when they graduate, most are thankful for the opportunity to work extraordinary hours performing sometimes menial but necessary tasks, so that they can learn what it truly takes to practice law, so that they can one day look back and realize that, indeed, they knew nothing about their profession when they got their law degree.

"The first thing I learned was that the only training was to watch, listen, and think about what to do and how to do it. I read the code of civil procedure, civil code, and evidence code, cover to cover at night. During the day I read papers and motions filed by other law firms and attorneys, digested countless medical records, discussed cases with expert witnesses, and attended hundreds of depositions."

The consequences of workers' prolonged exposure to more than a half-century's use of asbestos, in everything from furnaces and boilers to Linoleum and building insulation, became clear in the late 1970s. Inhaled asbestos fibers wreaked havoc with the lining of the lungs, remaining essentially dormant and inconsequential for years, but eventually causing a deadly form of cancer called mesothelioma.

"The second thing I learned was the culture of an insurance defense office. It was no place for a bleeding heart. Many asbestos companies had been aware of the dangers since the 1950s, before many of the gravely ill were exposed. Representing 'bad guy' clients required building emotional callouses, and that can threaten your sense of humanity.

"I started volunteering to attend the depositions of dying plaintiffs, which usually happened in hospital rooms, with a grieving spouse at the bedside."

As the asbestos litigation grew to a huge scale, the shear volumes of paper, reproduction tasks, and filing of ream-sized documents produced by this kind of litigation, were tasks for which a new attorney was perfectly suited.

It is also the kind of environment that can swallow an attorney for an entire career. Whatever else Ruggieri was willing to accept as a freshman attorney, he would not be buried under piles of motions and filings. It's necessary, but it can also be very limiting and isolating.

"It's easy to forget certain things as a young lawyer in that kind of situation, because you're doing office work, you're sending and answering interrogatories (questions that require answers from the other side of a case), and, if you're working on big cases, you could easily be doing that for the first twenty years of your career. People forget that there are real human beings involved."

"I met a lot of defense assholes, and I didn't want to become one. I could look around at other lawyers and see how easy it was to forget that there's a person lying there, in an oxygen mask, gasping for air, and his wife is writing his deposition answers because he can't lift his arm anymore, and he's trying to answer questions about things that happened decades before and these other lawyers are smirking when the guy makes a mistake, and I'm thinking, give the guy a fucking break."

"That's what I got when I went to those depositions, the wife sitting there crying, her husband dying right in front of me, and I have to ask a question like, 'You don't remember using my client's asbestos products, do you?'

"The worst asbestos-related injuries were very aggressive cancers diagnosed decades after asbestos exposure, and they'd often be terminal within six months of that diagnosis. I understood that litigation isn't just the game played by fake whiplash claimants or posturing business competitors. People suffer real and unbearable pain, and sometimes their only chance is a lawsuit, and their only hope is a lawyer."

He worked almost exclusively on the asbestos cases until he left to to take an associate attorney job in the San Francisco office of a massive, international insurance defense firm. The firm's attorneys represented a wide variety of well known companies and governmental agencies in a spectrum of lawsuits.

"I was a young attorney ready for trial experience, which I'd never gotten in the first firm. My new firm threw me into a products liability trial my first day."

The cases were huge, and although assigned to senior partners, Ruggieri was tasked with all phases of trial preparation.

"Many of the cases were defective product claims, and I spent a lot of time working with the experts we hired to evaluate the product and the failure. That was the best part, because I'm learning metallurgy one day, aircraft mechanics the next, then accident reconstruction, motorcycle failure, intersection design, milling machine safeties, things that all went right to the core of my own curiosities.

"Most of the cases settled before trial, but they all had to be prepared as if they were going to trial. It was as invaluable an experience as it was fun."

He worked hard and he worked smart. He also became

aware that there were poorly prepared and occasionally incompetent attorneys. He achieved a newly found confidence in his legal abilities. "I liked finding out that my instincts were right."

"Plaintiffs attorneys had some very strange ideas. Many would accuse the insurance companies of trying to stall the case so that the insurance company could earn more interest on its money before it had to pay the funds out to the plaintiff, but I learned it was just the opposite — the insurance companies wanted these cases settled, and at the earliest possible time."

It was in this firm that Ruggieri first experienced massive personal injury cases. He came to be assigned what were called "death or worse" cases. "Quadriplegia or brain damage were 'worse' from the insurance company viewpoint. Those cases involved lifelong full-time medical expenses and wage loss, in amounts that far exceeded the costs required to resolve most death lawsuits."

"Even cases in which it was very unlikely the plaintiff would prevail, those were ticking time bombs, because you never knew what a jury might do, and there could be tens of millions of dollars at risk." Insurance companies don't like uncertainty; they have to set future premiums based on past losses. "It was inconceivable that we would allow a quadriplegia case to go to trial without a significant and early attempt to settle for a known sum. It just wasn't good business, and insurance companies are all about business."

Quadriplegia, often shortened to 'quad' within insurance defense firms, is the commonly used term to describe someone paralyzed from the neck down. Someone in this condition may retain some ability to move an arm or their shoulders in a very limited fashion, but the paralysis is total and always permanent. Total paralysis impacts the entire physiology, every voluntary and involuntary bodily function. As an injury and long-term illness, its impact on the injured person, their families, and the healthcare industry are substantial, and it reaches into the very future of the paralyzed person, significantly shortening their lifespan.

Within the first few months at his new firm, Ruggieri was given a caseload that included two quad cases, in part because of his experience with asbestos-related defense work. The cases were in their early stages and Ruggieri had the usual tasks assigned to young attorneys, writing analysis and reports for the insurance clients, and preparing preliminary motions and briefs. As he read through the facts and briefs for both cases, he thought, *I can get these dismissed on summary judgment.*

A 'motion for summary judgment' is a request to dismiss a lawsuit without trial, either because it is baseless under the law or completely unsupported by any facts. It is an extreme and disfavored remedy, as it deprives a party of the right to have their case decided after a full trial.

Ruggieri took his idea for a summary judgment motion to the senior partner who supervised his work (every associate's work is always reviewed by a more senior attorney or firm partner), and the response was quick and emphatic.

No!

The delicate, seasoned strategy for trying a quadriplegia case was too important to let a young attorney try something that probably wouldn't succeed, would cost extra time and money, and, because quadriplegia cases were rarely tossed out on summary judgment, might look like a callous or even desperate ploy by the defense team.

Ruggieri dutifully returned to his work, but he

reviewed the cases again, and he was sure he was right. So, without any intended disrespect towards his superiors, he filed motions for summary judgment anyway, for both cases.

Both motions were granted.

He hadn't chosen to be a rebel, and he didn't think of himself as a hotshot attorney, he simply saw a legal weakness in the cases and judged that there was a good chance for a summary judgment ruling. He had won, and that muted any adverse reaction from the partners about doing something he had been told not to do. Ruggieri knew that if the rulings had gone the other way he might have been looking for a new job. Instead, he became the golden boy, the go-to kid for tough, emotionally charged cases.

In 1983, as Ruggieri walked past the office of one of the firm's partners, he heard, "Hey, Ruggieri, you're from Modesto, right? Take a look at this file and get ready for a meeting next week."

It was a life changing case.

A twelve-year-old boy had suffered a brain injury while riding his bike after he collided with an automobile at an intersection in Modesto, California. The driver and the city were sued, and the city's insurance carrier hired Ruggieri's firm to defend the city. The liability law favored the city, but the extent of the boy's injuries and potential financial recovery were off the charts.

The impact of boy's head on the pavement and resultant brain stem swelling had left him with locked-in syndrome.

"Our expert confirmed that the boy's thought processes were fine, but his body was so completely paralyzed that he couldn't breathe without a full time ventilator. The only movement he had was blinking one eye, and the condition was permanent."

The pressure on Ruggieri was enormous. This was the biggest personal injury damages case most attorneys would ever encounter. The accident and lawsuit were widely publicized. The local law firm representing the injured boy was working full time on the case and the client was Ruggieri's home town, where his father still had his law practice.

The insurance company was a major firm client, and the New York office had been assured that the case was receiving Ruggieri's full time attention, even as he was required to continue to carry his normal, full caseload. Both sides had retained dozens of experts, multiple motions were filed, and multiple lower court rulings were reviewed by the Court of Appeals. Two years of constant legal warfare had elapsed as the case slowly progressed to trial.

Ruggieri handled all phases of the case, including the deposition of the boy.

The boy's mother, father, the boy's attorney, and caregiver were there, as were attorneys for other defendants, and a court reporter.

"We were in his bedroom at home, which had been converted into a hospital room, and he was lying on the bed completely motionless, with a ventilator breathing for him, keeping him alive."

"The boy's parents were both medical professionals, but they could barely keep it together. We took considerable time agreeing on a procedure where the boy would only be asked yes-no questions and would respond by blinking either once or twice, and the first question he was asked was 'Would you please state your name for the record?' That screw-up released some of the tension, but the whole thing was brutal. He didn't remember anything about the accident and he clearly couldn't move, and he didn't know why. All I could think about was the movie Johnny Got His Gun, about a gravely wounded WWI veteran screaming in his head, because he's unable to speak, that he was a prisoner in his own body."

Everything changed a month before trial

Ruggieri was in the boy's attorney's office, attending a deposition about the case, when the attorney came in and interrupted, obviously upset. "We went into the hallway and he told me the boy had gone brain-dead after his ventilator tube clogged with mucus when the nurse stepped out for a cigarette. I was stunned. I literally couldn't think. This couldn't happen, the boy and his family didn't deserve this.

"I had absolutely nothing to do with his death and had done nothing to delay the trial, but I immediately felt guilt, screaming at myself for fighting the case so hard and long. Then I felt worse because I realized what a 'good' development this was for my client – the damages potential of the death case was only a tiny fraction of the personal injury case, and would be offset by the settlements already received from other defendants.

"I was a mess."

The boy was being kept alive on the ventilator, without brain function, "and the plaintiff's attorney wanted to negotiate now."

"I couldn't even talk to him, but I sorted out later that the guy could barely talk himself. He was a very decent guy, and he was caught in a jam. The family didn't want to keep their brain-dead child alive by a machine, and the attorney didn't want that either, but the *threat* of doing so was the only thing that gave the case any continuing settlement value."

Before the week was out, the family accepted a nominal settlement from the insurance company, the lawsuit was dismissed, the ventilator was disconnected and the boy received a funeral. "His family was devastated, the city was devastated, the attorneys were devastated."

"The insurance company was happy. It claimed a major victory for a very important client."

He left the firm less than a year later, taking with him a confidence that he knew how to handle the biggest and most difficult personal injury cases. He also carried painful memories, sorrows, questions and recriminations that would stay with him for life.

Over the next ten years, Ruggieri continued to practice personal injury defense with a partner in a two-attorney firm in San Rafael. There were big and little cases, nothing dramatic, but one particular client's legal trouble would expose Ruggieri to something with which he was barely familiar, but would loom much larger a few years later.

Their client got himself into some legal trouble. He was an avid gun collector and a gun club member, and part of the resolution of his trouble was that he could no longer own firearms.

"I cut a deal allowing him to donate most of his collection to his gun club instead of being destroyed. He was very grateful but had no money to pay us, so he gave me two handguns in a box. I had never shot a handgun, and didn't want them, so I offered them to my partner, but he didn't want them either. He had an idea, though, that we take them at lunchtime to a local indoor shooting range and give them a try."

They bought ammunition and targets at the range, were given ear and eye protection, and there were also a wide range of pistols that could be rented. "When I walked in I had no idea what the different levers and buttons were, or even how to load the guns. We kinda got carried away though, and when we left a few hours later, we had both shot various revolvers, Glocks, and Berettas, in different calibers. I learned that, at least for the inexperienced user, handguns, and especially semiautomatics, could be complicated and scary, while still mechanically impressive.

"We put the guns back in the box and stored it, and never took them out again."

In 1998, Ruggieri's partner decided to move his practice to San Francisco and Ruggieri remained in San Rafael, twenty minutes north of the city, moving into a smaller office across the hall and, for the first time, taking up a plaintiffs practice.

"It felt like something I should have done right out of law school. "

Doing good defense work had allowed him to grow as a lawyer, but now he discovered a passion for helping people in need. The change also allowed him to see that not all of the criticism of insurance companies and defense attorneys was unfounded. There was indeed a dark side, and he was reminded of the saying, "just because I'm paranoid doesn't mean they aren't out to get me.

"For years and years I staunchly defended insurance companies and insurance defense attorneys. Then I switched sides and I was in for a very rude awakening. My vantage point had been very limited. I correctly and staunchly defended the companies and attorneys I worked with, but, eventually, I got to know that there were other attorneys out there who didn't work the way I did, or think the way I did. Maybe it was because I had never been involved with them, or I was seeing them for the first time from the other side. There are a lot of fuck-heads out there, and there are a lot of really bad insurance companies going out of their way to avoid paying, even when it's a legitimate claim, using every dirty trick in the book, things I never did.

"A good litigator has to have a sense of humanity. You're dealing with people's lives, you have to have a sense of humanity, be completely honest, work hard and put your clients' interest completely in front of your own."

In March 2000, Ruggieri listened to messages on his voicemail. "Plaintiffs attorneys get lots of calls. People who don't even know what a plaintiff is, they feel that they've been wronged and they just need an attorney, and you get a lot of calls from people who are, well, they're just nuts, to be honest. You get even more calls, though, from people who actually have a legitimate beef, but don't have a hope in the world because legally, they don't have a case."

Clint Stansberry, from Willits, California, several hours north of San Rafael, had left a third message. He "needed to find a lawyer because he wanted to sue the police.

"That's a very common sort of message, one that I would not normally return. But he'd left three, so I picked up the phone and dialed his number."

Their first phone conversation wasn't very long. Clint explained what happened and gave him the background. Ruggieri would look into it and get back to him.

What Ruggieri found was a pattern. What had happened to Clint had happened to others. For some reason the county was ignoring the law specifically enacted to prevent a situation like Clint's. California law required that the word "arrest" be changed to "detention" on any record created when someone initially arrested is released without charges. The law also required a notice be provided to anyone in that situation, essentially, an official note that clarifies for any potential employer that while the person was detained there was no criminal charge.

Clint had unknowingly brought Ruggieri a civil rights case that had potential to become a class action suit. Over the next several months, Ruggieri built and presented Clint's case and settlement demands to the county. There were several meetings with Clint in Ruggieri's office and in Mendocino County, and during one of those meetings Clint first mentioned Brandon, an off-hand remark as the two men talked about the county's settlement offer.

"Yeah, I've had to deal with attorneys before."

"Why?"

"Because of what happened with my son, Brandon. He's a quadriplegic. He was accidentally shot by a friend of ours, about six years ago."

Clint described the accident and how everyone's lives had drastically changed, and how the "lawyer" had talked to him at the hospital.

"What firm?"

"A&B, in San Francisco."

Based on Clint's description, Ruggieri's initial reactions to Brandon's accident were "that it didn't suggest a viable lawsuit, and A&B firm dropping the case confirmed that."

"It did get my interest, because any lawyer, certainly any personal injury lawyer, would be interested, but at first I just kind of mentally filed it away."

An accident that causes quadriplegia "is the biggest kind of case there is."

Paralysis resulting from an accident or what should be an avoidable situation has 'big case' potential, legally and financially, but quad cases are especially significant. Any paralysis is life altering, but quadriplegia prevents someone from ever making an independent living.

Every Bay Area attorney knew of the A&B firm. Ruggieri thought, *if they say you don't have a case, you probably don't have a case*. The firm's reputation was solid. "If that firm takes a case, you take it a lot more seriously [if you're on the other side]." A&B was set up for big cases. Big cases require big resources, an infrastructure to manage, provide, and maintain everything from hundreds of filings and associated paperwork, to working with experts, taking multiple depositions, and the sheer volume of work involved in cases that can take years to complete.

A few weeks after first hearing about Brandon, Ruggieri went to the trailer home for a final meeting with Clint.

Brandon, then thirteen, was lying in bed with his headphones on, listening to a CD. Ruggieri waited in the doorway as Clint walked to the side of Brandon's hospital bed, lifted off the headphones and said, "Brandon, this is Rich."

"Hi Brandon."

"Hey."

"Nice to meet you."

"You too."

As Ruggieri was leaving, he told Clint he would "look into Bryco and its guns," but, for now, "I don't think there's anything I can do."

Ruggieri's practice was doing well and growing, with several wins and favorable settlements. There was no pressure to take on a case that at first seemed not just a long shot, but a case declined by one of the area's reigning plaintiffs firm.

"But it kept popping up in my head. I like mechanical challenges, I know products liability, and Brandon seemed like a nice kid. I liked him. I kept asking myself what if A&B missed something? In a way, I guess I was just arrogant enough to think I might find something they had overlooked."

He didn't have a specific stance regarding gun ownership or gun control. He had the general working awareness of guns, had that .22 rifle as a boy, and had taken those guns to the range.

"I was intrigued, and I had a healthy respect for those guns." His true appreciation wasn't for their dangerous power as much for their design and function. "The tolerances and precision of guns are impressive. I appreciate things like that."

Ruggieri continued to think about the accident. In Clint's brief description of the accident, the family friend was trying to unload the gun when it went off and insisted he hadn't pulled the trigger. Ruggieri had assumed the gun's safety was on, and wondered *if that was so, how could the gun have gone off?*

As Clint's case wrapped up, "whenever I had a few minutes of downtime, I looked for information on the Web about Bryco, and the Model 38 in particular."

As users knew it in the year 2000, the Web was barely six years old, far from the ubiquitous day-to-day presence it would eventually become. User-friendly sites of organized data were rare. Forums and group discussions about shared interests occurred on what were known as electronic bulletin boards, and online shopping of any sort of scale was embryonic.

Bryco was either one of the largest U.S. manufacturers

of semi-automatic handguns (in 1991, according to ATF statistics, Bryco led all other U.S. manufacturers in pistol production) or it had ceased to exist. It had produced different models over the years, but, early on, Ruggieri found "a lot of conflicting info about Bryco as a company, things that were misleading or simply wrong, nothing that helped me determine much of anything about them, and a lot things like a site that stated "*... Jenning's/Bryco Arms is now out of business, due mainly to new California laws...*"

With Sue and Clint's permission he obtained and reviewed the police reports on the accident, and contacted the A&B firm to arrange a time he could pick-up the gun. These were routine but critical first steps for any product liability case.

"The location of the gun is unknown..."

Ruggieri read the letter again, focusing on the word for which he hadn't been entirely unprepared, but that he couldn't easily accept: *unknown.*

The letter was the second from A&B. The first, from a partner who had worked on Brandon's case, had come a little over a week after Ruggieri's request for the gun. The gun should have been in the firm's evidence safe; it was not. The firm was searching for it, but there was a complication — Mr. Smith was dead, and he had been the last person to have the gun.

When A&B had decided to drop the case, Mr. Smith had been directed to pick up the Bryco from the gun testing facility, which he did. Shortly after, he was killed in a car accident.

This letter, sent a few weeks after the first, explained how the firm had reviewed the accident (nothing in any of the California Highway Patrol accident reports referred to a gun), interviewed Smith's family, and conducted a thorough search, but Smith's family and friends stated they hadn't seen the gun and didn't possess it.

Over the course of that summer Ruggieri implored A&B to continue its investigation and search. By July, A&B informed Ruggieri that while the firm understood the importance of the missing gun, it had exhausted all possibilities, the circumstances were unique and tragic, but there was nothing more to be done.

The Law Offices of Richard Ruggieri

Mr. Clint Stansberry & Mrs. Susan Stansberry

Dear Clients:

As you know, I previously looked into whether I would be able to do anything for your son Brandon. I contacted the A&B firm, reviewed their file, and tried unsuccessfully to find the gun...

By mid-August, Ruggieri hadn't found anything that merited much more serious work on Brandon's potential case, and, objectively, not enough to commit more time and money. A&B had probably already invested tens-of-thousands of dollars in attorney time, admin support, and gun tests before they decided to stop. Money and time are the realities by which every law firm lives or dies. Larger firms can more easily, but not always less painfully, absorb costs and expenses than can smaller firms and sole practitioners.

...I just wanted to tell you formally that I am not going to be able to help with Brandon's case...

Ruggieri's letter to Sue and Clint was a practical and self-protection necessity. Practical, because he hadn't uncovered anything to this point upon which he could build a case, and self-protective because although he wasn't ready to stop looking for information, he didn't want to give the family false hope or expectations, especially now that the gun itself had disappeared.

...Brandon is, however, still a minor, and the statute of limitations does not expire until his eighteenth birthday...it may be that some other attorney will be able to be of assistance either now or in the future...

The lost gun was a huge factor. How could you sue for a defective gun if that gun was 'lost'? Without it, its condition can't be proven, and not actually having it and not being able to explain its absence is suspicious. Moving forward with a case under the gun-is-lost circumstances would require proving that *all the guns of this model are defective,* rather than that single gun.

Ruggieri also had a serious administrative concern. Tasks like filing and scheduling might sound trivial, but in the context of what a lawsuit can become, the collecting, assembling, storing and retrieving documents, research, reports, notices, and schedules are all critical, and especially daunting for a sole proprietor. Misplaced or lost documents, a missed hearing, or missed filing deadline can put an entire case and all the time and expense of its associated work in jeopardy. Such tasks and their importance are the reasons that junior associates, paralegals, and good legal secretaries were always in demand. In a large firm, different individuals would have responsibility for scheduling (known as calendaring), filing, legal research, client contact, pre-trial court appearances, investigation, and trial.

Ruggieri had none of those resources.

Very few victims of horrific accidents can pay an attorney's hourly fees. Any lawsuit that would evolve from Brandon's accident would have to move forward on a contingency, all time and costs absorbed by a law firm, without guarantee of any renumeration at the end, even with a favorable judgment. Managing and financing depositions, tracking and being able to locate, record, and prepare evidence — which could encompass thousands of items and documents, from photos, to videos, reports, records, product models, tests, and testimony — for what could be years, are fundamental elements of litigation. A complex, drawn out, contentious lawsuit could easily break the financial back of a small firm.

Coming out on the wrong end of such a lawsuit could be professionally and personally devastating.

A decision to take Brandon as a client had to first consider whether Brandon had a viable case, and whether an attorney could manage the case and wrangle what could be such a massive, long-term task.

...I am sorry that I couldn't come up with anything to help.

For Sue and Clint, Ruggieri's letter was disappointing, but not overly so. With no expectations, their life's focus continued to be keeping Brandon alive, well, engaged with life and happy.

The letter meant nothing at all to Brandon. "I wasn't ever really aware of what Rich was doing then. I just knew him as a nice guy who did some something for my dad, and I didn't really know or understand what a lawyer did anyway. My school work was what I focused on, and my friends and stuff."

The family's daily life had improved slightly since the accident. They still lived in the single-wide, but Clint had built out more space; they had purchased a pre-owned van with a ramp for Brandon's wheelchair; Rocky and Trish were healthy and growing up; Sue had passed her certification and was working part-time as a CNA; and Clint was Brandon's full-time caregiver.

Even at the best of times, however, Sue and Clint

could never take Brandon's health for granted. Between 1994 and 2000, he had been airlifted to Oakland Children's hospital five times, his condition too fragile and problems too advanced for treatment in the community's smaller hospital. Each episode put a strain on the family and Sue was thankful for the support of her mom and close friends, all coming together to help. "We even got to become friends with Vivian, one of the paramedics who'd helped save Brandon and who came to get him for some of those flights."

Life was day to day, and Brandon was alive.

Despite his August letter to the family, Ruggieri hadn't really stopped looking for anything that might offer even the slightest glimmer of clarity on Bryco or the Model 38. Fall, winter, the Christmas holidays and New Year would go by before he would finally amass enough reliable research to believe "there might be something to the case."

Chapter 4

THE GUN

For ten months, Ruggieri researched and gathered information from discussion boards about Bryco guns, tracked the names of people associated with Bryco Arms, accessed public corporate records, and looked for snippets on the company, its guns and its owners. He found schematics, scans, and pictures, and began to understand that Bryco handguns were prevalent and well-known to many gun users, and, due to the preponderance of Bryco and Jennings Firearms guns connected to crimes, to law enforcement. User discussions and debates centered on whether Bryco guns were low-quality and dangerous, or good, inexpensive firearms.

As he sought information on the Model 38, he also came across a similar Bryco called the J-22, with a very confusing lineage, because it seemed to have been manufactured by one, two, three, or four companies: Jennings Firearms, a company called Calwestco, a company called B.L. Jennings, and/or Bryco Arms.

The J-22 fired a smaller caliber bullet, a .22 caliber instead of the more powerful .380 caliber fired by the Model 38. The J-22 seemed to have two different kinds of safeties, but there was nothing that indicated why or when a change was made, or whether a similar change had been made to the Model 38.

Ruggieri had lots of questions and no real answers. "Could you buy the gun and 'choose' one safety over the other? Was one kind of safety newer than the other? If there were different models of the gun, wouldn't there be different model names? If there had been a change, wouldn't Bryco have let its customers know?"

All the current models of Bryco pistols had the same kind of safety, so perhaps the differences meant nothing. Bryco pistols all had a mechanical safety, operated by a small switch on the pistol's left side, centered above the grip and just under the bottom of the slide, and that moved up and down. But a firm on the East Coast had tested a J-22 for a police department, and the firm's report included a copy of the J-22 instruction sheet, which described its safety as moving forward and back. These kind of details weren't part of the online discussions, and other than what direction the safety switch moved, there was nothing to suggest a change in the safety's operation.

Ruggieri had called Sue and Clint a few times since his "...not going to be able to help..." letter, both to check-in and ask about Brandon, and to reinforce "that there was't anything new or encouraging to talk about."

Questions, contradictions, and a controversial gun were very little to show for Ruggieri's months of preliminary investigation. The case, if indeed there was a case at all, presented an unintentional firing by an inexperienced user, who either did or didn't touch the trigger of a pistol that had been lost, a pistol that had been made by one or more of several companies, and had one kind of safety or another.

The friend, the babysitter, was trying to unload the pistol, mistakenly thought that the magazine had been removed and was retracting the slide to check for a cartridge in the chamber. The pistol fired when the slide slipped, but testing for slam-fire was negative. Operator error seemed apparent.

The question was, did the pistol contribute in any meaningful way?

Ruggieri himself had not even seen an actual Model 38. It was time to find one, hold it in his hand and evaluate it himself.

He pulled out the phone book and called a local gun store, asked specifically for a Bryco Model 38. The first store didn't have one. He called another store, and another. He called gun stores in San Francisco, then in the East Bay. Over the course of almost a week he called dozens of gun stores all over Northern California; none had a Model 38 in stock or for sale, and most responses included being asked, "why would you want one?"

He expanded his search, using the Web to find gun stores in an ever expanding circle that stretched twenty, forty, sixty miles from the Bay Area.

Nothing. It was almost as if every Model 38 had disappeared from Northern California.

He decided to drive to where the first domino of the tragedy had fallen, a place he had by now passed a half-dozen times on his trips to Willits. If he was lucky, he might even pick up a new Model 38 there.

Walt and his wife, now in their sixties, had owned Willits Pawn for over twenty years. It was still in its original location, on Main street just north of downtown, a small retail space crowded with everything from knives to guitars, dishes to jewelry, a store full of items waiting for their owners to return. Much of what was pawned would remain, to be sold eventually to someone looking for a bargain, or who couldn't afford the retail price, or someone looking for something that couldn't be found in just any store.

Like most pawnshops, however, there were also a few new items for sale, and that included guns.

It was a place Ruggieri had been destined to visit if he took the case, because if there was more to this case than Morris' negligence, any lawsuit would have to include "every link in the gun's chain of possession," the literal and figurative hands through which the gun had passed, from its assembly at the Bryco factory to Morris' hands. If there was a lawsuit, it would obviously start with Bryco, and at the end of the chain would be Clint, Sue, John and Jerry Morris. But between Bryco and the family there was Willits Pawn, and possibly others.

Ruggieri walked in to the small store and was immediately struck by the amount of stuff hanging, standing, stacked, and displayed everywhere. In the glass cabinet not far from the front door were several new handguns, but no Brycos.

Walt, who had sold Sue the gun, was behind the counter, as he had been almost every week for decades.

"Help you find something?"

"I'm looking for a particular handgun, a Bryco Model 38."

"Haven't had any for a while. Sorry. Think they might've stopped making them."

Ruggieri handed Walt his card. "I'm doing some research for Sue and Clint Stansberry, looking into their son's accident."

"Oh, yeah, Suzy. Yeah, read about her boy's accident, it was in the paper." Walt remained cordial, but now he became more guarded, more quiet as Ruggieri looked around.

"Do you remember selling her that gun, the Bryco Model 38?"

"I do, yes, I do. Cost me thirty dollars, brand new. Came with a lifetime guarantee. We had a couple of those, I think."

A row of new trigger locks in plastic packaging hung on the wall behind the counter, off to one side.

"Did they buy a trigger lock?"

"Nope. They're a good idea, I think. Keeps 'em safe."

"Pretty impressive amount of stuff in here. And you do have a few new guns, rifles too. Sell many handguns?"

"Every now and then. Not a bunch at all, though, really. Not something we specialize in, obviously, wouldn't really say we're in the gun business, y'know?"

"Any chance you'll be getting in any Brycos soon? Any on order?"

"No. Got these guns here, these rifles, that's it."

Ruggieri made small talk, said he wasn't really interested in any other guns. The conversation was civil, cordial, Ruggieri walked around the store for a few minutes, asked a few more questions, nothing intrusive, then said goodbye and left.

He had more information; he still didn't have the gun.

When he finally found a Model 38, it wasn't where he expected, and explained why his search had taken so long. He had been looking for it in gun stores, and while Willits Pawn didn't have any, he widened his search to other pawn shops.

Gun stores had seemed like the logical place to find a new gun. Even his visit to Willits Pawn hadn't suggested that he wouldn't find a Model 38 in a gun store. Now, after so many responses from gun store clerks — "...Why would you want that gun?..." — he now understood that the majority of Model 38's on the market were distributed through pawn shops.

He purchased the Model 38 and, like anyone who purchases a new gun in California, picked it up after the state's required waiting period. Back in his office he opened the box, held the gun, and, "the moment I had my hand on it and worked it, I thought, this is fucked, this is wrong."

It was his first realization that to move the slide, to look inside the firing chamber, he had to move the safety to fire.

It was an inexpensive gun and, like many products inexpensively manufactured, it adequately performed its most basic functions but lacked the operational smoothness and well-crafted feel of guns Ruggieri had handled before. The safety was a small tab that moved up and down — not back and forth — from 'safe to fire'. The tiny switch was the gun's only safety. Many guns have only one safety, but there are others that have a system of safeties, such as on the Colt .45 semi-auto, which has a safe/fire switch, a grip pressure safety, and, when the hammer is half-cocked, locks the trigger.

The Model 38 was surprisingly heavy for such a small gun. Ruggieri had made sure there was no magazine in it, moved the safety to fire and grasped the end of the slide. The slide itself was difficult to grip because it was narrow, the serrations at the end of the otherwise slick slide were too smooth to really hold and the tension of the internal spring made the slide surprisingly resistant.

The gun didn't have a hammer, which is, in the simplest of terms, the part that strikes the end of a cartridge when the trigger is pulled. A pistol's hammer can be on the outside, an external hammer like that on a revolver, which can be physically cocked (placed in a position ready to fire) by a shooter placing his or her thumb on it and pulling it back, and, conversely, un-cocked it the same way. A hammer can also be inside the gun, an internal hammer, or there might not be a 'hammer' at all, like the Model 38.

The Bryco's internal firing mechanism used the same principle of a hammer hitting the cartridge, but instead of a hammer, a bullet would be fired by what's known as a sear and striker, the striker being the part that serves the same purpose as a hammer. The Model 38 would be 'cocked' — like the hammer, the striker would be positioned to fire — whenever the slide was pulled all the way back and then allowed to slide forward. That same action also enabled the user: to get a clear look inside the chamber; load the first bullet; eject a bullet from the chamber; or when the gun was fired, would cause the automatic movement of the slide backward to eject the shell and feed the next bullet into the chamber as the slide moved forward again.

So, whenever the Model 38's slide traveled all the way to the rear and then moved forward, the result was a cocked the gun. To verify that the gun was not loaded, to unload it, load it, or fire it, all which required the slide be moved back and allowed to move forward again, which *always* cocked the gun, the safety had to be moved from 'safe to fire' for the slide to move.

Once the gun was cocked there was only one way to un-cock it: pull the trigger.

Unlike the stubborn, surprising resistance he felt as he had pulled back the slide, when Ruggieri pulled the trigger it offered little resistance and seemed to barely move before he heard a 'click.'

He turned his attention to the gun's packaging.

On the top of the square, light-blue box's cover,

printed in small but readable letters were "Made in the U.S.A."; on the next line below, in very large type, "Bryco Arms" with "Irvine, CA" directly under in much smaller type; "Extra Magazine Included" was on the next line. Under it all, the last line of text began *"Do not use this pistol until you have read the enclosed instructions..."*

An empty, gray magazine with a silver-colored base was in the gun. The other magazine, with a flat-black base, was in the box. Ruggieri released and pulled out the silver magazine, and slid the flat-black one into the gun. He stared at the bottom of the handgrip and recalled something he heard Detective Tripp say during a recording of Clint's interview:

...I did see one thing, though...that even when the officer picked the gun up, the way that magazine fits in there, it looks like a black hole...fooled him for a second... So, if it can fool an adult, it can fool a child...

He put the gun back in its box and picked up the instructions, a single, folded piece of paper. Square and slightly smaller than the box, it unfolded to a strip almost twelve inches long. Small, black text filled both sides of the paper.

Ruggieri read every word.

By late March, 2001, Ruggieri felt confident enough to commit, but not without managing his potential client's expectations, as he explained in a call to Sue and Clint, and reiterated in a letter a week later.

"... I am going to investigate whether and to what extent we can present any viable case on Brandon's behalf. This will be an uphill battle, so please don't get your hopes up, but I do think that it merits a fresh look on his behalf..."

He'd gone as far as he could without filing a complaint,

the first official, recorded step when someone sues another person, company or organization. His decision to move forward was without fanfare, had no dramatic moment of soul searching or self-interrogation. It appeared, based on records from the first law firm's gun test results, that those initial tests did not uncover any malfunction that had caused the now-missing Model 38 to fire on its own. But, that didn't mean it was a safe gun, and it didn't mean that there hadn't been something else about the missing Model 38, or several things, wrong with its function, design, or both.

If there had been a mechanical defect, it could obviously never be proven. If there was a defect, it would have to be a design defect, the only element that Ruggieri could base a case upon, and he'd still have to prove that *all Model 38's* had a design defect. Even though he now had an actual Model 38, he still didn't know if there were other Model 38s, and if there were others, the one he had might not be the 'right' one.

He had looked for and believed there were product design and safety issues that factored into the accident. And he had finally received documents and files relating to seven lawsuits filed over the last decade in which Bruce Jennings, Jennings Firearms, or Bryco had been named as defendants. The documents gave Ruggieri sorely needed context and insights into the man and company behind the Model 38. The research revealed a number of plausible product defect claims with which to justify the original complaints, but, from Ruggieri's perspective, the claims "weren't particularly compelling. They were the usuals, lack of a built-in slide locking device, no chamber loaded indicator, no firing pin blocks, the same list used in almost every previous complaint filed."

After years of defense experience and case analysis,

he had created a mental checklist for causes of action, those elements of negligence or fraud for which one party sues another. He now composed an analysis as if he were Bryco's attorneys, detailing Bryco's vulnerabilities, what the other side (Brandon) was probably going to assert, and the liabilities and legal consequences of those vulnerabilities.

He had almost everything he needed. There was nothing to be done about the original gun; of course he hoped it might still show up, but even without it there were ways to take Brandon's case to trial. There was, though, a crucial element that Ruggieri desperately needed, and in early April of 2001, a private investigator he had hired delivered welcome news: "I found Jerry Morris, and he's in Oakland."

No one in the family had seen Morris or knew his whereabouts since the falling out almost five years before. Whatever its cause, the incident or incidents had destroyed any bridge of friendship between the troubled young man and the family.

But Ruggieri needed him, not just for his testimony, but because Morris had to be included in the string of people, companies, and entities that would be parties in the litigation. It didn't matter from a civil legal perspective that no criminal charges had ever been filed or that Morris had no insurance or assets. He had been holding the gun when it discharged and Morris' culpability was without question. He had been negligent.

Locating Morris had been a priority, so it both excited and relieved Ruggieri that he'd been found, but to have found Morris in Oakland was, as Ruggieri described it, "a major stroke of luck because where he lived was so significant to where the case was filed."

A plaintiff — Brandon, the party filing a lawsuit —

can file where any defendant lives. Before finding Morris, Ruggieri would have been restricted to filing in Mendocino County, where the accident occurred, or Orange County, Bryco's location. Ruggieri's time and costs to try a case in either of those venues could have been substantial. Finding Morris in Oakland would allow Ruggieri to file in Alameda County, and the advantages that came with that were numerous, from home court advantage, to easy access to the Oakland airport, to the benefits of working in a sophisticated courthouse system, to the wider, more sympathetic pool of potential jurors. It was also where Brandon's doctors and medical records were located.

Morris had been adrift for the last six years. He had been in some trouble, been arrested and was now a nonviolent offender on years-long probation. His life had stabilized, and he was working part-time at a large department store, doing as well as he could. The private detective had tracked Morris to a halfway house in a neighborhood only minutes away from Oakland Children's hospital, where Brandon had received almost all of his medical services for the last six years.

Morris in Oakland was the upside; Morris in a halfway house and on probation was a downside. He had moved around, and although he might be settled currently, his history motivated Ruggieri to "file immediately, before Morris moved or was moved out of the county."

The halfway house residents all reported to a county social worker. Ruggieri called her, introduced himself and started to explain his relationship to Brandon.

"The young man from the family Jerry used to stay with," she said.

"Yes."

"I am familiar with Jerry's history, so I am aware of the accident. Has something happened to the boy?"

"No, it's not anything like that. I'm going to be suing the gun manufacturer on Brandon's behalf..."

"Really? That seems like good news."

"Well, we have a long way to go, but this also has to involve Mr. Morris. He has to be part of the suit. Since you know about the accident, you know that it was Mr. Morris who was holding the gun when it fired, so even though we're suing the gun maker, we also have to sue several other people who had a part in the accident. I know this sounds terrible in its own way, but I have to include Mr. Morris as a defendant."

"It does sound terrible."

"I'm not going to treat him like a monster, certainly, and although I obviously can't represent him and I am limited as to what I'm allowed to say, but before we go any further, we need to meet."

Two days later Ruggieri stepped off the elevator inside a large office building in a business and corporate complex directly opposite the Oakland Coliseum. Finding Morris had been a stroke of luck, but the reality of Morris could very well alter much of Ruggieri's case strategy.

"I needed him, but I'd never met him, seen him, interacted with him, so he was a wildcard. We had a major venue coup, because venue is so important, but now I needed to find out the kind of person he was, his attitude, how he came across socially, what he looked like, and how he felt about the accident. All of it could really impact the case.

"I needed some very particular, humanistic elements to be present in Morris. I needed to find out how verbal he was, and I had no idea as I stepped off that elevator what was going to happen… until I saw him through the glass of an office."

The social worker was waiting for Ruggieri in the reception area. Beyond her were several glass-walled offices, and he saw Morris, in profile, seated at a table in one of them, waiting. Morris was not overly big, but he was a decent-sized young adult of twenty-seven. His hair was longish, he wore glasses, jeans and a long-sleeve shirt. He didn't see Ruggieri.

The social worker was cordial, shook Ruggieri's hand, and said, "Jerry's ready."

But Ruggieri had already decided: "Wait, let's take a minute."

Whether it was a reconnection to his early work — *…I always worked to remind myself that these were people, not just numbers on pieces of paper…* — or simply an instinct, it had only taken a glimpse of the somewhat slouched, staring young man behind the glass for Ruggieri to decide that at least for now, he wouldn't talk to Morris. There would be time, there would be depositions, but with just his glimpse of Morris, Ruggieri sensed the weight of life's challenges Morris probably shouldered every day.

Ruggieri was relieved, for several reasons. He'd harbored another concern that if he did talk to Morris, it could come back to bite him because, "just as I would have thought about as a defense lawyer, any conversation or meeting I'd have with Morris at this stage could be construed as an attempt to coach or sway him."

Ruggieri suggested he and the woman talk first. She walked Ruggieri to a small, unremarkable office.

"Obviously, this is going to be a tough situation for everyone involved. I'll explain it to you, and I think it just seems that for right now, it would be fine if you could go over this with him. I don't really have to talk to him directly. I hope it's not too much trouble; I'm sure you have plenty to do without me adding to your workload."

"It's fine. If it affects him, which this certainly will, it's important for me to know."

Ruggieri explained how the lawsuit would work and that Morris would have to give a deposition. "And if this goes to trial, which I think is likely, he'll have to testify. All of this is the reason he'll need an attorney."

"Really? He works part-time, he stocks shelves. How..."

"I know, I understand. I don't want to recommend an attorney for him, but here's a list of several Bay Area attorneys whose practices match what Mr. Morris requires and who may be willing to take on his case without a huge fee. Call them and tell them the situation, give them my name, and they can call me."

They finished and walked out to the reception area together.

Including Morris in the litigation was a necessity, but for reasons that wouldn't be readily apparent to a non-attorney. "I needed him to be part of the case, and have an attorney, to prevent what's called the 'empty chair' defense." Without Morris as part of the litigation, or in attendance at trial with competent representation, Bryco's and Jennings' defense team would have repeatedly pointed to Morris' absence. The 'empty chair' in the courtroom would become the defendant's repository of full blame for the accident. The empty chair, as Morris, would be unable to defend his position or respond, and Brandon not having him there would be argued as unfairly piling on the existing defendants, i.e., *if he wants to be fair, why isn't Mr. Maxfield suing the guy who was at fault?*

An attorney for Morris would provide a defense for

the young man that, while not shying from participation in the accidental shooting, would serve to reinforce the correct interpretation of the law to the jury. Morris was but one link in a chain of circumstances that placed a defective gun in his hand, a gun made defective by Bryco Arms and Bruce Jennings.

As he waited for the elevator, Ruggieri took another quick look at Morris, still sitting at the table, now flipping through a magazine. He saw a challenged young man who had been involved in a tragedy. Morris didn't have Brandon's lifelong physical limitations, but the big young man did have challenges which would forever, in some fashion, keep him adrift.

Only Ruggieri had an educated idea of the legal work and obstacles that lay ahead when he called Sue and Clint in May, 2001 to tell them he was ready to file. To Sue, for all its importance, the call wasn't any different than dozens of conversations they'd had over the previous two years, except it was shorter than most. Over the course of his research year and, as Ruggieri would recall later, throughout and after the trial, Sue, Clint, and Brandon "were perfect clients, getting me information when I needed it, doing the things I told them they needed to do and in the ways I needed them to do it. They expected nothing, and were grateful for my efforts. They trusted me completely."

Sue was always ready. "I'd be making lists, he always had something he needed from us. After he decided to file the lawsuit, one of the first things he did, he bought us a fax machine, and he'd send us stuff or I'd have to send him some records or numbers. We went through a lot of paper, but I always got him what he wanted."

This time, however, when the conversation was over,

Sue hung up the phone and turned to Brandon, in his wheelchair and watching television. "Hey Brandon, Rich is filing papers to sue the gunmaker."

And Brandon responded in his usual subdued but sincere way.

"Excellent."

Even as Ruggieri filed a suit with the potential for a significant financial outcome — or for him, significant financial debt — the family barely focused on it.

Clint continued to add-on to the single-wide, a perpetual process of making room not just for Brandon but for the growing family. Sue was close to finishing her nurse's assistant training, although she was already well versed and experienced in many of the same tasks she was studying. In a report to Ruggieri from Dr. Robert Haining, who had overseen every hospitalization of Brandon since the accident, he noted that while there had been "some nursing assistance through the years...the family has shown themselves to be remarkably good caretakers, although this has been extremely wearing on the family in general."

Brandon, while doing well for a teenager in his condition, had been admitted to either Willits' Howard Memorial or Oakland Children's Hospital no less than twice a year, every year, from 1995 to 2001. He had been treated multiple times for pneumonia, pressure ulcerations, and had several operations, from spinal fusion to hip and leg procedures. A Medi-Cal summary of Brandon's hospital bills up to November 2001 showed a total amount of almost $2.5 million.

In May, 2001, Ruggieri filed a general negligence and products liability suit against a half-dozen defendants, including numerous John Doe defendants, people or entities unknown at the time of the filing that could be added to the suit later. Morris was actually the first to be 'served', the process of giving notice by delivering copies of the summons and complaint to an individual, business, or business entity that they are being sued. The owners of Willits Pawn were served a few weeks later, but it was several more months, after getting the pawn shop's records which identified the distributor, before the East Coast company that had distributed the gun, and which had since gone into bankruptcy, could be served.

It would take another three months to properly serve Bryco Arms, and to locate and serve Bruce Jennings, owner of B.L. Jennings, Inc. and named in other suits as an owner — again, or not — of Bryco Arms, and serve, as president of Bryco Arms, Mr. Jennings' ex-wife Janice Jennings. During that same period Ruggieri received documents and transcripts of several previous lawsuits against Bryco and B.L. Jennings, Inc., then the sole distributor of Bryco's guns, which enabled him to replace John Doe defendants and serve an additional half-dozen Nevada and California financial trusts in the names of Jennings' children but directly controlled by Jennings; serve RKB Investments, a partnership of three trusts, controlled by Jennings (the letters stood for the first name initials of Jennings' children), and that owned the Bryco manufacturing building; and serve another ex-wife of Jennings, Anna Leah Jennings.

While Ruggieri anticipated degrees of push back and delay, these early efforts to uncover business locations, ownership, and assets were mere harbingers of the depth and breadth of evasion that would confront him for the next twelve months. In one particular motion asking the court to overturn an Orwellian secrecy order that prevented Ruggieri from accessing the files of a 1997 lawsuit against Bryco, Ruggieri wrote, "the order is *so* secret that the order *itself* is secret".

Over the next year Ruggieri would wage an unrelenting campaign of motions, correspondence, and investigation that would cost him hundreds of thousands of dollars, and consume his time morning to night, usually seven days a week. In return, Jennings and his attorney would respond in ways familiar to Ruggieri, obfuscating, ignoring, and sheltering truth, documents, and money.

Nothing was revealed voluntarily, and nothing came easily.

Bruce Jennings had yet to be beaten by the legal system, thriving and then surviving personal and industry turbulence. In the time since Brcyo Arms had 'gone bare' and dropped its insurance, Bruce Jennings had personally managed all lawsuits against his companies, moving his attorney into offices within the Bryco manufacturing facility, and being part of phone conversations during any important calls involving his attorney. He had been pursued but never really caught, figuratively struck but never really wounded.

He had almost four decades of experience in avoiding responsibility for the chaos his products had caused, and had pocketed millions of dollars. But Jennings' escape-and-evasion strategies were, for the first time, about to fall apart.

Ruggieri had discovered a book while researching Brandon's case that provided invaluable context for Jennings' legacy within the California handgun industry.

The book's author, Dr. Garen Wintemute, a California emergency physician and researcher, had also been prominently featured in a 1997 episode of Frontline, an award-winning PBS investigative series. The episode,

"Hot Guns", featured Wintemute and expanded upon his research on a particular class of guns' increasingly negative impact on society. The handguns were being manufactured by a group of Southern California companies, of which Bryco and its founder, Bruce Jennings, held prominent positions.

Wintemute's book was published in 1994, the year of Brandon's accident. Its title was also the phrase Wintemute used to describe the gun companies which encircled the Los Angeles area, evoking the similarity to a region of active volcanos encircling the Pacific ocean and identified by the same phrase: the Ring of Fire.

The Ring of Fire companies' existence had grown, ironically, from an opportunity created by the passage of the country's first major gun control bill. In the wake of the Kennedys' and Martin Luther King's history-shaking deaths by assassination, the 1968 Gun Control Act enacted a broad series of laws and controls to regulate the firearms industry, firearms distribution, and sales. It placed new restrictions and controls on everything from interstate commerce of all guns, to who could and couldn't legally possess guns, and banned the importation of certain foreign-manufactured guns, including non-sporting handguns. The Act now included a grading system of dimensional measurements, features, and firepower to determine if a non-sporting handgun could be imported from a foreign manufacturer. Foreign-made handguns not much bigger than a person's hand, with short barrels and high firepower for their size, would no longer be available in the United States.

George Jennings, Bruce Jennings' father, owned a Southern California-based machine shop when he became aware that the Gun Control Act's import restrictions had dried up the country's inventory of cheap, small handguns. As described by Bruce in one of the "Hot Guns" segments, his father "was quite an inventor and a very interesting man, but most of his ideas were a little bit on the odd side. He doodled on paper continuously, though, and developed his first gun."

George Jennings established Raven Arms in 1970 and produced what is widely accepted as the country's first, homegrown Saturday night special style gun made after the Gun Control Act, the Raven P-25.

From the early 1970s and continuing for the next two decades, the Jennings family, relatives, and their friends branched out and created a dozen gun companies north, east, and south of L.A., all less than an hour's travel from the city. Those companies produced handguns that shared as many design and manufacturing traits as the companies shared family members and associates. Many models sold for $500 to $800 less than handguns from traditional and well-established companies like Smith & Wesson and Colt.

By the time a fire destroyed the Raven company building in 1991 and its designs were sold to another Ring of Fire company, Raven had produced an estimated 3,000,000 guns.

Ring of Fire guns flooded the marketplace. The companies heavily marketed their guns' allure as affordable self-defense / offensive protection weapons, priced for "the working man." Each company's guns shared similar design, mechanical, and production elements. Reliance on low-grade materials kept manufacturing costs low, while the guns' small size and light weight made them easy to carry and conceal.

And the guns were cheap.

But those same elements also contributed to troubling

situations ignored, denied, or derided by the manufacturers.

The small size and short barrel made the guns wildly inaccurate at distances past ten feet. The low-quality metals (zinc and pot ash, alloys with much weaker structural integrity than steel), and low-price / mass-market approach to everything from design to manufacture, made the guns notoriously unreliable. On the streets their easy concealment, wide availability, and low price made them the gun-of-choice for crime. Bruce Jennings insisted in an interview that "The concept that our guns would be used more in crime is incorrect. Our products are used the same as anybody else's products."

Crime statistics indicated otherwise.

Between 1968 and 1971 the phrase 'Saturday night special' appeared in several newspaper articles and as part of a crime study's report, but a gun historian has traced its origin as far back as the 1800s, when men carousing the town on a Saturday night would carry small guns, like Derringers, in their vest pockets. By the 1970s, the phrase was widely accepted as describing the growing, insidiously pervasive use of the small handguns in street crimes, robberies, and assaults. Another description of the guns also became widely used among police departments: junk guns.

The troubling rise of the Saturday night special as a 'crime gun' was highlighted in the Hot Guns episode and would be widely revealed to the general public in 2002 when Time magazine featured a list of "top-ten guns used in crimes" from an unpublished study by the Bureau of Alcohol, Tobacco and Firearms agency (now known as the Bureau of Alcohol, Tobacco, Firearms, and Explosives, BATFE). Six of the ten listed guns were manufactured by Ring of Fire companies.

Bryco Arms made two of the guns on the list, a nine-millimeter and the Model 38.

By the year 2000, Bruce Jennings was virtually alone atop the crumbling, cheap handgun industry his father created nearly thirty-five years before.

Bryco Arms was Bruce Jennings' second gun company. Or it might have been his third company. Or, as he would go to exaggerated lengths to point out years later, it wasn't 'his' company at all.

As a young man Bruce Jennings worked for his father at Raven Arms from the company's formation in 1970. He left in 1978 to create Jennings Firearms, where he created his first gun, the J-22, a twenty-two caliber semiautomatic, which he designed based on the Raven Arms J-25 caliber. In depositions years later, Bruce Jennings would insist his father had designed the Raven J-25 by borrowing much of the gun's internal operations — including the safety mechanism — from an early-1900s German handgun.

Jennings Firearms' J-22 would sell well, become infamous, make Bruce Jennings wealthy, and give rise to the Bryco Model 38 a decade later. That decade also brought the Jennings family unwelcome media attention, law enforcement scrutiny, litigation, and domestic troubles.

From 1978 to 1985 Jennings Firearms sold an estimated 600,000 J-22s. In the same time period, Raven Arms had sold 1,000,000 of its gun. Two other Ring of Fire companies had barely gotten off the ground by '85, giving Raven and Jennings Firearms virtually the country's entire small handgun market.

As his guns blanketed the country and law enforcement agencies began to see the guns' prevalence on the streets, Jennings did something that placed his future as a gun manufacturer in jeopardy and forced him to adopt a new strategy to maintain his role as a leading purveyor of cheap handguns.

In April of 1985, Jennings broke his second wife's jaw. A plea deal reduced the original felony assault charge to a misdemeanor, but he was suddenly a "prohibited person" in the view of the ATF. He could no longer hold the Federal Firearms License (FFL) required of anyone who sells or manufactures guns, could no longer hold or own a firearm, and could no longer control a gun company... at least, not in a legal way.

Jennings acquired Jennings Firearms in a divorce from wife Janice, assisted his plant manager in setting up a new corporation, Calwestco, then sold the assets of Jennings Firearms to Calwestco, which continued to produce the J-22 pistol, now with both companies' names stamped on the gun. Simultaneously, Bruce Jennings incorporated B.L. Jennings, Inc., installing himself as the sole shareholder and non-controlling 'consultant,' and obtained an FFL in the name of the corporation and its manager.

Calwestco made the J-22s and sold most, if not all, of its products to B.L. Jennings, which served as Calwestco's national distributor and set all prices, paid profits to its sole shareholder, and funded itself and Calwestco with money loaned back personally by Bruce Jennings, as a 'secured creditor.'

Even as Calwestco pumped out the J-22s, Jennings incorporated another gun company, Bryco Arms, with Jennings' ex-wife Janice as president. The stockholders were Janice Jennings and Nevada trusts in the names of Janice and Bruce's children, with Janice and Bruce as the trustees.

Calwestco closed in 1991 and Bryco Arms began putting out its own J-22 — through B.L. Jennings, Inc.

— and the Model 38, identical to the J-22 but with more firepower.

His business configurations and distributions kept Bryco Arms and B.L. Jennings from retaining much in the way of profits. Between B.L. Jennings, Inc. distributions and loan repayments to Jennings himself, Bryco Arms' distributions to Janice and the Nevada trusts as shareholders, and Bryco's rent payments to the partnership of California trusts that owned the Bryco Arms building, through Bruce Jennings as manager and trustee, neither Bryco nor B.L. Jennings, Inc. kept much cash in reserve, nor, after 1994, carried liability insurance.

Jennings remained in the gun business and lived well. A 1991 news release by the nonprofit Violence Policy Center proclaimed that based on production figures obtained from the ATF, Bryco "led all other U.S. manufacturers in pistol production," the company's almost 203,000 pistols [*not revolvers*, however] far surpassing the output of "traditional industry leaders Sturm, Ruger, and Smith & Wesson."

Through Calwestco and then Bryco, Jennings kept his money flowing and beyond the reach of several lawsuits filed against him and 'his' companies. He was not, however, beyond the reach of the media.

A 1992 Wall Street Journal feature illuminated not just the family's gun dynasty, its hard light lit up everything salacious about the family, from the growing use of Jennings' guns by criminals to Bruce's excessive lifestyle, family and domestic troubles. Two years later a scathing Philadelphia Daily News piece focused on the J-22's position as having "been confiscated in more criminal investigations [based on data from from state police records] than any other weapon since 1989." The article highlighted Jennings' mass produced J-22, "molded from zinc-alloy so soft its rough edges can be shaved with a knife," in contrast to "finer examples of American craftsmanship, the hand-tooled, stainless-steel design, and perfect balance and unfailing mechanics of Colt, Smith & Wesson, Remington and others that cost $350 and more."

According to the article, gun experts estimated Jennings' company could produce a handgun in under five minutes, with unskilled labor, "for about $15 in parts."

The article concluded with a quote from the director of the Violence Policy Center, declaring that Jennings knows "exactly what the inner-city buyer wants. They've built a gun that's very concealable, very inexpensive... These guns are tearing up the market."

By 1998, the Ring of Fire companies were facing increased public and political scrutiny, new state-enacted laws restricting or banning the sale of junk guns, and steeply rising liability insurance premiums. Bryco had allowed its liability insurance to lapse four years before.

That year, Jennings also filed for a renewal of his FFL as president and shareholder of B.L. Jennings, Inc. As a court document would reveal later, Jennings answered "No" to the application's question of "Have you ever been convicted in any court of a misdemeanor crime of domestic violence?"

Congress had amended the Gun Control Act in 1996 to now include anyone convicted of misdemeanor domestic violence — a change from what previously had been a felony conviction — as prohibited from shipping, transporting, possessing, or receiving any firearm or ammunition. Jennings would argue for many years that because his misdemeanor conviction had been expunged he no longer had a misdemeanor conviction. The court ultimately disagreed.

The year ended with the cities of New Orleans, Cleveland, and Chicago suing dozens of small handgun manufacturers, including Bryco Arms and B.L. Jennings, Inc. (unsuccessfully), for a combined half-billion dollars. Eleven California cities and counties also sued Bryco, B.L Jennings, and other gun companies. New California state and county restrictions made it increasingly difficult to manufacture and sell junk guns throughout the state. The OC (Orange County) Weekly, reporting that Bryco was being sued by the family of a boy who had been shot in the face when a Bryco discharged, included the disparaging results of tests on Bryco's line of guns by *Gun Tests* magazine. Several models performed so poorly and dangerously that the magazine couldn't complete the tests. The article also noted that an ATF study had concluded "Saturday night specials blow up in their owners' hands at a higher rate than any other gun…"

As the year 2000 approached, several Ring of Fire companies had gone bankrupt or were out of business, the junk gun industry's sales were in steep decline while gun industry insurance premiums were quickly rising. A new company, Shining Star Distributors, Inc., was incorporated in Texas, with Janice Jennings installed as sole shareholder and president, but it would be a few more years before it was used for any business.

While certainly affected by it all, Jennings continued to reign over his industry as Ruggieri researched and built Brandon's case.

Jennings had boats, sports cars, a private jet and a glimmering, silver P-51 Mustang, with the name Saturday Night Special painted on its fuselage. Based on who asked him and under what circumstances, his answers to questions indicated: that he spent the majority of his time living and working in Southern California, whenever in the area he lived on a 'shore boat', which in Jennings' case was the small boat he used to get to and from a yacht he owned and docked either in Costa Mesa or Newport Beach; he had a Nevada and a Florida drivers license, and claimed to be domiciled in Florida where he lived part-time on another yacht, his 'home', valued at over a million dollars; his Oregon-registered company, Jennings Racing, owned another jet, cars, and a boat registered in Guernsey, an island overseen by the UK and known for its low to non-existent tax rates for high-wealth individuals and business.

It would come to light in later depositions that much of what Jennings said was misdirection, his attempts to hide assets — including a multi-million-dollar home — from yet another lawsuit.

He had been named in at least a dozen lawsuits, filed by several of the country's largest cities, and while there is no accurate or official record of his legal costs, those costs were arguably minute compared to his personal profits, which he minimized on paper by passing cash and ownership responsibilities through his maze of straw men, straw women, and trusts.

Through it all, he kept his figurative get-out-of-jail-free card, ready to use if sued, as he explained in a 1999 BusinessWeek magazine interview: "...Bankruptcy is the likely way many of the West Coast [gun] companies will deal with any litigation. "It doesn't mean they'll be gone forever," Jennings says. "They can file for bankruptcy, dissolve, go away until the litigation passes by, then reform and build guns to the new standard — if there is a new standard..."

CHAPTER 5

DISCOVERY, DISCOVERING, AND UNCOVERING

Most people never enter a courtroom or are involved in a criminal or civil trial, and many of the public's assumptions about legal procedures, lawsuits, or trials have likely come from news articles, news shows, TV, film, or John Grisham novels. The complexities of civil law, combined with dramatized depictions of trials and attorneys, foster a litany of misguided beliefs and misunderstandings. The most ignored elements, arguably, are the massive expenditures of time, effort, and evidence-based work necessary to properly prepare for a big trial.

From March 2001 to his opening statement at trial in March, 2003, Ruggieri worked on Brandon's case every day, with the exceptions of September 11th, 2001, Christmas, and New Years. He had no administrative support of any kind and hadn't since he'd chosen to open a solo practice in the late-'90s, and although he realized the sheer magnitude of the administrative-related filing, documents, logistics and travel tasks that lay ahead, he never hired even a temp. "I had seen how big firms could screw up a case, I understood what was needed and knew I could do better. And from a practical point of view, I knew the costs were going to mount and I was watching every dime. But, even as I did some manual tasks that I abhorred, I never considered bringing in more help. I knew I could do it."

Over that same two years, opposing counsel took all available steps to defend their clients, blunting Ruggieri's unrelenting work as best they could by fighting discovery requests and going to great efforts — again, to absurd extremes in Jennings' case — to avoid, misdirect, and obfuscate.

Ruggieri's process began as many personal injury lawsuits do after potential defendants have been notified: serving document and other discovery requests; locating, scheduling and taking depositions from parties and witnesses; retaining experts; and maintaining the continuous stream of written communications between opposing counsel.

"By the time I filed Brandon's case I only had one other case, and I wouldn't have had the time to do this the way I did if I had any other cases. Early on and for quite awhile, I was getting up to seven faxes *a day*, with opposing counsel trying to screw me around in seven different ways."

"But I knew how it was, because what these guys were doing was standard insurance defense practice."

If not for the life altering importance of the stakes, what was happening could be described as a paper game.

"I kept the pressure on, and I began to drown *them* in faxes. Usually, if a plaintiff serves discovery or a demand to identify or produce documents, when the defense finally does respond it gives them a sense of relief, because now they have some breathing room, because the calendar has been reset. The defense feels like they have time to not think about things. It's the way they slow everything down, drag things out.

"But as soon as I'd get something from them, usually their refusal or objections, I'd hammer out my response and it would be sitting on their fax machine the next morning, and suddenly the calendar issue is back on them, they're forced right back into it." Early on, this kind of paper play made for ten or twelve-hour days, then "I'd go home and do research in bed."

Pre-trial work is an eclectic mix: a large part stamina, large part intelligence and knowledge, and a mix of spy vs. spy, drudgery, euphoria, gamesmanship, and luck. The tasks can extend for years. The work and its results, i.e., information revealed during depositions, product test results, professional experts' evaluations, new leads extracted from financial records, etc., all build a trial's foundations and inform an attorney's case strategy. And, as is *usually* hoped for by both sides, it is where the possibility of settling a case grows or vanishes.

It's a process that is ruled by calendars, paper documents, and formats for different legal motions that are served to the 'other side' and filed with the court in specific ways and within mandated time periods.

Ruggieri was unrelenting during this twenty-month phase. Stonewalling is a routine defense tactic, something Jennings and his attorney might have done with any requests from any attorney. It was certainly a tactic used in numerous previous lawsuits filed against Jennings. But by accelerating the pace and, through hundreds of letters to Jennings' attorney documenting Ruggieri's constant frustration at the delays, Ruggieri was also building credibility that would favor him in future hearings.

The court denied every motion Jennings filed to stop Ruggieri's discovery requests. As file box upon file box were delivered to Ruggieri's office, the copies of Jennings' financial documents, the absence of certain records, and transcripts of other Jennings trials conveyed just how far Jennings would go to avoid revealing anything other than the most superficial parts of his business and personal finances.

By October 2001, Ruggieri substantially expanded the number of gun defendants, and by November, through details revealed in subpoenaed documents and from information obtained in depositions, he had identified what would be called the "alter ego" defendants, the people behind the figurative curtains.

"There were three groups: those nominally involved with the gun; those who were alter egos of those nominally involved with the gun; and those involved in the fraudulent transfer of a multi-million-dollar property."

They now included Bruce Jennings, Bryco Arms, B.L. Jennings, Inc.; two ex-wives; three trusts in California; three trusts in Nevada; the partnership that owned the Bryco Arms building; a distributor that sold the Model 38 to Willits Pawn; the pawn shop's owners; and Jerry Morris.

Bruce and Janice had direct control of the trusts (set-up, as asserted by Jennings, for his children) as trustees.

Matt Newberg, Jennings' attorney, represented Jennings, Bryco Arms, B.L. Jennings, Inc., Janice Jennings, and all the alter ego defendants except third ex-wife Anna Leah Jennings. A combined four other law firms represented the remaining defendants.

Barely two months after filing Brandon's suit, Ruggieri's office phone rang.

"Richard, it's Matt Newberg. I received your fax yesterday asking about the status of my clients' insurance coverage."

"Uh-huh. Best to get that sorted out right away."

"My clients have no coverage. I have us on speakerphone with Mr. Jennings here..."

"I'm not going to talk about anything at this stage with Mr. Jennings. If you want to discuss this with me, that's fine, take me off speakerphone so you and I can talk."

"I think it would benefit us if..."

"Matt, take me off speakerphone."

Jennings spoke. "Richard, it's Bruce Jennings..." Jennings was direct, saying there was nothing to get, no insurance, no cash, and if Ruggieri continued the case Bryco would simply file bankruptcy.

Ruggieri, without another word, hung up.

Subpoenaed documents would eventually reveal that in March 1993, three major insurance companies had declined coverage before Bryco secured liability insurance from April 1, 1993 to April 1, 1994.

Bryco Arms had already made millions for Jennings, and sales projections of Bryco guns were for millions more.

In March of '94, Bryco's insurance agent received a letter from the carrier asking about the design of the safety mechanisms on Bryco guns, including, "What upgrades in the safety mechanism has the insured made since last year, both in current production and modifications to existing models?"

Carriers were raising rates significantly for all handgun manufacturers and declining to insure those manufacturers with products that either by design or function were too dangerous to cover. Insurers were closing ranks, demanding assurance from insureds that their guns functioned correctly, with features designed to keep the user safe during normal operation of the guns.

On April 5th, Bryco's insurance broker scribbled a

note on his formal reply to the carrier, *"It is my feeling [the] insured will not be renewing with us. The insured feels the cost is too high."*

Going bare is a term used to describe a company that chooses to operate without insurance. A well-funded company may plan for such a situation by creating a cash reserve specifically to self-insure the company. If there is no cash reserve, going bare leaves a company completely vulnerable, with limited available options should a company's product or negligence cause serious harm to the users of its products. Bankruptcy is often the only option.

Some companies may go bare during hard financial times, when business is bad and funds are low. But Bryco's decision to go bare pushed all risk for responsibility downstream, to distributors, to vendors like Willits Pawn, and to victims.

Greed was the driver of Jennings and Bryco going bare — no money in the company, nothing to lose if sued. Statements from many sources and media over the years revealed Jennings' stoic yet subtle arrogance when defending his Constitutional right to provide inexpensive handguns to people who couldn't afford more expensive guns. It was also his right not to be held accountable if someone got hurt using his gun, because Jennings believed that no matter the circumstance, anyone injured using a Bryco or a Jennings had only themselves to blame; the malfunction was the *user*, always.

Going bare and bankruptcy were essential parts of Jennings' business plan.

With direct financial support from Jennings in the form of loans to his gun companies, there was always just enough money to keep the companies in business, and beholding to him for enough funds to stay in business. He controlled the distribution pipeline, the ebb and flow of Bryco products. Everything was Bruce Jennings.

The reality of how Jennings had distanced himself and his money from the reach of anyone who might be harmed by his gun was far different than what he had described in the 1997 PBS Hot Guns episode. Jennings responded to a question about his family's dominance of the industry with the contention that his companies needed to make higher profit margins than other gun companies, because that money needed to be there and "support" the gun for years after it was made:

Q: When you mean support it, you mean pay for litigation that comes from it?

Jennings: I mean support it by replacement parts, warranty repairs, and litigation. One of the biggest problems of the firearms industry circles around product liability insurance.

[I]t's a very large cost of doing business. That cost is an unforeseen number because of the number of years that you need to support the insurance for that product. Even though you may have sold the gun last year or two years ago, you may be facing litigation and product support fifteen or twenty years into the future. And even if the company is no longer building firearms in quantities... we still have to have enough capital available to support the product liability, litigation and claims.

Even as he answered the question, neither of his companies had actually had any "capital" available for years, and his statements also offered proof that he knew how important it was to have insurance or capital, that he understood his obligations.

Yet, he bled his companies dry.

Bryco's lack of insurance didn't shake Ruggieri. "I wasn't too surprised, really. If anything, it fueled me." In August 2000 he sent a letter to all parties' counsel, stating he would be "joining parties {adding defendants} as necessary to ensure a judgment fund..." and advising "if anyone intends to file for bankruptcy, they should do it sooner than later."

It was good advice that none of the defendants acted upon.

In late October, attorney Newberg received a four-page letter from Ruggieri. Ruggieri laid out the strengths of his case against Bryco and Jennings, "and I wanted to tweak him a bit, to convey that I understood just how successful this case could be, and what that could really mean for his client. I wanted to be sure they understood how this was an all or nothing case for them."

The letter blended the legal with the colloquial, tongue-in-cheek with in-your-face:

I always make an early attempt to see if a case can be settled. Cases driven by business decisions often can, while those driven by emotions rarely do. Still, I always make the attempt — and this is it.

Although there is a great deal left to play out in this case, I think we can all see the handwriting on the wall... all the usual design defect issues (ie: lack of warnings, trigger locks, chamber-loaded indicator, slide lock, yada-yada...) are involved. California law does't require me to prove fault or negligence, only that the product could have been designed safer, failed to meet reasonable consumer expectations, and/or lacked adequate warnings. The law then imposes strict liability on the product defendants, in effect taxing them instead of society at large to pay the full freight.

{Ruggieri shared his logic for a significant outcome for Brandon}

...The case obviously has present settlement value. The only question is can it settle presently. You may want to wait and see if I get discouraged by all the poor-mouthing and just go away. I won't. The case is fully financed, the experts are hired, the dice

are rolling, this is what I do, and (to be perfectly candid) I think there is a ton of money there anyway.

You may also want to wait until I go through the whole exercise, figuring that when I do find the skeletons, you can always settle just as cheaply and shut me up with one of your secrecy agreements. You can't. I never agree to seal files, keep secrets, not represent other clients, destroy or return documents, etc. I never do it, period. To avoid getting jammed by a conflict, all of my clients sign off on this at the time I am retained. (You don't defend products actions for 20 years without learning something.)

...The numbers in this case are huge and the way they fall entirely on your clients is shocking. There's nothing I can do about that. Either way, we are talking millions — the only difference may be whether we are in single or double digits.

Chapter 6

THE DEFECT REVEALED

Depositions are where lies go to die. Could be instantaneous or by a thousand cuts, but few lies get out of depositions alive.

The Bruce Jennings that Ruggieri met was different than the Jennings he'd seen in the PBS Hot Guns video. Jennings' fairly composed and almost understated demeanor in the Frontline interview segments was a more conservative Jennings than the one Ruggieri faced in a half-dozen deposition sessions over the course of a year.

Jennings, at about five-feet ten-inches, often wore loose fitting, untucked aloha-style shirts over a well-fed belly and had the skin tone of someone who spent time outdoors. "He was a salesman, a casual, unworried bull-shitter. He'd greet me acting all cheery, with something like, 'gonna beat me up again today, huh?' He was confident and certainly wasn't stupid."

The deaths of Jennings' lies, though, often played out like scenes from a Monty Python farce. In the comedy troupe's 1975 film, *Monty Python and the Holy Grail,* an enemy knight is gravely wounded repeatedly during a sword fight, losing first an arm, then a leg, the other arm, the other leg, until he is left standing, so to speak, on stumps. He remains vitriolic and taunting, refusing to acknowledge his fatal condition even after the white knight stands back and says, *"but I've cut off your legs!"*

"No you haven't."

Most people will never be deposed. A handful of brief, now somewhat famous video segments from taped depositions have been aired on news shows or investigative-themed programs, the most historical being the infamous clip from President Clinton's impeachment deposition as he answers a question about his assignation with an intern: *"It depends on what the definition of 'is' is..."*

Depositions, a crucial element of the process known as discovery, are question-and-answer interviews, under oath and often videotaped, of parties to a lawsuit, witnesses, and experts. Because those deposed are under oath it's as if a witness is being examined and cross-examined in trial. The onus of being under oath can make the process uncomfortable, nerve wracking, or, as in Jennings' depositions, difficult and contentious.

All parties' attorneys attend each deposition. Objections are made if a question is asked improperly or seeks an answer that is privileged. An attorney can instruct a client not to answer, although the client is often allowed to answer anyway, leaving it to the judge to strike or allow the response.

The end results come out in trial. Courtroom testimony should match deposition testimony, and if there's a difference witnesses have to explain why or risk losing credibility. If a witness doesn't, won't, or can't be compelled to appear at trial, a party can introduce that witness's deposition testimony into evidence at trial.

There were dozens of depositions between 2001 and

2002, the attorneys obtaining information to use in trial, and informing, changing, or reinforcing their perspectives. In addition to Jennings and his ex-wives, depositions were taken of several current and former Bryco employees; gun and safety engineering experts; and of Clint, Sue, John, Jerry Morris, and Brandon. Ruggieri travelled between his Marin County office and several states, and made a dozen trips to Costa Mesa, the Southern California location of Bryco.

An undercurrent of culturally ingrained perspectives about guns indirectly influenced several elements of Ruggieri's case, as notably demonstrated by the opinions of his retained gun experts.

There was the industry-entrenched perception, continuously parroted by Jennings, that guns were protected by the Second Amendment from any legal actions. Only a year before, Democratic Senator Carl Levin had proposed amending a bankruptcy bill to prohibit gun manufacturers from evading accountability for firearms deaths or injuries, but Republicans defeated it, labeling the action as anti-business.

Several gun experts contacted by Ruggieri all expressed similar perspectives about Brandon's lawsuit, Jennings, and Bryco: the gun was crap but there was nothing 'wrong' with it.

Ruggieri would have to find a way to present the gun at trial as a product that should have the same user-safety requirements as other products, but that approach was a challenge. "I couldn't find a legal theory that I liked, and didn't like what many of the groups suing gun manufacturers were pushing, things like the lack of a chamber-loaded indicator or a slide lock. They were legitimate, not unreasonable safety features that arguably should be used, but as a basis for litigation they hadn't worked in other cases, and I kept looking for something else.

"I needed an 'oh my god' argument, not a technical argument".

Jennings' defense had to portray the accident as a simple mishandling of the gun by an inexperienced user, entirely out of the gunmaker's control.

Jerry Morris' only defense was to admit but minimize his involvement, and shift some focus onto the other defendants. Sausalito-based attorney Joe Hoffman had realized from his first meeting with Morris that the young man had "serious, serious challenges."

After talking with Morris' social worker, Hoffman had said he would consider taking on Morris' defense and arranged to meet the young man in an East Bay restaurant near Oakland. He found Morris waiting in a booth, reading an earth-against-aliens graphic novel. As they talked, and in subsequent meetings to prepare Morris for deposition, Hoffman knew "Mr. Morris couldn't really grasp the gravity of everything that was to come."

Jennings was no stranger to depositions. He was being deposed in another Bryco/B.L. Jennings lawsuit even as Ruggieri was investigating Brandon's case in 2000, and had been deposed numerous times going back as far as the early '90s. Those lawsuits, however, had either been dismissed or settled for minimal amounts, and Jennings had never gone through persistent, intense, detailed examinations like Ruggieri's.

None of the half-dozen defense attorneys in the case had anywhere near Ruggieri's deposition experience. "Depositions are one of my strengths, asking questions and being able to build questions and answers into a case. You have to know where you're going every time, every question you ask. In the depositions there's a balance of what I find out versus what I can present. You build a case, then start focusing on the trial and on who you can *get* to trial. But you have to be able to pivot, you take what you get and channel that, lead it to where you want or need it to go."

Ruggieri first deposed Janice and Bruce Jennings in December of 2001, and soon discovered just how far Jennings would go to keep his businesses stripped of records that might provide insight into his interchangeable company business dealings, agreements, inventory, or profit/loss.

Jennings routinely filed for protective orders before acquiescing to any discovery motions. He had insisted on obtaining confidentiality agreements with settling parties of prior litigation, a process which made any financial or business information uncovered in those cases virtually impossible to obtain. In cases where he had been forced to disclose significant information in discovery, he had insisted — and the parties had agreed — that upon settling, plaintiff's attorneys turn over all the case files to Jennings, which Jennings then destroyed, along with his own files.

Jennings kept the barest-to-no written records of business arrangements or relationships: no written business plans, no shareholder reports, asset statements, or financial reports.

It was during one of the earliest depositions that Jennings described how he had done a "house cleaning" and destroyed almost a decade of records and documents. These were reportedly the same documents he had been ordered to provide in another case, documents that court was still waiting to receive.

Despite Jennings' efforts, Ruggieri's countless hours

pouring over public records, old depositions, and court pleadings for other Jennings/Bryco-related lawsuits, and his fortuitous acquisition of several deposition transcripts, gave Ruggieri solid information on the complexities of Jennings' financial and business networks.

By October, three months before the trial, document discovery and the depositions had solidified that:

— Clint never wavered from his belief that the safety had been on and the gun uncocked when he put it back in the box after firing it for the last time before the accident, despite the defense's speculation that, based on the somewhat inconsistent description by Morris of his own actions, the safety might have already been in the fire position; Clint acknowledged blame for having the gun, with a loaded magazine in it, in a dresser drawer instead of a locked gun box.

— Sue blamed herself for allowing the gun in the house and everything that occurred thereafter.

— While John's adolescent judgment had been poor when he took the gun out of the dresser drawer, he had ceded control of the gun to Morris, an adult; he remained consistent in his description of Morris' attempt to unload the gun, in contrast to the defense suggestion that Morris might have deliberately pulled the gun's trigger to see if the gun was loaded.

— Jerry Morris was negligent in handling the gun but remained insistent that he had not intentionally pulled the trigger. Attorney Hoffman accepted that his client Morris inadvertently had his finger on the trigger and had pulled it accidentally in the process of attempting to check the chamber to see if the gun was loaded.

— Willits Pawn had trigger locks for sale, and while the owner believed every gun should have one and promoted the locks to customers, he hadn't recommended, offered, or even mentioned them to Sue when she inquired and subsequently purchased the gun. The business was uninsured.

— The national distributor that sold the gun to Willits Pawn had insurance, but refused to make a settlement offer.

— Anna Leah, Jennings' third ex-wife, had participated in a divorce from Bruce to facilitate transferring and sheltering assets and real estate, including a million-dollar house;

— Janice, Jennings's second ex-wife, was president of Bryco Arms and had become its sole stockholder, but had little direct involvement in the business or grasp of even the most basic Bryco operations; and had direct involvement in the creation and manipulation of trusts in the names of their children, that were controlled by Bruce, largely for the purpose of sheltering assets.

— As for Bruce Jennings: he was the sole person responsible for every decision made by Bryco Arms, Jennings Firearms, and B.L. Jennings Inc.; neither he nor the companies had insurance, even as he was placing millions of guns on the street; and as the case progressed to trial, he had undertaken a considered plan to remove his assets from the reach of the court and any possible judgment.

It was time to go after the gun.

Without a compelling argument why the manufacturer should be held liable for the apparent gross negligence of a twenty-year old, Jennings' record of avoiding responsibility stood a chance of remaining intact.

That argument revealed itself to Ruggieri only a few months before trial, and, although Jennings didn't realize it as it happened, it came out of the mouth of Bruce Jennings himself.

On a beautiful fall afternoon, October of 2002, Ruggieri waited to board his flight back to the Bay Area after several days in Orange County deposing Jennings. These final three deposition sessions with Jennings, each lasting a full day, had been the most contentious of all. Newberg, Jennings' attorney, had objected so many times — hundreds over the three days — that Ruggieri finally said, "I'll stipulate that you object to all my questions just to get you to stop saying objection."

For two years Ruggieri prepared Brandon's case on what he had described in his early letter to Newberg as the "usual" gun-as-product safety weaknesses ("… *all the usual design defect issues... lack of warnings, trigger locks, chamber-loaded indicator, slide lock …*"). But throughout those years he had also been bothered by, searched for an explanation of, and sought an answer to why and when the design of the Model 38's manual safety had been changed from that of its predecessor, the virtually identical J-22.

Now he knew. During the depositions, Jennings had revealed something so significant that as Ruggieri walked up the ramp and boarded his flight home, he thought, *I just won this case.*

Throughout Jennings depositions, Ruggieri elicited crucial testimony by making it seem that the Model 38's design and mechanics were beyond his ability to grasp. "Bruce's depos were the hardest I'd ever taken. Sometimes it was like banging against a brick wall. Other times, I'd get something good out of him, some critical admission, something he'd say offhand, then I'd leave it, come back later and play dumb. I'd say, 'I'm not sure I understand this…' and get him to give up more detail about something that I already, absolutely understood."

That wouldn't work with many witnesses, but "Jennings had a certain arrogance that left him vulnerable."

"At the end, he left happy and I was happy."

The mystery of the Bryco Model 38 started with the Raven pistol designed by George Jennings, evolved into Jennings Firearms J-22, and formed the basis for Bryco Arms' first pistol, the Model 38. Nothing uncovered or revealed in these final depositions, neither the Model 38's history, the designer's identity, nor, indeed, even the very existence of the gun's designer, were readily forthcoming:

You worked for your father's company?

I did.

And you left your father's company and opened your own company, called Jennings Firearms, Inc., a California corporation, correct?

That's reasonably accurate.

Jennings Firearms, Inc., a California corporation, started manufacturing a firearm called the J-22?

That's correct.

Who designed the J-22?

I made the drawings for the J-22, and I used the Raven exemplar as the basis for the firing system.

. . .

Was the J-22 an exact duplicate of the Raven?

No, it was not.

The changes in the design of the J-22 that you started manufacturing from the Raven design, who was responsible for those changes?

An employee of Jennings Firearms Corporation.

Who?

That would be the president, Bruce Jennings.

Is that somebody other than you?

In a legal sense, probably.

Well, when you are sick, is Bruce Jennings, the former president of Jennings Firearms, Inc., sick?

Jennings Firearms, Inc. has no longer got a president. So if I am sick, I am sick.

So you, Bruce Jennings, designed the J-22 acting in your capacity as an employee of Jennings Firearms, Inc., is that what you are telling me?

I am telling you that Bruce Jennings, acting in his capacity of Jennings Firearms, Inc., a California corporation, is the individual who made the design drawings based upon the Raven pistols.

Can you distinguish in your mind between a design and a drawing of the design?

Yes, I can.

You have told me about who made the drawing of the design. Who made the design?

The design existed in the pistol that was being copied.

Portions of the design existed in the pistol that was being copied?

That's correct.

But the J-22 was not identical to the Raven?

No, it was a combination of two different things.

The Raven and the Sterling?

That's correct.

And who was it — whose brain was it that put together elements from the Raven and Sterling into a design, which you then committed to paper?

Bruce Jennings, an employee of Jennings Firearms, a California corporation, took the two guns and incorporated the firing system from the Raven and the exterior appearance of the Sterling and made the drawings for that.

That same Bruce Jennings designed the J-22, didn't he?

In my opinion, no.

Okay. Who designed the J-22, in your opinion?

I think the design was already there from the Raven and in the Sterling.

Did anybody besides you participate in the design of the J-22 and the committing of that design to paper?

I don't know of anybody else that made drawings on that project.

I am not going to fool around about this anymore. I have read your depositions. I have seen you dance around on this. This is very straightforward. I want an answer to this. You took the Sterling and the Raven, you took elements from each, you put them together, and you made a design for a J-22, true or false?

Inaccurate.

Tell me why it's inaccurate.

Because I don't consider myself a designer of an existing product just because I made the drawings of the product.

Who came up with the concept for the J-22? Wasn't it you?

I had a vision of what it would be.

And who took elements from the Sterling and from the Raven and put them together into a final vision of what the J-22 would be, wasn't it you?

I made those drawings.

Nobody is asking you about drawings.

Bruce Jennings, an employee of Jennings Firearms, a California corporation, made drawings from the Sterling pistol and the Raven pistol, and the pistol contained the firing system of the Raven, and the exterior appearance of the Sterling, and I was the person, as the employee of Jennings, that made those drawings.

So we are absolutely crystal clear, then, that you Bruce Jennings, it was your — are you right-handed or left-handed?

I am right-handed.

It was your right hand that held the pencil that actually made the drawings of the J-22?

That's correct.

And who told you how to move that right hand when you drew the J-22? Who said the command to that right hand? Come on. It was you, wasn't it? It's not that hard. It was your brain telling your right hand how to move and how to make those drawings, wasn't it?

I am not sure if the question even deserves an answer.

Well, good. Let's have the answer.

As we sit here today, you are asking me to take and testify that my brain is connected to my hand, and that's going to be part of the evidence in this trial?

Mr. Jennings, I am going to play all of this for the jury, and they are going to see you dancing and bobbing around on this. The simple question is, wasn't it your brain that made the decisions that your hand incorporated into the drawings for the J-22?

My brain, yes.

Thank you. Who designed the Model 38?

I made the drawings on the Model 38.

Your right hand?

Correct.

Your brain containing the ideas that your hand translated to paper for the design of the Model 38?

The Model 38 was drafted by my right hand, and it's a copy of the Model J-22, and it was only enlarged dimensionally to accept the larger barrel.

Other than that, it's identical, just dimensionally enlarged?

Pretty much.

Any changes of significance besides dimensional enlargement from the J-22 to the Model 38?

I think that there was a different safety system incorporated.

And anything else of significance?

Not that I recall. By the way, that was made by an employee of B.L. Jennings, Inc., a Nevada corporation. I do not do firearms work in any capacity as an individual.

Now, we are talking about the drawings that were made for the Model 38, right? Isn't that what we are talking about?

That's what we are talking about.

And you are telling me that except for the safety, the Model 38, at least at its inception, was simply a dimensional enlargement of the J-22?

That would be reasonably accurate.

The stated purpose of 'discovery' is to promote settlement, and to prevent surprises at trial — known as 'trial by ambush' — if settlement cannot be reached. The process includes a pre-trial exchange of evidence and documents between parties, and is governed by a detailed set of rules which lawyers in a seriously contested case spend significant time and expense trying to evade. Production of evidence and documents will be delayed for as long as possible, and when the defendant is finally forced to produce them, it is often by 'document dump', wherein the one or two documents important to the plaintiff are buried among stacks of boxes full of irrelevant papers, in the hope that the important documents will be overlooked.

One document dump from Jennings contained a single, undated page, with two seemingly irrelevant, unimportant, and puzzling sentences: "IMPORTANT – Pistol should not cock, or feed a cartridge into chamber with the safety on safe(s). However, the pistol will feed a cartridge into the chamber with the safety in safe(s) position, if previously left in a cocked condition."

Baffled but determined, Ruggieri showed Jennings a

copy of the document. Jennings identified it as something from the Calwestco gun company:

Why is this a Calwestco document rather than a Bryco or a Jennings Firearms of California?

Well, the warning up here that says important, it says that the pistol will not feed a cartridge into the chamber if the safety is in the safe position. On a Bryco firearm the safety locks the slide, so you can't pull the slide rearward with the safety on, but early Calwestco's could. That's the clue.

What about the Jennings Firearms of California? The original J-22?

The original J-22 would do that also.

I didn't understand what you said about this. What is the warning at the top of this pertaining to?

It pertains to a person attempting to chamber a round into the barrel when the pistol is uncocked and the safety is in the safe position. What it tells you is that the gun will jam and will not feed the cartridge into the barrel, so by reading this instruction the individual would learn about the operation of the firearm.

Do you remember that this was a problem with some of the earlier guns or is that just what you're telling me from reading this?

This was an instruction that was meant to stand out from the regular instruction sheet so that people would see that and understand it.

When this was packaged with a, I guess a J-22 or a Calwestco 22, this was in addition to whatever the original instruction sheet was?

That's correct.

I don't see in here anything about that a cartridge would jam if you tried to feed it. Can you explain what that means?

I think the document probably speaks for itself. It says

the pistol should not cock with the safety on. However, the pistol will feed a cartridge into the chamber with the safety in the safe position if it was previously left cocked, so what it's really saying is that you cannot cock the gun with the safety in its on position. You must take the safety off in order to cock it. That's what it's saying. But as a practical matter, it had the ability to take and partially feed the round out of the magazine resulting in an uncocked gun that was partially fed.

And jammed?

Yeah. It would be inoperable.

Well, was that considered to be a problem?

I don't think it was much of a problem. It was a situation that was resolved when Bryco added the plastic safety that moves vertical because that eliminated the problem of putting a cartridge in the barrel without the firearm being cocked.

Was that the point of the change to the up and down safety?

Yes, it was, but, you know, I'm not saying that it was a problem with the early gun. I'm just saying that the up and down safety, that was one of the reasons that it was incorporated, to alleviate that particular condition.

And that was felt to be significant enough to include a special notice about it?

Yes, it explained in detail.

...

You're telling me that the first Model 38 made had the up and down plastic safety? Correct?

That's correct.

But that it wasn't until sometime later that the J-22s were switched over to the up and down safety?

It wasn't until sometime later that Bryco started making J-22s, and when Bryco started making it they used the plastic safety from the model 38 and incorporated it into the new J-22 that Bryco was building.

Other than the issue, then, addressed in [the document] under the heading 'important', was there any reason for the change from the back and forth safety to the up and down safety?

All Bryco pistols have the up and down safety.

Did you have any input into the Bryco safety?

Yes, I did.

...

Well, your company, B.L. Jennings, Inc., was going to be the primary purchaser of the model 38s, right?

That's correct.

So did you or B.L. Jennings, Inc., have input then into the decision to incorporate an up and down plastic safety on the Bryco pistol?

Yeah, B.L. Jennings has the ability to make the suggestions. Of course, the manufacturer has the ability to decline the suggestion or find it infeasible.

And in the case of the up and down plastic safety on Bryco guns, did B.L. Jennings exercise that ability that it has to influence those decisions?

B.L. Jennings concurred that that safety would be the best safety to put in the gun.

The up and down plastic safety?

That's correct.

When you say B.L. Jennings, you were involved in that personally as Bruce Jennings, correct?

No. I was involved as the president of B.L. Jennings. I don't do any decisions as a private individual.

Well, was the carbon organism known as Bruce Jennings, the breathing, living, eating, blood pumping organism, involved in the decision-making process? Why did B.L. Jennings, Inc., through its president, Bruce Lee Jennings, concur in the decision for the Model 38s to come out with the up and down plastic safety? What were the reasons?

We knew that with the early design it would be possible to take and jam a gun by attempting to cock a gun with the safety on, and we also knew that the steel sliding safety had a tendency to go from the fire position to the safe position during heavy recoil of a larger caliber, which made the gun fail to cock, so with those considerations, and the convenience of the vertical moving safety, it was decided that it was an excellent design.

Any other reasons?

Superior design. That's all I can think of at this time.

...

The revelation that the safety had to be taken off 'safe' and moved to 'fire' to unload forced Jennings to take nonsensical, absurd positions:

Do you believe that anyone has ever been injured or killed with a Bryco pistol because they thought it was unloaded?

No.

Do you believe that anybody has ever been injured or killed with a Bryco pistol because they thought it was uncocked?

No.

Do you believe that anyone has ever been injured or killed after pulling the trigger on a Bryco pistol without intending to pull that trigger?

No.

And to this day have you ever become aware of anyone being injured or killed by the unintentional discharge of a firearm?

It's my opinion that most often there have been intentional discharges and I could not say that I know of any one particular instant of an unintentional discharge.

Mr. Jennings, do you believe as you sit here today that any-

one has ever been injured by the unintentional discharge of a firearm?

Well, I can understand that it may happen. I'm just not aware that it does.

Well, do you believe that it has happened?

I don't have a strong belief one way or the other.

Do you acknowledge that people have been injured or killed by the accidental or unintentional discharge of any Bryco pistol ever?

Accidental, yes. Inadvertent, I don't know.

Has anybody ever shot themselves without intending to shoot themselves with a pistol made by Bryco?

See, the problem we're having with this inadvertent word, this — handgun inc. style word that's been invented for this conversation, we're having —

Okay. I'm going to withdraw the question, sir. Then we won't use that word. Okay? If you are having a problem with it, we won't use that word. Do you believe that any human being has ever been injured or killed by a projectile that was emitted from a Bryco pistol when they did not want to be injured or killed by that projectile?

No, I don't. Well, with the exception of a broken gun or — or a drop, and the reason that I'm stating it this way is that anybody that's handling a firearm knows that when you pull the trigger it's going to shoot if it's loaded and cocked, and if they shoot themselves in the foot or they shoot themselves in the hand, it's not an inadvertent shooting. It is a direct and deliberate act of pulling the trigger.

So do you disagree that it's foreseeable that some persons probably because they're unfamiliar with the function of handguns can make that mistake?

I don't think that's foreseeable.

...

And after you heard of Brandon Maxfield's injury, you considered whether or not the design of the gun, in general, might have contributed to that injury, correct?

Yes.

...

And have you reached a conclusion as to whether or not the design of the firearm played any role at all in causing Brandon Maxfield's injuries?

I believe it did not contribute at all to the injuries.

Not one percent?

Zero percent.

Not one one-hundreths of one percent?

No, nothing.

Have any changes been made to the design or features of the Model 38 as a result of learning of Brandon Maxfield's injuries?

No.

Have any changes been made to the packaging or warnings or instructions with the Model 38 as a result of learning about Brandon Maxfield's injuries?

No.

...

How much of the fault for Brandon Maxfield's injuries is it that you feel rests on the head of Mr. Morris?

As I sit here today, with the knowledge that I have currently, I would fault him one-hundred percent.

Do you fault Brandon Maxfield for anything in connection with his injuries?

As I sit here today, I am not certain what activities, what role he played in the overall scheme.

So as you sit here today, you don't fault him because you don't know what role he played in the overall scheme?

I cannot fault him at this time because I don't have knowledge of what he did.

Okay. But you are leaving the door open to the possibility that as you gain additional knowledge you may decide that Brandon Maxfield was partially at fault for his injuries?

There's that possibility, yes.

...

Ruggieri had a fresh, new direction as he boarded his flight home. He had been looking for a theory of liability that could pierce Jennings' and the gun industry's time-tested strategy of *blame the user.* Without the actual gun that injured Brandon, there was no way to prove that pistol had operated other than as designed. And Ruggieri had been repeatedly assured, by Jennings and others, that no American jury had ever ruled a firearm defective because of an unsafe design as opposed to a physical failure. They reasoned that unlike other products a gun's design was, frankly, 'designed' to cause injury.

Numerous design claims alleged in Brandon's suit had been advanced unsuccessfully in past lawsuits, even though the design claims all made logical sense, but none had the emotional impact or power to overcome the *blame the user* defense.

In deliberately padding his document dump with irrelevant pages, Jennings had inadvertently included the one paragraph of text that, when looked at in context, could change everything.

Jennings had admitted that the Model 38 was essentially the same as the J-22, except for the larger caliber and a change in the safety. Millions of J-22s had already been sold with explicit instructions cautioning the user that "to unload without firing" the safety should always be placed on safe. That same instruction sheet now accompanied the Bryco Model 38, but the new safety designed for the Model 38 locked the slide and could not be placed on 'safe', and had to be moved to 'fire' before unloading the gun. The cautionary instruction not to unload that way could no longer be followed and, as Ruggieri had discovered by comparing the Model 38's instructions to the J-22's, had to be deleted from the Model 38's instructions.

A design change that contributes to an accident is 'defective' if its dangers outweigh its benefits. The benefits of the Model 38's new safety design might seem obvious. A gun had to fire when it was needed for defense, and a jammed pistol could mean instant death. But, the increased risk of not allowing the user to unload on 'safe,' as Bruce Jennings himself had cautioned the prior users of, essentially, the same gun, also seemed obvious.

There was ample precedent for a slide locking safety. The Model 1911 .45 caliber semi-automatic pistol used by U.S. troops in WWII was an obvious example. Colt Arms and other major firearms manufacturers that continued to use the design employed stables of firearms engineers. Bruce Jennings, Jennings Firearms, Inc., Bryco Arms/B.L. Jennings, Inc., however, had never in their history employed or consulted any engineer of any kind to design, evaluate, create, or test any aspect of their firearms.

"The bottom line — and a thin line it was — was that IF there were no better, cheaper, easier way around the *now admitted* jamming problem, then the safety change was arguably necessary, but this new path might again lead to failure. If it's a choice between the gun failing to fire when needed to save your life, and the chance of being injured when you are unloading, which are you going to choose?

"But if the safety was deliberately disabled just to hide a jamming problem that could have been easily and readily fixed without violating millions of prior warnings, then, well, 'oh my god.'"

The case was now product liability based on design defect. The other aspects of user safety that had been relied upon in other gun-related litigation — the lack of chamber loaded indicator, magazine loaded indicator (also, specific to the Model 38, its black-bottomed magazine) — would still be included in Maxfield's causes of action, but Ruggieri finally had the anchor strategy he'd been so desperately seeking.

"Still, though, I had to prove this through Jennings, not just because I didn't have the original gun, but because his asset sheltering and business structuring established the mindset of someone aware that his actions could result in legal consequences. Here was someone so calculating that he had everything in place to avoid giving up one penny to anyone hurt by his product, pennies he declined to invest in a gun design that would work properly."

Jennings had become wealthy by creating products destined to harm the products' users. "Brandon's accident was the inevitable result of every choice Jennings made as a gun manufacturer."

Ruggieri pulled together the case of his life, and Jennings did what he had done throughout his gun-manufacturing life — planned an escape.

Chapter 7

JANUARY 2003

It might be assumed (again, as reinforced by popular dramatizations) that a trial begins and moves along continually to some kind of decision.

And such an assumption would be wrong, especially in Maxfield vs Bryco.

As with every other aspect of the case, the trial's beginning was contentious, with over eighty pre-trial motions, many having to be decided by the presiding judge even before jury selection could begin. Trial started on January 17th, but another two weeks would pass before a jury would be selected, with motions presented right up to opening statements in March.

The trial judge, John "Fritz" Kraetzer, was a Harvard and Stanford Law School grad and had practiced law for thirty years before being appointed to the bench in 1992. As a judge he was known to be fair and smart, as a man, friends and family described him as a wise, kind gentleman.

Every objection made (and there were hundreds) during any segment of a deposition that was going to be used in trial required the judge's ruling. Disagreements over mountains of evidence, terms and descriptions the defense attorneys felt were prejudicial or should be excluded, and procedural issues, took weeks to complete. Arguments for and against written motions were presented in front of Judge Kraetzer, and after all sides had their say he ruled on many of them immediately, others a day later.

Each side made its case for evidence that the jury would see or hear, and how the evidence itself would be displayed or explained. The motions ranged from trying to exclude witnesses to a defense motion to prevent Ruggieri from using a certain phrase.

Newberg didn't want Ruggieri to use a photograph of Bruce Jennings' strikingly beautiful, bright silver P-51 mustang racing plane, parked, with Anna Leah Jennings in white shorts standing on its wing and smiling for the camera. Newberg argued that the name of the plane, *Saturday Night Special,* prominently painted on the fuselage just behind the plane's nose, was prejudicial.

As Judge Kraetzer looked down on the attorneys from his elevated bench, the chin of his poker face resting on his hand, Newberg said "Mr. Jennings no longer has the plane, it had been his personal plane, and the pejorative, prejudicial name had been painted on prior to Mr. Jennings acquiring it."

Ruggieri could barely contain his exasperation. "Your honor, this photograph was used by Bryco, printed on a postcard that included the Bryco name and product information, and given to dealers. Mr. Jennings not only referred to the picture and the plane itself by the name, he testified in depositions that he was the one who had the name painted on it. Regardless of what the defense may wish, the phrase Saturday Night Special is known and used throughout the gun industry, by law enforcement, by gun buyers, and by Mr. Jennings and Bryco to advertise and promote their guns."

Judge Kraetzer allowed the picture and phrase to be used, but also went to great lengths to keep everything fair, cautioning Ruggieri on a related issue. "Don't use the phrase 'junk guns' just for the sake of description."

California counties and cities, including Oakland, had gun ordinances that used that phrase, but the judge wasn't going to let that bleed into this case. "Don't broad brush the quality of the guns by simply describing them all in that way."

Other important motions involved information about Morris that had no direct relevance to his involvement in the accident; the details about Jennings' criminal conviction, and the loss of Jennings' Federal Firearms License due to that conviction.

But one initial ruling by Judge Kraetzer so threatened Ruggieri's strategy that Ruggieri almost lost the trial before it really began.

Newberg handed the judge two sheets of paper. "Your honor, we would like the court to exclude these pieces of paper that plaintiff purports to be instructions for a gun that is not a Bryco, not a Model 38." These were copies of the J-22 instructions presented to Jennings in depositions. "Mr. Ruggieri describes it as a document, but it is obviously not, it is simply two pieces of paper upon which are draft or in-progress descriptions for an unnamed gun. It's not a proper document and has no relevance to this case. We don't even know where these came from."

"Oh, for the love of god," Ruggieri blurted out, "Of course they're documents."

Judge Kraetzer's eyebrows went up slightly. "Mr. Ruggieri?"

"These pieces of paper came right out of Bryco's file cabinets, your honor. They are word for word and typeset exactly as the instructions provided with every J-22 sold.

Their relevance is unquestionable, directly relevant to instructions that were boxed with every Model 38, including the one purchased by the Stansberrys. Bruce Jennings declared that he had no originals, but recognized this as the language that could have been included with the J-22, and had we not obtained these through discovery we might not have ever seen them."

Newberg kept his focus on the judge. "There's nothing on those copies that indicate these are anything other than an internal work in progress, some draft language."

For one of the few times in his career, Ruggieri became anxious, feeling that a key piece of evidence was slipping out of his grasp, evidence too important to surrender.

"Your honor, it's from their files and matches the Model 38's instructions exactly, with one small exception, and that exception is vital, your honor. That exception is why the defense wants to exclude this document."

Newberg countered, "It has nothing that indicates that it was used as plaintiff contends."

Judge Kraetzer studied the copies. "I'm going to find for the defense on this one."

Ruggieri went from anxious to stunned. "If that's your ruling your honor, you've just gutted my case."

The remark caught Judge Kraetzer by surprise. "What?"

"My whole case is right there, your honor. After everything else the defendant did to put his gun on the market, the last thing he did was copy instructions from the gun that Bruce Jennings himself described as just a smaller caliber version of the Model 38. But because the Bryco didn't work right, he had to remove one of the most important sentences from the J-22's instructions before he could use them with the Model 38, because what he instructed the user to do couldn't be done with his new, defective gun."

The judge took a few more seconds to look at the words.

Ruggieri pressed on. "Your honor, it's evidence of the defendant's direct knowledge that he was hiding a dangerous defect in the gun's design."

The judge scooped up the papers, stood, and as he stepped toward his chambers said, "We'll recess for ten minutes."

They were ten of the longest minutes in Ruggieri's career, and he spent them spinning through thoughts of defeat.

Judge Kraetzer stepped out of chambers and returned to the bench. "That ruling was partly wrong. I'm going to allow plaintiff to use the description of the words, and use the words, but not allow showing the documents themselves to the jury. Can you live with that, Mr. Ruggieri?"

Relieved, Ruggieri said, "I can, your honor, and thank you."

All the defense's deposition objections were overruled for every video deposition of Jennings that Ruggieri would use, and "those were all key, because Jennings had moved to Florida. I couldn't subpoena him, couldn't compel him to appear, and the defense was under no obligation to let me know if or when he'd be here. His depositions would be my go-to whether I got him on the stand or not."

While Ruggieri knew Jennings would certainly do everything possible to avoid being at the mercy of the law, it would be almost another year before he would know the full extent of what Jennings had already done before the trial had even begun.

In 2000, during the early stages of Brandon's case, Jennings and Bryco were already being sued by the family of a Georgia teenager who had been accidentally shot and killed when a jammed Bryco 9mm discharged after it was dropped.

That case was still glacially making its way through the system as Ruggieri filed Brandon's case. It's possible that with the Georgia case and Brandon's case happening almost simultaneously, Ruggieri's eventual, successful acquirement of the deposition documents that revealed the extent and make-up of Jennings asset sheltering, and California's widening, pervasive constraints placed upon the Saturday night special style of guns, Jennings may have finally decided to permanently flee the West Coast.

In December 2001, shortly after Ruggieri first deposed Bruce and Janice Jennings, and six months after Jennings was served with notice of Brandon's suit, Jennings met with Florida bankruptcy attorneys. Less than a week later he put down $25,000 and signed a contract to buy a house in a 'fly-in' neighborhood of multi-million dollar houses, most with attached hangars for residents' planes. He deposited over $500,000 into one of the trusts a few days later, paid a $5,000 retainer to his bankruptcy attorneys "for legal services regarding Florida residence, domicile and exempt assets..." and signed a Florida declaration of domicile.

By February 2002, the Bryco plant was listed for sale and Jennings purchased the Florida house for $925,000 cash. He also transferred a multi-million-dollar Southern California home to his third ex-wife, transferred hundreds-of-thousands of dollars to a Florida account, and purchased a half-million dollar annuity.

He proceeded to liquidate two trusts, sold his yacht, and sold the Bryco plant, collectively totaling $5,000,000, money which he moved into other trusts and his Florida bank accounts.

By the start of the trial Bryco was still operating out of its Southern California building, and still selling guns, but Jennings had financially liquified, transferred, and moved most of his California assets.

CHAPTER 8

TRIAL

It was the first courtroom he'd appeared in as a young attorney almost twenty-five years before. Now, as he pulled the small wheeled cart behind him to his table, Ruggieri was ready to begin the trial of his career, fully recognizing the risks. He had told a close friend, "I blow this case, I lose, and I just might have to take a short walk off a tall bridge."

He knew this room, had been part of many cases tried here, and as he had with every aspect of every case he left no detail unaddressed. Over the last few days he had come in at least once a day when the room was empty to set-up and test his laptop's video playback through the courtroom's projection and sound system.

Now, he unpacked his document bag, pulled out his ever present legal pads, and arranged everything neatly on the table. Then, just as he had yesterday and the day before that, he plugged in, checked the power and video connections, cued the files he needed on his laptop and was ready to go.

The voice came from behind him.

"Uh, hi, could we have a minute to hook up our system, see if we need to adjust any of your cables so that…"

"Who are you?"

"I'm with Mr. Millsteen, setting up his AV."

"Well, you go ahead and set up whatever you'd like but I'm not about to move anything."

"What?"

"You might want to ask the clerk or the bailiff what you have to do, but you're not about to touch any of this."

The young man turned and went back the few steps to the defense table, where the gaggle of six attorneys and a paralegal bumped around and rearranged chairs and tried to fit at a table sized at best for two or three people.

Matt Millsteen was the defense attorney for Jennings' third ex-wife. A tall, good looking San Francisco attorney, he had irked Ruggieri by unnecessarily complaining and posturing over the woman's inclusion in the litigation, even after documents revealed her participation in Jennings' asset sheltering.

As the AV assistant walked away, Ruggieri thought, *he probably thinks I'm an asshole, but his problem is not my problem.*

Judge Kraetzer's voice floated over the room noise. "Mr. Ruggieri, is there some sort of problem brewing with the use of the projector?"

Ruggieri saw Millsteen standing by the bench. "I don't have a problem at all, your honor. I've been coming in for days to test and make sure I have everything set up so I wouldn't take any valuable court time fumbling around. I'm about to make an opening statement in an important case, I'm prepared and set up, and considering how fickle these systems can be, I'm not about to take a chance on them changing something that will screw up my presentation...your honor."

"This the first time in my court for your AV person, Mr. Millsteen?"

"Yes, your honor, we..."

"Have him take a seat until after Mr. Ruggieri's opening statement."

Ruggieri glanced up as Bruce and Janice Jennings walked into the room and sat in the row behind the defense table. As soon as they sat down, Ruggieri headed out of the room, waving hello to Joe Hoffman, Jerry Morris' attorney, seated at a small table behind the other defense counsel. Hoffman's client might have been a defendant, but Hoffman wasn't about to squeeze in among the six attorneys elbowing for room at the defense table, especially since much of their strategy was to push all responsibility for the accident onto Morris. And Hoffman couldn't sit at the plaintiff's table, so the court had placed him where it could. Hoffman was fine with his "kid's table" location, which would maintain a psychological distance from the 'real' bad guys.

Out of the courtroom, Ruggieri walked down the short corridor. Clint, Sue, her brother John, who would be a witness, and Brandon were waiting just around the corner, out of sight, as Ruggieri had instructed. He wanted Brandon in court as the jury filed in, and had asked the bailiff to keep the first row of seats available for the family so Brandon didn't have to be in the room until everything was ready, which also meant not until Bruce Jennings had entered and was seated.

It was the only time that Ruggieri knew for certain Jennings would be there.

Court convened at ten that morning, which meant the family had left Willits at five a.m. It was two-and-a-half hours to Oakland, but the logistics of getting Brandon up, fed, dressed, in the van, driving during the morning commute, then getting out of the van and into the building, added at least another two hours. Brandon slept part of the trip, but "I was kind of excited and kind of curious. This seemed to be a big deal."

As Ruggieri came around the corner to get them, "Sue had her game face on," a mom whose sole task in life was to take care of her son.

Clint, in a short-sleeve dress shirt and tie, looked as serious as Ruggieri had ever seen him, the man's expression and physical size emanating a vibe that could part a crowd.

"Ready?"

It was Brandon who answered. He was upright in his chair, his spinal curve giving him a slight lean to his right as his round, young face looked up at Ruggieri. "Yeah, let's go."

As Ruggieri held the door open, Clint wheeled Brandon in, Sue behind them, and everyone except Bruce and Janice turned and watched. Brandon couldn't see the entire room, so he couldn't see Joe Hoffman, who he'd come to know from the depositions and when Hoffman had come to the house with several of the defense attorneys to see the accident scene. But he could move his head enough to see most of the room, the cluster of defense attorneys, a few people people he didn't know sitting in some of the seats, and the judge. Brandon hadn't seen pictures of Jennings and didn't know he was actually looking at him as Clint wheeled Brandon to the front row.

Brandon was "used to people looking at me, but this was different, because they're all looking, and it's really quiet for a couple of seconds, and it's a small room. A little weird."

Sue, John and Clint sat in the front row, Brandon's chair beside Clint. None of the family looked at Jennings, in a suit and no tie, no more than twenty feet away, and Jennings never looked at them.

There were some brief discussions at the judge's bench with Ruggieri and the distributor's attorney about a last minute settlement offer from the insurance company, then Judge Kraetzer said, "Bring in the jury."

Seven men and five women, shouldering the weight of Brandon Maxfield's future, walked into court through the door of the jury room and took their seats in the box.

It had taken six days to select these twelve and six alternates from a pool of eighty people, and another month had passed before they convened today. The youngest was twenty-three, the oldest seventy, the others between their early thirties and early sixties. They were single mothers, widows and widowers, working and retired, several had relatives in law enforcement, at least two owned guns, one owned several and had a concealed carry permit.

Almost all believed jury awards in lawsuits were usually too high.

Their opinions on gun ownership, gun regulation, and personal responsibility were mixed, with a few jurors on each end of the spectrum. All agreed that manufacturers had a responsibility to make products safe. Most were skeptical how this could apply to a gun and were inclined to blame the user. One juror believed that the more complicated the style of gun, the more effort the manufacturer should put towards user safety.

Together they were fairly representative of the country's views and opinions.

The jurors glanced around the room, familiar by now with the attorneys, and saw Brandon reclining in a wheelchair. All noticed the awkward, uncomfortable closeness of the attorneys huddled around the defense table.

Judge Kraetzer began. "Good morning, ladies and gentlemen. It's been a while, but thank you all for returning and we'll get started with this trial in just a little bit. I want to say a couple of things.

"There are some of the participants in the courtroom today who will be here from time to time, but not all the time. They can't necessarily be here everyday, so that is something that you need not concern yourself with. Another thing, I'm not sure it was made clear to all of you, is that this is strictly a civil trial in this case. There are no criminal aspects regarding any of the defendants involved in this. This is strictly a civil matter.

"I'll also remind you that you are not allowed to speak to anyone, including your fellow jurors, about the case. No discussions at all, because discussions might cause you to form conclusions before all the evidence has been presented to you.

"We'll start with opening statements. Each counsel will tell you what they believe the evidence is going to show, but what they say in their opening statement is not the evidence. The evidence comes from witnesses, from documents, those kinds of things.

"Plaintiff's counsel will give his opening statement, we'll take a brief break, and then it will be defense counsel's turn."

Each attorney introduced himself and his clients, then Ruggieri stood and stepped toward the jury. As he spoke he alternated between taking a few steps back and forth along the front of the jury box, moving back to his table for different exhibits and to glance at his notes. How he spoke and moved here weren't much different than in other environments, and he was still occasionally humorous, but this was the litigator Ruggieri, and the two most important aspects of the trial would be the evidence and the jurors, and he was about to begin a construction process, building a bridge to each person in the jury box.

During his opening he would swing from eloquent to familial, conversational to professorial, and he would make sure to engage each juror.

This was the culmination of two years of research, work, travel, and a still growing debt which would reach $400,000, all built on Ruggieri's belief that this wrong could be made right.

"Thank you, Your Honor. Good morning, ladies and gentlemen. Brandon Maxfield, my client, is a quadriplegic.

"He's sixteen, paralyzed below the neck, paralyzed when he was shot in the face at age seven with a Bryco .380 caliber pistol fired while a twenty year-old, Mr. Morris, was trying to unload the gun for the purpose of making it safe.

"It was an accident that could have happened anywhere, could have happened to anyone.

"This gun, a Bryco gun, was produced by a company that has been producing guns from the late 1980's to the present time. They're still producing guns. They brag that they have churned out at a maximum six-thousand guns a day. We're going to follow one of these guns to Willits.

"The gun was an accident waiting to happen. It happened during what's called the administrative handling, that time you're doing anything other than shooting the gun. We'll have experts here to tell you, and this may surprise you, that the time you're actually shooting the gun is the safest possible time for you the shooter and the people around you.

"It's not a particularly safe time for who or what you're aiming at, obviously, but the reason administrative handling is the most dangerous is that when you're shooting the gun all of your concentration is on the gun. You're planning for the gun to go off. You're focusing on the gun. That turns out to be the safest time.

"All the other times, when you're unloading the gun, putting the gun away, holstering it, cleaning it, unloading it, disassembling it, that's a time you're not expecting it to go off. You're not completely focused on the gun, and that's the time you need safety features on the gun.

"Now, I'm going to show you a gun like the one that was used in this accident."

Ruggieri went to his table, picked up and brought back the blue box and gun to show the jury, telling the jury that "this and any guns we bring in during the trial will be checked by professionals to ensure that they're empty, and left in an open condition so they can't fire."

"This is an exemplar gun, an example. The main thing I want you to see is it has a little manual safety on it, a little switch that goes up and down, two positions, and little words on here, fire and safe." He stepped and paused, stepped and paused, his finger resting next to the safety, glancing at the individual jurors to ensure they had actually looked at the switch before moving again.

Now he took a step away, held the gun up and moved the switch. "Put it in the fire position, the trigger can be pulled; in the safe position, the trigger cannot be moved, you can pull the trigger all you want, the gun cannot go off."

He put his finger on the trigger, gun pointed to the floor, but even with his assurances about the gun's inoperability, he noticed several jurors wince as they watched him.

He paused a moment before continuing.

"Sue and Clint Stansberry, the owners of the gun, failed to fully appreciate the danger of this product, underestimated the danger of owning it and of storing it.

Mr. Morris was handling the gun. He particularly underestimated the danger of trying to unload the gun to make it safe.

"Bruce Jennings' name is on this side of the gun," he pointed to one side, then the other. "The Bryco name is on this other side. Bruce Jennings and Bryco Arms *fully* understood the danger presented by this gun.

"They forced the user to put the safety on 'fire,' making the trigger fully operable, before being able to try to unload the gun, forced the user to put this gun in a lethal condition where it could go off and seriously injure or kill someone.

"And they intentionally and deliberately built-in that danger for the sole purpose of increased profits. They intentionally disabled the only safety on this gun so it couldn't be put on safe during any administrative handling.

"And you'll hear evidence in this case that Bruce Jennings didn't care."

He placed the gun back on his table, and in a paced but easy manner recounted Jennings' creation and production of the J-22, and the evolution from that gun to the Model 38, and the massive sales of the same gun but with different names. "Three million guns sold to people all across the United States under different names, names you'll hear throughout the case. You'll hear the name Raven, his father's company, where Bruce Jennings worked at a time Raven was churning out guns. You'll hear the name Jennings Firearms. That was Bruce Jennings' next company, and he owned it.

"You'll hear that Bruce Jennings designed and sold three-million J-22s, functionally identical to the Bryco Model 38. A user trying to make the J-22 safe, to disable it, to unload it, like the intent of Mr. Morris in this case, on all those J-22s, the safety was enabled so you *could* put the safety in the 'safe' position, just as you'd expect, and then unload it.

"And every one of those guns was sold with a little instruction sheet. I don't have it here, but," he picked up the folded paper, "it was very similar to this little one-page instruction sheet that came with this Model 38.

"Mr. Jennings and his companies and the people that put out three-million guns specifically recognized the danger of an accidental discharge when the gun was being unloaded. And they put in their instruction sheet a specific warning that said, *to unload without firing, put the safety in the 'safe' position*. You could put the safety on 'safe' with every one of those guns, so that if you accidentally pulled the trigger while you were trying to unload the gun or the gun slipped out of your hands, nothing would happen. It couldn't go off.

"Why? Because the safety was on safe."

He transitioned to how Jennings first discovered that "the Model 38 had a jamming problem. Bruce Jennings has testified and has called it an annoyance, just an annoyance."

"There weren't any engineers on staff at Bryco, and no consulting engineers. Bruce Jennings is not an engineer. Bryco could not fix the jamming problem, or the jamming 'annoyance.' This is absolutely undisputed in this case. So what did they do?

"They decided to hide the jamming problem. Decided to hide it. We'll have an expert walk you through the mechanics of this later; if the Model 38 was uncocked and the safety was on, when the user tried to pull back the slide, that's when the gun would jam.

"And they didn't know how to fix it.

"Their reasoning was, *We can't fix that, therefore, let's not let the user pull the slide back when the safety is on, and that circumstance will never arise.* It jams when you try to pull the slide back with the safety on, we can't fix it, so we won't let you pull the slide back with the safety on.

"That is undisputed. That's how they tried to hide the problem."

Prior to the Bryco guns, "Jennings specifically warns every single purchaser of three-million virtually identical pistols under different names to put the safety on 'safe' before you try to unload the gun. Now they put a gun on the market that you have to put the safety on 'fire' in order to do any of the things recognized as being dangerous when handling the gun.

"They forced the user to move the safety to 'fire' before being able to pull back the slide, which is what you do to unload the gun, and how you look inside the gun to make sure there's not a bullet in there.

"But, what about the warning in that instruction sheet?

"They deleted it. Took it out. Took the words out, those words that I quoted, 'put the safety on 'safe' before trying to unload the pistol.'

"The instruction sheet was almost identical to the J-22 sheet, but those words are gone from the Model 38 instructions. That is also undisputed in this case. They had *made* this gun more dangerous than the prior guns. They had actual and superior knowledge about what they were doing, and they did it on purpose, knew they were doing it, knew what the consequences were.

"They did it anyway because they didn't care."

Now he shifted to the 'case'.

"This is a product design case. You're going to hear that design decisions have to consider the market. This is a low cost, low quality firearm sold primarily through pawnshops. And you'll hear testimony that this gun is sold primarily to people who have little or no experience or training.

"This gun defines its own market, because people with experience or training don't buy guns like this, because it's low quality. It's a cheap gun. But Bruce Jennings knew hundreds of thousands of inexperienced users would be the people using this gun, users who only wanted to make the gun safe, and now had to take the safety off 'safe' and put it on 'fire.' They had to put that gun in a lethal condition before even *trying* to make it safe."

He paused, reached into his pocket, and pulled out a nickel.

He held it up as he walked along the front of the jury box. "The edge of this nickel, the thickness, is the margin of error, the distance the trigger has to move for the gun to go off. This is the margin of error they allowed the user — the edge of a nickel. They'll say the trigger is too hard to pull, that it's *impossible* to accidentally pull the trigger.

"Approximately a tenth of an inch, that's all they give hundreds of thousands of inexperienced and untrained users of this low-quality gun.

"That's how much chance Mr. Morris had of avoiding this accident.

"And yet with all the horrors that this gun brought, you're going to hear from experts that the cost of fixing this problem instead of just hiding it would be less than a nickel." He looked at the nickel, and looked at the jury. "Less than a nickel."

He paused again, glanced at Bruce Jennings before he looked back and scanned the eyes of each juror. "The cost now? Brandon Maxfield."

He shifted to "responsibility," explaining the case was about "personal responsibility, corporate responsibility, and about the personal responsibility of the those who are responsible for their corporations.

"The issue in this phase is joint responsibility for Brandon's injuries. You'll hear that Brandon's family accepts responsibility. They'll never escape it, live with it everyday. They underestimated the danger of this gun.

"Mr. Morris especially underestimated the danger of trying to unload a gun, trying to make it safe. It didn't occur to him that in trying to make the gun safe, he'd be forced into a position to make it the most unsafe that it could be.

"They've all taken responsibility.

"Bruce Jennings and the companies that made and distributed this gun refused to take any responsibility for this accident."

The jury was with him, listening intently, eyes following him, only leaving whenever Ruggieri, by body language or by turning his head, focused on Brandon or Jennings.

It was time for a photo. He walked to his laptop.

"Bruce Jennings, Bryco Arms, and B.L. Jennings, Inc. proudly market these guns as Saturday night specials. Let me show you what I mean." All eyes in the room, except Jennings', shifted to the projector screen. "This is a P-51 Mustang that Bruce Jennings had restored; it's polished aluminum. The name of the airplane is the Saturday Night Special.

"In common usage, ladies and gentlemen, the term Saturday night special refers to a gun of low quality, a crime gun, a throwaway gun.

"To the defendants that term was a marketing slogan. This photograph was emblazoned on an oversized postcard and sent to distributors and dealers around the country, and handed out at gun shows. This is how they marketed the Bryco line of guns.

"This airplane made its appearance at air races, and Mr. Jennings will tell you himself that it was a marketing tool. It brought his product to the attention of people who are potential customers. It was his Goodyear blimp."

Now Ruggieri began to link Bruce Jennings not just to the design of the product but to Jennings' views, views at odds with reality. "He doesn't think that guns are unsafe, says it's impossible to accidentally pull the trigger on one of his guns, and he'll tell you he has no idea what training and experience the purchasers of these guns have. Bruce Jennings is going to tell you he's a businessman. He has no engineering training, no safety training, no design training, no products training.

"And he will tell you he doesn't care."

"He'll tell you he doesn't know of anyone being injured by an accidental discharge of a gun, that *he doesn't think, despite his three-million warnings to always put the safety on safe before you try to unload it, that it's unsafe to unload one of these guns*. He doesn't think there is any safety advantage to putting the safety on safe before you try to unload it.

"And you'll hear him admit his design decision forces the user to violate one of the ten commandments of gun safety — to always, always, always leave the safety on safe until you're ready to fire the gun.

"Mr. Jennings will tell you he is not going to change the design, and will not acknowledge even one percent responsibility for Brandon's injuries. Believe it or not, they are still selling the same gun today. The design has not been changed.

"You still cannot unload the gun on safe.

"But the instruction sheet has been changed — again.

They put something back in. Remember I told you they deleted something? Now it says, always keep the safety on safe — pardon me, I'll quote it exactly."

He slowly, deliberately picked up the instructions from his table. *"Always keep the safety on until the pistol is pointed at a safe target and you intend to fire."*

"Always keep the safety on. Good advice, advice they know to a certainty that you cannot follow with this gun. It shows they know that it's important, and yet they know you cannot follow that advice. They intentionally prevented the user from following the advice, but they know it's good advice so they put it back in.

"There is something else now on the current instructions to show what they know. Remember I told you Bryco Arms is going to say you can't accidentally pull the trigger on one of these guns?

"Since Brandon's accident they added these lines — "Keep the chamber empty and the safety on to avoid accidental discharge if dropped *or if trigger is accidentally pulled,* something which they claim cannot happen."

Ruggieri paused, head bowed for a moment. When he continued, his volume was the same, but his tone softer.

"It is my honor to represent Brandon, one of the bravest, strongest people you'll ever meet, and someone I admire.

"He's here with his parents Sue and Clint Stansberry. I wanted you to meet Brandon at the very first opportunity so you could see who this case is about." Ruggieri looked at Brandon for several seconds. Brandon smiled, his eyebrows arching, and in Ruggieri's peripheral vision he saw several of the jurors smile in return. "I'm sure that you can imagine this is probably the most important thing going on in a 16-year-old boy's life, right now, and maybe for the rest of his life.

"It's only natural that Brandon wants to be here every single day, but when I'm done talking today, I'm going to kick Brandon out of here. I'll bring him back later when we talk about him, his injuries, his needs, his future and his plans. He's attending regular high school in Willits, California. He wants to graduate with his class, and he wants to go to college with the other kids.

"Brandon has no memory of this accident. And during this trial we're going to talk about a lot of things that he doesn't need to hear."

He now explained that the trial would be divided into "three phases, sort of like three little mini trials.

"The first is liability. Most of the evidence you're going to hear in this first phase will be about the gun and the accident; the causes or significant factors of the accident, including testimony about defects in the design of the gun, testimony about how the accident happened, testimony about the negligence of the defendants.

"The second phase will be about Brandon's damages. Most of the evidence in that phase comes from doctors, rehabilitation experts, from educational experts, and it will concern Brandon's medical condition, his medical care and expenses, his earning capacity, ability to get a job, things like that."

He gestured with a wave of his hand at the defense table as he said, "The third phase — who are all these defendants? You've heard a big list of defendants and trusts and partnerships and whatnot, and we're going to talk about who they are, to what extent each of them are responsible for this pistol that bears the Bryco Arms and the Jennings name, and the interrelationships, if any, of these trusts, partnerships, people, corporations."

He described the kind of evidence the jury would see, documents and witnesses, but, "there are some people outside California and we can't force them to come in with a subpoena, nor do we want to, so we've videotaped their depositions. And we'll show you video on this screen."

There was a break for lunch, then Ruggieri concluded his opening. "Ladies and gentlemen, I have some more to say. I've been waiting to talk to you a long time, and I won't get to talk to you again until the end of the case." He described the events that led to the accidental shooting; how one of his expert witnesses had created two different ways the Model 38 could be altered at little cost to allow for unloading with the safety on; explained the different aspects of the laws on which Brandon had relied upon to sue; and finished with an explanation of what created a "design defect."

"Causation means 'the substantial factors contributing to this accident', and the law recognizes there can be more than one cause. 'Who' has acted unreasonably is the negligence action. Again, the law recognizes that it can be more than one person who acted negligently in respect to an accident.

"Did the gun fail to meet reasonable consumer expectations of safety? That's called 'defect', product defect. A 'design defect' is if the risks of the challenged design of the gun outweigh any benefits that design may have.

"I want you to be clear in understanding there's no issue of manufacturing defect in this case. A manufacturing defect is a product breaks, the gun breaks in half, the trigger falls off; it was made improperly. The gun that injured Brandon Maxfield was in the exact condition that the manufacturer wanted it to be in."

He picked up the exemplar gun. "The reason I'm showing you a sample here, is because the actual gun has been lost. Brandon had another attorney a long time ago, and the attorney's paralegal was the person who last had the actual gun. That paralegal was killed in an automobile accident years ago. We were never able to find the gun.

"Before the gun was lost, though, it was tested twice." Ruggieri told of measurements and other tests performed on the original gun, which found "no modifications, nothing was changed, nothing damaged. No issue of manufacturing defect.

"But no one evaluated the *design* of the gun. It's all about the design. The design that they 'engineered', and I put that in quotes, into this gun. The issue of product defect in this case is entirely the *design* of the gun. Yes, the gun worked the way you designed it, but that design was bad, or it was stupid or it was unsafe. But it worked the way you designed it.

"And I want to tell you right now so you don't hear it for the first time later, there are plenty of guns that as part of the overall design have a safety that locks the slide closed. Most of those have a specific military or police purpose and are sold to people with a lot of training or experience, and most include a comprehensive system of safeties.

"But, even though there are other guns that have this one feature, you will hear that not one non-Jennings gun was designed that way so an annoying jamming problem could be *hidden*.

"Not one other gun that you'll hear about had the safety disabled for the sole purpose of curing an annoying jamming problem.

"Not one other gun company took the *only* safety on the gun, the only safety, not part of a system of safeties, and disabled it, made the safety unusable instead of getting an engineer or a safety expert to look at it.

"And not one other gun company revised their warning when they made this change, just erased the warning to always put the safety on safe before trying to unload the gun."

Now as he moved back and forth in front of the jury, he looked from the gun to a different juror every time he said the word "zero."

"The total amount spent by Bruce Jennings, Bryco Arms and B.L. Jennings on engineering for this gun? Zero.

"Total amount spent by Bruce Jennings, Bryco Arms and B.L. Jennings for human factors ergonomics analysis? Zero.

"Following safety developments in the industry? Zero.

"Following failures of the product? Zero.

"Exploring modifications or improvements? Zero.

"Exploring alternatives to hiding the jamming problem? Zero.

"Exploring ways to fix the jamming problem? Zero.

Ruggieri paused, allowing the pile of "zeros" to settle, glancing at Jennings before looking back to the jury, and slowing his delivery as he continued.

"How much money did they spend to minimize the dangers of this gun to users and people around the users? Zero.

"How much money did they spend determining the number of people killed or injured? Zero.

"The evidence in this case is going to show that as between the user and the manufacturer, one was in the best position to know the risks and dangers, the common mistakes, the nature of the market for this gun, what types of people buy it, their experience or training.

"Who as between the users and the manufacturers deliberately eliminated the one safety on this gun and who just didn't care?"

He placed the gun back on his table. "I'm going to sit down, and you're going to hear from attorneys for the defendants. I won't get back up and respond right away. I'll talk to you at the end of the case.

"For now, you'll have to imagine what plaintiff's evidence would say in response. The fundamental truth here, ladies and gentlemen, is that this gun was defective in design. The manufacturer and distributors were negligent in selling it. The victims were the purchasers, the users, the handlers. If the defendants had accepted any responsibility, *any responsibility,* personal responsibility, corporate responsibility, personal responsibility of the persons responsible for the corporate decisions, this one gun would not have destroyed this family, we wouldn't be here today, and Brandon would walk anywhere he wanted to."

Judge Kraetzer called a ten-minute break.

Ruggieri sat down and took a deep breath. In a few minutes the defense would have its first say. Ruggieri knew what much of it would be, and he was prepared, but that didn't stop him from thinking about what had occurred just a few weeks ago.

He and Edith were at a small gathering of family and friends. As he described the case and the upcoming trial, someone had asked, "If the ATF and the FBI can't do anything about this guy, what makes you think that *you* can?"

He had tried to laugh it off, but hadn't shaken it, and reminded himself where he was right now. There was no going back.

The attorneys representing the distributor, Willits Pawn, Anna Leah Jennings, and Janice Jennings, each gave opening statements that sounded like separate parts of the same defense: a straight-forward case of negligence on Brandon's parents and Jerry Morris, and a gun with no defect, a gun with a safety that worked as it should:

"...Mr. Ruggieri spent a lot of time talking about deception in the pistol. It's like any other firearm. You pull the trigger, it goes bang and something comes out the end of that tube at a very high rate of speed. Mr. and Mrs. Stansberry knew what that was. There was nothing deceptive about what they were getting ready to buy...

"It's an awesome responsibility, parents have, to watch out for our children so they don't hurt themselves. Now, in this case, there were four children under the age of thirteen that lived at that trailer up in Willits. And when Clint and Susan Stansberry chose to buy that lethal weapon and bring it into that home, they knew who was living there. And they undertook the responsibilities to store it safely...

"So whether you like handguns or you hate them, whether Mr. Jennings is somebody you would choose to be with or not, those issues are totally irrelevant in this case.

"What is at issue is whether or not that pistol caused this accident. And the testimony that we will be offering to you will demonstrate that it did not..."

Jennings' attorney Newberg was direct and to the point:

"First thing I'd like to say, the evidence is going to show that there is absolutely no design defect with the safety mechanism of this firearm. That's what the evidence is going to show.

"And the evidence is going to show you that absolutely there was careless and reckless handling in the storage, management and use of this firearm. It's plain. It's simple. That's going to be my position throughout this trial.

"I'm going to ask you to find zero liability for my

clients. Not a half a percent, not one percent, not two percent, not three percent. Zero liability.

"And that is going to be difficult, because we saw Brandon Maxfield here today, a quadriplegic. I'm sympathetic to his position. I certainly am. But we also need to talk about my clients who are here today.

"Earlier Mr. Ruggieri talked about a margin of error, showed you a nickel, said it was about one-tenth of an inch on the trigger pull, and it may or may not be one-tenth of an inch. I don't know.

"But what you have to observe and understand is that the firearm that was involved in this accident and the other Bryco Model 38s have approximately an eight-pound trigger pull.

"A hair trigger that's used in target shooting is approximately two to three pounds. It takes very little effort to move it, and that is very specific for target shooting.

"The evidence will show you wouldn't want it on an ordinary gun, because it's too light. By using the extremely heavy trigger pull, Bryco Arms has the highest in the industry. It forces the user to think and to pull the trigger. It's eight pounds of pressure.

"Imagine eight pounds of pressure. Other firearms, like the Beretta, may be about four to six pounds.

"That's going to be an important fact in this case. Why? Because Mr. Morris, as you will see him in his deposition testimony, had both of his fingers outside the trigger guard. There's no way that firearm can discharge. That's what the experts will tell you. If he didn't put his finger on the trigger, which is evidently what I guess we're going to hear now, he would have to make an intentional pull on that trigger to discharge that firearm.

"They don't go off accidentally with an eight-pound trigger pull. You're going to hear Mr. Morris testify that he knew if he pulled the trigger on fire, it is going to discharge a bullet. There are just no two ways about it."

Hoffman, a fit man with tight, curly hair and an energetic oratorial delivery, gave his opening last. As Ruggieri had anticipated, the only way an attorney could defend Morris was to accept a portion of responsibility, and focus on the other defendants as links in the chain of causation.

"Ladies and gentlemen, I represent the condemned in this case. Mr. Morris. When one represents the condemned, one has to be very careful to make sure one never loses the credibility of the jury.

"And one must also be very careful to always bring what all the other lawyers say about the evidence back to the true evidence. The true evidence in this case that you will know after ten weeks will demonstrate to you, irrefutably, that every single defendant, including my client, is responsible for the gun injury to Brandon Maxfield, responsible for condemning that boy to a wheelchair for the rest of his life.

"Now, let me tell you what you will never hear from me. Mr. Millsteen referred to this gun as a tube which fires a projectile. For me, it's a gun. Under the law, it's a gun.

"Many things have been said about Mr. Morris, which I'm going to take all the time I need, and I apologize to you for that, but I think it's only fair if everyone's going to condemn him that I have a chance to defend him."

He glanced at Jennings. "This gun started out being designed by that man there who is not an engineer, who did not bother to consult with a safety engineer, who did not bother to consult with a human factors expert. That man back there designed the gun with no concern nor consideration about safety.

"The law of California demands that every person who designs and sells and manufacturers a handgun has the duty of safety."

At one point in attorney Newberg's opening, he had stated to the jury that based on the circumstances of this case, there should be "no judgment" against Jennings. Hoffman specifically addressed that point:

"You also heard Mr. Newberg talk about no judgment. You know what, it's totally irrelevant. You're the ones who are going to decide the case. It doesn't matter what somebody else thought about some other evidence at some other day. Don't be misled by those things. Stay on the path of the truth."

Newberg objected, unusual but allowed during an opening statement; Judge Kraetzer overruled.

"And don't be bothered by objections. Stay on the path of the truth.

"What was it that Mr. Jennings designed? He designed a gun that is a Saturday night special, a gun which must be placed in the firing position in order to be made safe.

"Mr. Morris had nothing at all to do with that decision. What about manufacturing control? This gun was sold by Bryco. Did Bryco consult with a safety engineer to make a safe product? No. Did Bryco Arms consult with a human factors expert to make a safe product? No.

"Who controlled Bryco Arms? You see the president sitting there, Ms. Jennings. She didn't control Bryco Arms. Bruce Jennings controlled Bryco Arms; the same man that designed the gun controlled the company that manufactured the gun.

"Now, one of these lawyers talked about the awesome responsibility that parents assume when they buy a gun. Yeah. That's right. It's an awesome responsibility. It's the same responsibility that the manufacturer had.

"Who has more awesome responsibility under the law? The law doesn't say you have a more awesome responsibility or they do — the law says we all do. But in the case of a gun, the responsibility rests on the designer and the manufacturer and all the distributors. They had the responsibility. It wasn't just Mr. Morris.

"So let's stay on the path of the truth. Mr. Jennings controlled Bryco Arms. His title was consultant, but he had the power to fire, had the power to hire. He made the decision not to put any safety device on this gun, except the one that had to be disabled before anyone could use the gun.

"Now, the law is that all those people who are substantial factors in causing the injury are responsible. During our questions to you when we were selecting this jury, many people spoke about ultimate responsibility. The law that the judge is going to give you is not the law of 'ultimate' responsibility. The law of California is shared responsibility."

"The substantial factors? My client, Jerry Morris, was a substantial factor in causing this child's condemnation to a wheelchair.

"Bruce Jennings was a substantial factor. All of these clients here were substantial factors...

"Someone made the comment about the sole responsibility of the owner. That's not the law. It was the responsibility of everyone of these people to protect that child, and they all failed. They all failed. My client failed, too...

"Did he have his finger on the trigger? Probably. Probably he did. But it was predictable, predictable to a person unfamiliar with that gun. It's very difficult to pull that slide back, very hard to do. It's Mr. Morris' fault his finger was on the trigger, but the design of that gun, knowing that you had to pull the the slide back when the thing was in the fire position, it was foreseeable, it was predictable."

Hoffman's pace in front of the jury had been steady, not rushed, and an energy came across in the way he spoke, his volume, emphasis, and gestures. Now he stopped, took a deep breath, and scanned the jurors faces.

"Mr. Newberg said that when Jerry Morris pulled the slide, he probably put a bullet in the chamber. There's no probably about it. He did. He did. Because if there had already been a bullet in the chamber when he pulled that slide, the bullet would have ejected. And unfortunately but true, my client is the one that took the safety from the safe position and moved it to the fire position…

"I hope that I've been able to impress upon you the fundamental truth of this case. The fundamental truth that you will all know after ten weeks of testimony is that we, the defendants, we are all responsible. Thank you."

Twenty-four witnesses testified over the next ten weeks, the family and experts in person, Jennings and a few other witnesses on video. Witness testimony was never less than hours long, several witnesses were on the stand for two days, and experts' testimony was often technically complex. Almost two-hundred documents, photos, charts, posters and other items would be shown to the jury. The testimony of each side's gun experts would be key, as would that of the medical experts — with substantially different opinions — on Brandon's future medical costs.

Ruggieri would hold back Brandon, his star witness, until the end of the trial.

It would be months, however, before Ruggieri would find out that it would be his first witness that had the most influence on the jury, a witness not involved in the case and who Ruggieri had subpoenaed only weeks before. The witness had nothing to do with Brandon's accident, but he would educate the jury about guns, gun-related lexicon and nomenclature, gun handling and general safety.

The first witness would be, essentially, Guns 101 for the jury.

Plantiff expert witness Sergeant T.

"Your honor, plaintiff calls as their first witness Sergeant Gary T."

Ruggieri made a few quick notes as tall, fit, in a black Oakland Police uniform, Sergeant T. walked to the witness stand and was sworn in. The defense table vibrated with murmuring between the attorneys. Even though the defense had deposed him, they had no idea what he was about to say, and as Ruggieri glanced at them before walking towards the stand, "they were going ape shit because he showed up in uniform."

Ruggieri had no personal or professional relationship with the officer. "I'd seen him on the local news. Finding him was huge, and deciding to list him as what's called a non-retained expert witness turned out to be a very wise decision."

The distinction of a 'non-retained' expert witness was important. Both sides in a trial can use expert witnesses, but a retained expert witness is a professional, paid for his or her services and trial appearances. Such experts are sought out by one side or the other for specific expertise, to study the case based on information shared with them by the legal team, present their findings in depositions and, almost always, in person at trial. Ruggieri's gun experts and the defense gun experts were compensated, as were the medical and economics experts.

A non-retained expert witness, like Sergeant T., is not compensated, may or may not appear voluntarily, and is allowed to state his presumably unbiased opinions. Such a witness can be a great advantage in a contentious case.

"Putting him on first rattled them, they had no idea what I was going to do with this guy. Frankly, neither did I when I first contacted him. But the defense's opening statements gave me direction.

"He was a good way to attack the other side's stupid positions."

The defense team seemed intent on piling all responsibility on Morris, Clint and Sue, and had been direct about it in their openings, which included several absolute statements. Newberg in particular had looked the jurors in the eyes and said, "...By using the extremely heavy trigger pull, Bryco Arms has the highest in the industry. It forces the user to think and to pull the trigger. It's eight pounds of pressure...They don't go off accidentally with an eight-pound trigger pull..."

Successfully refuting those statements so soon after the jury had first heard them could call into question not just the statements themselves but the credibility of the entire defense.

Sergeant T. was a SWAT tactical operations supervisor, range master (overseeing officers on the firing range) and former supervisor of the department's weapons unit, the detective in charge of investigating "illegal possession, illegal purchase or illegal acquiring of firearms. We also provide experts from the department who testify for the city. Those duties also include becoming the department's expert on new gun laws."

Ruggieri began:

Sergeant T, you have been called as a witness here under subpoena today?

Yes.

Do you view yourself as aligned with one side or the other in this case?

No. I have no reason to have any involvement in this other than being subpoenaed.

Are you receiving anything over your regular pay for being here as a witness today?

No.

Are you anti gun?

No. I'm probably just the opposite.

Did part of your duties require you to gain familiarity with different weapons, and be involved with firearms on a daily basis?

Yes, every firearm listed on the assault weapons ban.

How many weapons is that?

Hundreds now. I have fired over 100,000 gun, handgun, shotgun, and machine rounds. I estimate that number [of different weapons I've fired] to be about 250. I also teach a lot of courses.

Your resume lists total hours of instruction that you have received on firearms, as 796; is that right?

Yes. It's probably a little bit more than that.

Have you had experience with the Bryco Model 38?

Yes.

Where have you seen the Bryco Model 38?

At the Oakland Police Department, at the property section.

In what context?

They were recovered as either evidence in a crime or found property.

...

Are you familiar with a Jennings gun called a J-22?

Yes.

Outside of your duties as a firearms expert, have you ever had any involvement with a Bryco pistol, ever used one hunting or carried one as your own weapon?

No.

What experience have you had shooting a Bryco Model 38?

I believe it was twice.

And how many times have you handled this particular model?

Half a dozen times, I believe, or more.

Have you seen this particular model in the course of your work?

Several dozen.

Have you disassembled this gun?

Yes.

…

You told me you have some opinions about the Model 38. For what purpose would you recommend the Model 38 Bryco?

Would I recommend this gun to be purchased by anybody?

Yes. Let's start with that.

My personal opinion is no.

What about your expert opinion?

That would be a no also.

…

During his testimony, Sergeant T handled several guns provided by Ruggieri, including a J-22; with each demonstration, he always ejected each gun's magazine and did a thorough chamber check; he now explained the differences between a revolver and semi-auto.

Some of the guns you've been showing us have a double-action trigger pull and a single-action trigger pull. What about the Model 38?

It just has a single-action pull.

(Note: generally, a double-action trigger pull is one in which pulling the trigger causes the hammer to pull back

— making it 'cocked' — and then release forward to strike the shell and fire a round; a single-action only releases an already cocked hammer, in which a separate action, such as pulling back the slide of a semi-auto gun, has already cocked the hammer.)

The gun has to be cocked before it can go off?

Yes.

And there's only one distance that the trigger travels?

Yes.

And is that a long distance or a short distance?

In this particular model you've given me [the Bryco 38], it's a fairly short distance.

We're going to hear evidence in this case that the trigger pull on the actual gun in the case was measured at eight to nine pounds. Can you tell me where does that fall in the range of trigger pull that you encounter?

I'd say that's about average. Some manufacturers, as I said earlier, have twelve pounds — could be up to twelve. Some have as little as five pounds, three pounds of pull.

Do you have an opinion as to whether or not it's possible to accidentally pull an eight pound or nine pound trigger?

Yes.

And what's your opinion?

You can do it easily.

...

The defense opening statement had compared the Bryco's design as analogous to the venerated Colt .45, a model known also as the 1911, a large semi-auto used by the military in WWII, familiar to much of the general public, and capable of being carried into combat "cocked and locked."

That's the Colt 45 we see in the World War II movies?

World War I, World War II movies. Modern police

agencies and some special forces in the military have gone back to that weapon. The original model was the 1911.

What does that Model 1911 signify?

That was the year it was accepted by the U.S. military.

And presumably designed sometime before that?

Yes.

What is the purpose of cocked-and-locked carry then?

Because it is a single-action weapon with an exposed hammer, you keep a round in the barrel and ready for action, so it is cocked already and then it's locked for safe carry.

Is that considered an aggressive style of carry?

Very.

What would an officer have to do with such a weapon if he didn't carry it cocked and locked to prepare it for firing?

He or she would have to remove it from the holster, reach up, pull the hammer back and then shoot it.

So by carrying it cocked, the only thing left to do is take off the safety?

That's correct. And shoot.

And pull the trigger. Is that appropriate in your opinion for civilian use?

No.

Why not?

It's extremely dangerous to carry that that way. You have to be highly trained so you don't shoot yourself or someone else accidentally.

Are you aware that in 1992 there was no training required to buy a pistol in the State of California?

Yes.

You told us at your deposition that with respect to the untrained civilian market, you felt that semiautomatic pistols were too complicated. Can you explain why?

Yes. There are too many parts, too much manipulation. You have to handle the weapon too much. And in some cases, in the firearm itself, something is under tension. A revolver is inert. Once I put five rounds into this [revolver] and I lay it right here, nothing is under spring tension. It is also simple to load because I can see the bullets that I put in it.

And once I pull the trigger, I can see the hammer function and it's easier to train with. It doesn't look sexy, but for untrained people, I recommend the revolver versus an auto pistol.

...

Is it possible for someone, by virtue of human error, to accidentally pull a trigger that has an eight to nine pound tension on it?

Yes.

Is that a mistake that is made solely by inexperienced users?

Unfortunately, no.

Can you explain that?

Yes. Police officers have done it, and I know that because I have trained a lot of police officers, that they do every once in a while pull the trigger accidentally.

Even on a gun with an eight to nine pound trigger pull?

Yes.

Is this the type of mistake that you would predict with all your experience that would be more common among inexperienced users?

I would say yes.

And how is it that in a police department where you have officers handling firearms everyday, what steps, if any, do you take to guard against the accidental pull of a trigger?

We train our police officers to treat firearms for what they are, deadly weapons. And the second mechanical thing we teach is that they index their finger, their finger goes along the side of the weapon outside of the trigger guard.

All right. I've seen that on television and in movies. This is called index?

This is called indexing. Yes.

When do you train officers to index? In other words, at what time in the handling of a gun are officers trained to index?

Always, unless their intention is to pull the trigger.

And what is the reason that the officers are taught to index?

We don't want them pulling a trigger accidentally.

Is that something that's just taught by the Oakland Police Department?

No. This is worldwide now. Indexing your finger's just about worldwide.

Is there any reason why indexing is taught worldwide except to combat the possibility of an accidental trigger pull?

Not that I can think of.

...

Have you seen inexperienced users of handguns pick them up for the first time?

Oh, yes.

Is it the natural thing that they index their finger?

Index, no. Put the finger on the trigger would be the natural thing. That's what everybody seems to do, not index.

Do you find that in training your officers to index, is it the kind of training you tell them once and they always do it? To what extent is drilling and repetition involved in training officers to index?

It's constant and ongoing. Today when I leave here and I go put my SWAT gear on, we're going to have SWAT training. Part of my responsibilities as a team leader when I'm doing training is talk. And when we're talking, I look down at those fingers to make sure they're indexed. And we're carrying machine guns and all sorts of things that can hurt people.

The SWAT team officers, officers you serve with are the most experienced in the department?

Yes. I would say they're on the top.

Yet, you are still on guard for one of them pulling the trigger before they're ready to fire?

Yes.

Do you find officers who make that mistake?

Yes.

Do you have to emphasize and caution officers to index their fingers?

Yes.

Even experienced officers?

Yes.

…

In their opening statements, several defense attorneys had ridiculed Ruggieri's suggestion that Jerry Morris didn't realize there was a magazine in the Bryco. Ruggieri explored that with Sergeant T.:

Let's talk for a minute about the magazines. One of the issues in this case is a possible failure to detect that there was a second magazine in the handle of the gun. Do you have any experience with users making mistakes about whether or not there's a magazine in the handle of a gun?

I have had some experience, yes. In fact, I've had police officers not know how to remove the magazine, or if there was, in fact, a magazine on certain weapons.

On certain weapons, it's true, isn't it, that whether or not there's a magazine in the handle of the gun can make a critical difference as to what you've just done when you cycle the slide?

Yes.

If there's no magazine in the handle of the gun and you cycle the slide, you've presumably unloaded the gun?

Yes.

If there's a magazine in the handle of the gun and it's got a cartridge in it and you cycle the slide, that very same action you've presumably loaded the gun and made it ready to fire?

That's correct. I could inadvertently have reloaded the weapon. That's correct.

In the law enforcement field, is that considered an important issue to pay attention to?

Absolutely.

Do you find that experienced officers make mistakes about this subject?

Yes.

...

Ruggieri used a Beretta Model 92-F, nine-millimeter, as a comparison to the Bryco in addressing the design of the manual safety. The Beretta's use is widespread, and a military version of the gun replaced the Model 1911 as standard issue in the armed forces:

Can a user attempt to unload the Beretta with the safety on?

Yes.

And if the user of that gun were to inadvertently pull the trigger while attempting to unload the gun and the safety was on, would the gun fire or would it not fire?

It would not fire. I have the mechanical safety on, and you can see that with the mechanical safety on, the trigger is neutral or inert.

Can you show me with the Bryco Model 38, the exemplar of the gun involved in this case, can a user attempt to unload that gun with the safety on safe?

No.

Why not?

Because the safety locks the slide to the frame.

Is there a way to release the slide and allow the user to unload the gun?

I could take the safety off.

And put it in the fire position?

Yes.

Assuming we've got a semiautomatic pistol and assuming it is equipped with a safety, and the manufacturer has designed it so the user has an option of using the manual safety or not, do you recommend for safety reasons that the user attempt to unload the gun with the safety on safe or the safety on fire?

The safety on safe.

For a civilian user, especially perhaps an inexperienced user, do you recommend that if they're going to have a semiautomatic weapon, they have one with a manual safety that can be left on while they are trying to unload the gun?

Yes.

And is the reason for that safety?

Yes. Hence the name.

Is the reason for your opinion that the user might accidentally pull the trigger if they lose control of the weapon while they're trying to unload it?

Yes.

...

Are you familiar with the term Saturday night special?

Yes.

Is that a word that you use?

We use the term junk gun.

...

Sergeant T. testified for two days, during which the defense focused on the poor storage of the gun, but overall, his testimony eviscerated several defense claims regarding the "impossibility" of an accidental discharge.

Ruggieri's second witness also left a lasting impression on the jurors, both because of the testimony and because after appearing in the courtroom on the first day of trial, he never attended the trial again.

By the time trial began, Bruce Jennings officially resided out of state and was, therefore, beyond the reach of a subpoena. Ruggieri couldn't compel Jennings' attendance, but, still, it had never occurred to Ruggieri that Jennings wouldn't voluntarily show at trial. "Whether it was because he was a loose cannon and someone advised him not to come — although Jennings never struck me as someone one who took advice from anyone, especially lawyers — or because the defense thought forcing me to play his deposition videos would bore the jury, or whether it was something else entirely, his non-attendance was a huge mistake.

"Someone in Jennings' position should have been there every day, front row. Show up every day looking like you care." The only two possible justifications for his absence would be that there was no need for him to explain anything in the case, or that he would surely be destroyed on cross-examination.

But Jennings couldn't avoid testifying even by staying out of the courtroom. Select portions of his videotaped depositions were entered in evidence and played for the jury. Jurors watched and listened for several hours on the courtroom's large monitor, his appearance and expressions ranging from stoic to disinterested, bemused to aggravated. At one point a red-faced, frowning Jennings froze on the monitor for ten or fifteen seconds, which seemed like ages to the defense.

Jennings' videotaped testimony established his long history in the industry; that he had created several gun companies, including B.L. Jennings, Inc. and Bryco, and, regardless of others who had served in Bryco's director or executive positions, that he solely directed and oversaw all business operations and made all corporate decisions; that he had been the sole designer of the J-22 and its next iteration, the Bryco Model 38, a model identical to the J-22 save for being enlarged internally to accept a larger cartridge; that the first versions of the Model 38 jammed during testing, and that Jennings was the sole decision maker in choosing to alter the safety mechanism of the gun, which did not fix the actual cause of the jamming situation, and to then produce, distribute, and sell the gun while knowing that the altered design made the gun unsafe even when used in foreseeable ways; and that Jennings was not an engineer, had never taken any engineering classes, and had never brought in any kind of mechanical or safety engineer to evaluate, test, or consult on any of his products.

The video testimony and Jennings' lack of attendance in court had placed his defense team in a very difficult position. They had not questioned him at depositions and had no favorable deposition clips to present. By not appearing, the defense had no opportunity to offer favorable testimony, but had they called him as their own witness it would have defeated what seemed to be their misguided strategy, because it would have allowed Ruggieri to cross examine him.

Plaintiff gun expert Tom Butters.

Ruggieri had hired several of the country's leading gun experts, including Tom Butters, to evaluate the Bryco Model 38, then design and implement, if possible, a fix for the safety. Butters had become controversial to pro-gun advocates for his occasionally high-profile work as a plaintiff's expert witness in several gun-related lawsuits, including testifying in what became a decades-long legal battle with Remington.

What was your goal after you were contacted and asked to do some work on this case?

Well, I was assigned the task of designing a modification to this Bryco .38 that would enable the unloading of the pistol on fire or on safe and certainly the loading and unloading on safe, and also to do it in such a way that it would not induce a jam with an uncocked pistol.

And have you done that?

Yes, I have.

Can you tell us, in pursuit of that assignment, what have you done?

I obtained a number of Bryco .38 pistols and examined them for form and function. So, once having determined the general configuration of two separate types of modifications that were possible — there may be more, but at least two — I took an unmodified pistol and I fired 600 rounds to determine what could I expect from a factory pistol. Then, I installed the modified parts in the pistol and attempted to determine whether or not the modified parts would create any problem in and of themselves.

Before we get to the results of that work, let me ask you — in connection with your work in this matter, have you reviewed any written materials?

Yes, I have.

And do those include the several days of deposition testimony by Bruce Jennings?

Yes.

And you're familiar with the explanation that he gave as to why he designed the Model .38 so that the safety locked the slide?

Yes.

Do you have an opinion as to whether that decision was reasonable?

The decision he made was unreasonable, given the exposure and the defect that was generated by his design choice.

And what was that defect?

He was getting jams when he was trying to load the pistol with an uncocked firing pin, in other words, where the firing pin protruded. Now, it has to be pointed out that this particular pistol uses the firing pin as an ejector. When the pistol is fired, the slide comes to the rear and the extractor pulls the fired cartridge case from the chamber; as it does so, the firing pin causes the cartridge case to be pivoted out to the right and out the ejection port. The firing pin is what is used as a means of clearing the cartridge case from the pistol after the round has been fired.

Under those circumstances, if an attempt is made to feed a round from the magazine with a protruding firing pin, the rising cartridge that is supposed to come up and go into the chamber jams under the firing pin and creates a disabled firearm. In order to prevent that type of jam from taking place, Bruce Jennings elected to prevent the loading of the gun when it is on safe, [because the tip of the protruding firing pin is, essentially, in the way]. He simply locked the slide closed so that you couldn't perform that operation.

Did that cure the problem or did that hide the problem?

No, that just covered it up.

...

As an engineer, Butters was able to readily identify the cause of the Model .38's jamming problem, and considered Jennings' cover-up as creating a new design defect. Butters created two separate alternatives that actually fixed the jamming problem, while allowing the pistol to be unloaded in the 'safe' position. The first involved a simple modification of the firing pin; the second required that the safety's slot in the slide be slightly extended.

He prototyped both alternatives, and in both designs

the defect was fixed, and the jamming problem solved with no increase in production costs.

To test the unmodified Bryco Model 38, Butters used a portion of the California testing protocol, which requires that a pistol be able to fire 600 rounds with minimal failures. He described what happened during the tests:

"Deterioration was rapid throughout the tests, affecting not only the ability to cock securely, but the ability to extract and eject securely and the condition of the chamber and the barrel. The barrel got loose, the chamber swelled up, the slide became loose on the frame, so that the firing pin struck off center, thereby affecting the reliability of discharge as well as the security of engagement between the firing pin and the sear.

"And the face of the slide battered out so badly, that the cartridge that was being fed into the chamber was misaligned so far, that the reliability of ignition was thereby affected. It was remarkable to see the degree of the deterioration as these tests proceeded."

...

Were you nevertheless able to engineer a solution?

Yes.

And you've told us that each of these prototypes costs you nothing. You have enabled the gun to be unloaded on safe.

That's correct. The modifications are functional, workable, they're technically feasible, they are affordable and they certainly are desirable from the standpoint of safety and functionality of this particular mechanism.

There's one thing that I would want to change on prototype 2; and that would be to change from the plastic safety to a sheetmetal safety, because I don't think the plastic safety will survive very long due to the physical force that's applied to it.

If we were to take that additional step and replace the plastic safety with the metal safety, could you give us an estimate of what that would cost?

It costs less than a dime.

...

If we take your modification and apply it to the Jennings Model .38, does the feeding on it work any differently than it did on the millions of J-22s that Bruce Jennings had sold before?

No. They're functioning the same. They do exactly the same thing, feed the same way.

And with your modifications you can also, like the J-22, now unload the Model .38 on safe?

Yes.

Plaintiff witness, the owner of Willits Pawn

Walt, the owner of Willits Pawn, admitted on the witness stand that although he had insisted during depositions that he had offered, shown, and recommended a trigger lock to Clint and Sue when they bought the gun, he actually had no specific recollection of that conversation. When informed that another customer who bought a Model 38 from the store only a few days later had offered sworn testimony that he was never shown or informed about trigger locks, the owner was dismissive, claiming the man was a "certified alcoholic... with a memory that wouldn't last longer than what he could see in this room..."

He also admitted he did not know the safety had to be moved to fire to unload the Model 38 — "I think they all work like that, generally..." — and that while he had sold other Saturday night specials, he actually had no familiarity with how any of them 'worked'.

Plaintiff witness John, Sue's brother

Sue's brother John had been in and out of the family's

lives since Brandon's accident. On the stand he described how Sue "was more of a mother to me" than a sister, and had always interacted with Brandon as a brother rather than a nephew. Ruggieri played tape recordings of the sheriff's deputies conversations with John after the accident, giving the jury a sense of John as the little boy who witnessed the accidental shooting. Through John's deposition and courtroom testimony, he came across as honest, straightforward, and accepted blame for his part in the accident.

The defense attempted to have John admit that he in fact knew there were two magazines with the gun, and that he knew the gun was loaded. He denied both claims.

On Ruggieri's redirect, John said he actually had no recollection of even speaking to the deputies on the day of the accident, and that what he had testified to in court was consistent with deposition testimony he'd given almost a year before the trial.

Judge Kraetzer had been strict but fair to both sides. In a hearing without the jury in the room, Ruggieri now argued that he should be able to admit an exemplar J-22 as an evidence exhibit, because it was the same gun as the Bryco Model 38. He also argued that jurors should be allowed to handle the exemplar Model 38, a motion the other side fought against vigorously.

"I think it's apparent by now this case is most certainly about the J-22. The J-22 was the safer, alternative design we're contending they should have stuck with. They should not have moved to the Model 38. Obviously, we don't have the actual gun. Every witness that has taken the stand has identified the Model 38 as being identical to the pistol that was sold.

"I retained custody of it. Anyone has the opportunity to request and do any testing on it they want to.

"This whole case is about the handling of a Model 38, the jury needs to know the look and feel of it. As far as the spring or trigger tension, I think the jury can be admonished that pending some foundation, this is not necessarily the exact trigger tension and they're not to experiment, but they need to hold this gun in their hands.

"I don't think the defense can stay back, a year passes without them coming up with anything to suggest it's in any way different, and now they just stand up and object that it's not the gun."

The defense responded, saying, "It's not our obligation to lay the proper foundation for evidence that's being offered by the plaintiff. They've had a year to lay the proper foundation and bring in a witness to testify that it functions the same way as the subject pistol. There are two people, [expert X and expert Y], who tested the subject pistol. If they thought it was so important, they could have laid the foundation the pistol operated just like that one, it had the same trigger pull, same spring tension. The fact they didn't do that is not our problem, your Honor, so it lacks foundation and it's not our burden to overcome that."

Judge Kraetzer barely took a moment to reach a decision. "The J-22 will not be admitted and the Model 38 will be admitted. It will be rendered, and we'll figure out how, it will be rendered inoperable. I'm satisfied there has not been a foundation laid with respect to how hard or easy it is to move the slide and how much trigger pull there is. The trigger will be inoperative. The slide will be inoperative.

"The jury will be allowed to handle it, and there was testimony when you pick it up you automatically put your finger on the trigger, so I don't have a problem with that. I think enough foundation has been laid for it as an exemplar. But with respect to things like tension on the slide and on the trigger, no, they'll be instructed not to operate it."

Plaintiff's witness Jerry Morris

Jerry Morris had by now been estranged from Brandon's family for many years. Guilt from the accident had followed him into adulthood. Where John evoked warmth and respect from the jury, Jerry drew sympathy, and perhaps pity.

The defense focused on his inability to remember and numerous minor inconsistencies between his statements to the deputies, his deposition testimony, and his trial testimony, pushing their questions at him almost as statements: had he known there was a gun in the house; how did it get in his hand; who had stood where; how he held the gun; what was he thinking; where was his finger on the gun; why couldn't he remember?

The defense questions emphasized to the jury, with some success, that Jerry was a mess, his testimony was a mess, and they attempted to portray Jerry as irresponsible and evasive. But that was negated as Ruggieri drew testimony from Jerry that painted a mental picture of Jerry on his knees beside Brandon, covered in Brandon's blood as Jerry gave the boy CPR, out of his mind with horror with what had happened.

There was no connection between those images and conclusions the defense hoped the jury would draw, that Jerry had been playing with the gun and had intentionally pulled the trigger, even inferring that he had intentionally shot Brandon.

Instead of proving Jerry to be a liar and reckless, the

defense attack reinforced the feeling that he was a person to be pitied, who found himself in a bad situation, had not been well treated in life, and was understandably confused and inconsistent. Some jurors would later comment that Jerry and his life made them think of, "There but for the grace of God..."

Ruggieri felt that "Jerry's testimony was his testimony, nothing more or less, and I believed it wouldn't be a crucial consideration in the jury's deliberations."

Plaintiff's witness Sue Stansberry

Sue took the stand and Ruggieri began by having her recount her upbringing, marriage and family, and going through the events leading to the accident. She held up well through the early questions, but shed tears as she described Brandon right after the accident, and how she didn't know if her son would live or die. After a break for lunch, the defense questioned her about knowledge of the gun, Clint firing the gun, if she had ever read the gun's included instructions, and the phone call to John, when she had told him to unload the gun but admitted she had no reason to believe John knew how to do that.

Sue was the last plaintiff's witness, and after her time on the stand Ruggieri rested the plaintiff's case, having presented his evidence and dozens of witnesses to prove this first phase, liability. The defense would now present its witnesses and evidence to refute the plaintiff's case, and Ruggieri would be the cross examiner.

Defense witness Mr. Boyd

Mr. Boyd was a a senior criminalist with the California Department of Justice, one of two people who examined the original Model 38. He was a non-retained witness, subpoenaed by the defense. He examined the original Model 38 after receiving it from the sheriff's department shortly after the accident, reporting that "it operated only in a proper manner."

On cross-examination, Ruggieri was able to put that original, early conclusion in proper context:

Mr. Boyd, did I hear you correctly? You did not take this gun apart?

That's correct. I did not.

...

And you don't consider yourself a gunsmith?

No, I do not.

You don't consider yourself a design expert?

No, I do not.

When you wrote the words, "it operated only in a proper manner," did you intend that to be a comment on the design of the safety?

No, sir. That is a comment that I use as referring to a consumer's approach to a weapon; that it would operate as would be expected by a consumer or a person who would buy the weapon and take it to a firing range or to use for home defense.

Or by the manufacturer?

Yeah. I suppose.

I told this jury in my opening statement that this gun operated exactly as Bryco intended it to when it left the factory. Can you confirm that for us from your examination? Did this gun work exactly as Bryco knew and intended it would when it left the factory?

I don't know the exact specifications they have, but it would be likely that it operated as they specified it would.

...

As far as you noted, there were no modifications?

That's correct.

There were no changes?

Not that I was aware of.

There was no damage?

It did not appear to have any damage.

There were no add-ons?

No.

As far as you know, the gun that you examined was exactly the way it came out of the box when it was sold new?

No. Slightly older, somewhat used. But it was in generally the same condition.

And the gun that you examined, you had to take the safety and put it on fire in order to move that slide, didn't you?

Yes, sir, I did.

...

One of the defense witnesses, an engineer with experience in firearms, testified about the modifications made by Butters, Ruggieri's expert, opining that in some respects Butters' alterations had "made a mess" of the gun and potentially added to the probability that something else could go wrong. During cross-examination he admitted that he was also an expert witness for several other 'junk gun' manufacturers in lawsuits. Ruggieri then led him through a series of admissions.

It was during this testimony that Ruggieri had to deal with a pro-gun platitude so often repeated and so widely known by the general public that he had devoted considerable effort thinking about his response. "I knew it would come up, and no one had ever really rebutted it before."

You had done no testing on any firearms in connection with your work on this case?

No. But I had looked at guns and handled them. I hadn't done actual test firing, no.

You have made no evaluation of the reliability of a Bryco Arms Model 38?

Right. Because there's no claim in this lawsuit that the gun didn't work reliably. It did exactly what it was supposed to do.

Of course reliability is something, in your overall engineering analysis, you want to take into account. An engineering feature, as you just told us, has to be considered not only with respect to what it does, but what unintended consequences it may have?

Of course. The particular issue is not the reliability. There's no claim on the part of you folks that this gun didn't do what it was supposed to do. It fired as designed.

Sir, let me ask you, you had a meeting in Denver, did you not?

Yes.

And met with Mr. M., and Mr. S, [both defense expert witnesses] and Mr. Bruce Jennings?

Yes.

And, sir, you told me at your deposition that that meeting was not important to your opinions. You had formed all of your opinions before that meeting; isn't that right?

It didn't change any — I mean, it's possible that if I learned something new it would have changed them. I didn't learn anything new.

But you had reached your opinions before the Denver meeting, hadn't you?

Pretty much.

And you didn't reach any additional opinions as a consequence of that meeting, did you?

No.

And you didn't change any opinions you already held as a consequence of that meeting, did you?

That's right.

. . .

And the Denver meeting was the first time you had ever held a Bryco Arms Model 38 in your hands?

I believe it was. Yes.

Having once reached an opinion, for example, a design is adequate and reasonable from an engineering point of view, learning that other people do it this way or other people don't do it that way has no more significance to you than people jumping off a cliff, does it?

It might if it proved that I was wrong. Anyone can make a mistake.

Just the fact that one person jumps off a cliff doesn't mean we should all do it?

No.

The fact everybody's jumping off a cliff, even in engineering terms, doesn't mean we should do it?

Right.

You're not a safety engineer, are you?

No.

You agree, do you not, with the general engineering principle that any risk of serious injury or death is always unreasonable, and unacceptable, if a reasonable accident prevention method can eliminate, or minimize, the risk. Agree with that?

Sure.

And you agree that a firearm holds a risk of serious injury or death?

Right.

And you agree that under basic engineering philosophy if that danger can be eliminated by mechanical means, it must be if possible and feasible?

Sure.

So, and that's true even if the danger is something caused by human error?

Right.

So let me ask you about this accident a little bit. First of all, this is a self-defense gun in your view?

Yes.

And it's very foreseeably going to be purchased by homeowners?

Yes. I would think so.

Very predictably going to be owned by people of all ages, educations, socioeconomic classes?

Sure.

You're not aware of any law enforcement agency in the world that uses this, are you?

Not certainly as a primary weapon. I would assume some that use it as a backup weapon.

Aside from what you assume, you're not aware of any law enforcement agency in the world that uses it as a backup weapon, are you?

No.

This is clearly a gun that's designed for people who don't want to spend a lot of money?

Right.

. . .

And you've also gone on record saying that it can be a perfectly reasonable practice to put a firearm on the market without having any engineering review?

Yes. And in this instance, we're looking at a gun that functioned exactly as it was intended to, regardless of how many safety reviews or hazard analysis or anything else was done on it, or product audits. It functioned exactly as it was intended to function.

It functioned exactly as it was intended to?

Right.

Was Brandon Maxfield the intended target of the user of the gun?

It's impossible for the manufacturer to determine the

intended target. That's the point at which the responsibility of the gun handler comes into play.

How about you, sir, you're the one who just said the gun functioned exactly as it was intended to.

Yes.

Was Brandon Maxfield the intended target of the projectile from the gun in this case?

No. As I say, it's impossible for the gun manufacturer to determine what the intended target is. It's up to the user of the gun to determine what the intended target is.

Does a gun function exactly as it was intended if the gun discharges and shoots someone that the user did not intend to shoot?

Unless there was a malfunction of the firearm, that's exactly what it did.

So in my car, if I press on the gas pedal and the car goes, but it goes in a direction I did not intend it to go, does that function exactly the way the car was intended to function?

No, it does not.

And so simply with a gun, if I am manipulating a gun and it shoots someone that I, as the user, do not intend to shoot, is that part of the gun operating exactly as it was intended?

They're completely different. The reason the car doesn't go where you want it to, you don't have the steering wheel pointed right. That's your problem. Unless the steering mechanism is broken, it goes where you pointed it. Just like a bullet goes where you point the gun.

Sir, let me ask you about some testimony by you: "Is there mechanical technology available to prevent the discharge by an unthinking albeit perhaps intentional trigger pull?" You said the manual safety will do that, for instance. Remember that?

Right.

Remember this question and answer, sir? "QUESTION: Assuming that Mr. Morris pulled the trigger on this Model 38 without thinking about it, as we've discussed, your opinion is that he pulled it without thinking about it? ANSWER: Well, what I'm really certain about is that he pulled it. How much he thought about it is certainly nothing I can ever finally determine. I know he pulled the trigger on it. QUESTION: All right. Once his finger was on the trigger, was there any safety device in place to prevent him from pulling the trigger without thinking about it? ANSWER: If he had the manual safety engaged, it would be, yes. QUESTION: Other than that? ANSWER: No." That was your testimony, wasn't it?

Right.

Let me refer you to another little block of testimony. "QUESTION: What about operations that you can anticipate someone's going to want to do with a handgun? What about checking to see if there's one in the chamber? Is there a hazard at the time somebody is checking to see if there's one in the chamber that if they pull the trigger the gun might go off? ANSWER: That's a hazard. Yeah." Remember that?

Yes.

That was your testimony?

I also say, again, it relies on the human being to engage the safety.

Of course. That's why we call it a manual safety.

Right. It's not an automatic system.

How about, "QUESTION: Does a manual safety have any function to serve on a firearm that's being checked to see if there's a cartridge in the chamber? ANSWER: It could. QUESTION: And that function would be to prevent accidental discharge? ANSWER: Yes. It could do that." That was your testimony?

Yes.

And then "QUESTION: Does the manual safety have any function to serve while someone is unloading a gun from an engineering point of view? ANSWER: It could, depending on the particular design. QUESTION: And that function would be preventing accidental discharge? ANSWER: Yeah." Do you recall that?

Yes.

And then one more. "QUESTION: Does a manual safety have any function to serve while the firearm is being loaded? ANSWER: Yeah. It can. QUESTION: And that function would be to prevent accidental discharge? ANSWER: Yeah." That also was your testimony?

Right.

We were talking here about the pros and cons of the safety locking the slide. Do you recall that?

Right.

I asked you about the cons. Let me just read this into the record. "QUESTION: How about the cons. Let's list the cons. Are there any disadvantages to this design having the safety lock the slide when it's in the safe position so that it has to be put in the fire position to manipulate the slide? ANSWER: I think I mentioned that to begin with, that in order to manipulate the slide, you have to have the safety in the fire position." You still agree with that?

Sure.

"QUESTION: Okay. What's the severity of that con? Is that an annoyance con, or is that something more serious? ANSWER: It's a con that can easily be neutralized. Don't pull the trigger. Nothing could be simpler. If you don't want to shoot the gun, don't pull the trigger." That was your testimony, wasn't it?

Right.

"QUESTION: That's a human solution? ANSWER: That's a human solution. Right. QUESTION: So we can make up for the absence of a mechanical solution then by human solution, don't pull the trigger." And your answer was "right"?

Right. But of course the non-slide locking safety is

also a human solution since we do need to have the person engage that safety.

Do you still agree it's a con that can easily be neutralized? Don't pull the trigger, nothing could be simpler?

Oh, yeah.

That's your opinion?

Yeah.

Your expert opinion?

Oh, yeah.

Just don't pull the trigger?

Yeah.

It was time.

The jury had simultaneously reached an end and a beginning, a crossroads where they would decide the future path of a young man. Ruggieri had told them this moment would come and they would *"have to commit, make a decision based on the evidence presented by both sides, guided by the law and the judge's instructions."*

As they sat around the large table, "...We really didn't discuss much right away, we all agreed we'd go ahead and do a straw vote. But just before the vote the foreman, he was kinda thinking out loud, he said 'Well, there's nothing wrong with that gun.' I gotta say, the rest of use were stunned, really, and then it seemed like one of the other jurors was leaning a little that way. We didn't jump all over him or anything, we were all civil about this, but the rest of us reacted pretty quick and reminded him, asked him to remember how the whole reason the safety worked like it did was because Jennings had a gun that jammed and didn't fix it..."

"...Jennings didn't care enough to show up, he didn't care about the people who bought his guns, and anything he could have done to make his guns better, anything, would have been better than what he did, which was nothing..."

The first vote came up as nine agreeing that the gun's design was defective and Bryco/Jennings bore a significant percentage of responsibility.

"...so we all reviewed the evidence and pointed out that it wasn't just what the witnesses and the experts had said, it was Jennings himself in the videos who said that he had changed the safety, and that he had done that because the gun jammed..."

Overall, none of the jurors were impressed with or much swayed by the defense.

One juror summed it up as, "we were all together, we all found that the parents had made their mistakes, the father had left the gun in an unlocked drawer, left it loaded, there was fault everywhere, and we had some of the longer discussions about percentages. We had to compromise, though, because we didn't want it to be a hung jury."

Among themselves, they reached agreement on everything with very little to no drama. "We all came from different backgrounds but we all got along pretty well. This was a jury made up of people with good common sense; everyone had their attitudes and feelings, but no one hit anyone over the head with them."

Deep in thought and leaning against the jury box, Ruggieri jumped as a loud, ragged buzz, like an old doorbell, sounded behind him.

It was the jury room buzzer. It could mean any number of things, that there was a question or an issue, something about a witness's testimony, or clarification was needed about the judge's instructions. It could be that a juror was sick, or that the jury was ready for lunch.

It could also mean a verdict had been reached, or the jury was deadlocked.

The bailiff walked from his small desk and crossed to the other side of the near-empty courtroom. Ruggieri watched him open the jury room door slightly, someone in the jury room said something, the bailiff closed the door and walked toward the judge's chambers.

He glanced at Ruggieri as he walked past, and said, "They're ready."

The jury had reached a verdict on the first phase — liability.

Ruggieri went to his table, sat down and closed his laptop. Two days and a morning of deliberations were better for Brandon, short deliberations would have been better for the defense, but until the jury was in the room with a decision, 'better' meant nothing. Ruggieri refused to be optimistic.

He had remained in the courtroom each day until the jury went home at night. "I had a superstition about not leaving the courtroom. It was something I had always felt, and the one time I *had* left while a jury deliberated it bit me in the ass, the only time a jury came back with a decision that blew up my case.

"By being in the courtroom, being available for anything, I at least felt I could retain some modicum of control, even though I had just divested myself of almost all control by throwing my life and Brandon's life to the jury.

"I spent the days thinking about the case, worrying about it, thinking about all the different scenarios and ways it could go. What did I miss? What if this, what if that?

"The jury needed to come back with at least one-precent responsibility assigned to Bryco-Jennings, because under California law that's all we'd need to put Jennings on the hook for Brandon's medical costs."

The defense attorneys returned, moving quickly to their table. They were relaxed and smiling, apparently convinced of an imminent victory. A few minutes passed before Judge Kraetzer came out of chambers, sat at the bench and had the jury come in.

Ruggieri worked hard to appear composed, fighting stomach-churning anxiety. He glanced at jurors, and some returned the glance, but most were stoic as they filed into the jury box.

"Has the jury reached a verdict?" Judge Kraetzer asked.

The jury foreman, older and more conservative than many in the group, stood, answered "We have, your honor," and handed the special verdict form to the bailiff, who walked it over to Judge Kraetzer.

Formality ruled, suspending time as Judge Kraetzer read all ten pages of the form. After what seemed to be at least a minute, he looked at the jury and asked, "This is your verdict, you are all in agreement?"

"Yes, your honor."

Judge Kraetzer flipped back to the form's first page and read out loud. "We, the jury, find the following special verdict on the questions submitted to us…"

The liability verdict was based on the jury's answers to five questions given to them by the judge. The questions began with '*Was there a defect in the design of the Bryco Model 38,' and 'was there a failure to warn of the defect in the Bryco Model 38 pistol?'*, followed by '*Was a design defect a cause of injury to the plaintiff… Was a failure to warn defect a cause of injury to plaintiff… Was plaintiff's injury caused by a use of the product that was reasonably foreseeable?'*

The jury's answer to each question was '*Yes*'.

By the time Judge Kraetzer reached the fifth 'yes', Ruggieri exhaled as he realized he was close to winning. But there were still two specific negligence questions — '*Was any defendant or other person negligent... Was the negligence of any defendant or other person a cause of injury to plaintiff?*' The answer to each was also 'yes', which required the jury to assign percentages of negligence, totaling 100%, to all the involved defendants and non-partys.

Clint and Sue were assigned 32%, Morris, 20%.

Ruggieri jotted the percentages next to each defendant's name on a legal pad. For Ruggieri, the percentages not only represented how well or how poorly he had presented Brandon's case, they would point to the defendants the jury considered most responsible for creating Brandon's missed-and-never-haves.

No Little League, no playgrounds, no playing with dad, no playing with anyone, no hugging mom, no *tag, you're it,* no recess, no swings, no slides, no crude but love-inspired crayon drawings on the fridge door, no setting the table, no doing dishes after dinner, no dances, no holding hands, no buying and eating ice cream, no tree climbing, no driver's license, no adolescent sexual exploration, no running just for the hell of it, no biking down a steep hill just for the hell of it, no getting yourself dressed, no first fast food or grocery store or 'gofer' jobs, no walking home on a late summer night, no first car, no water balloon fights, no independent means, no continual good health.

Everything Ruggieri had ever done as an attorney had propelled him here. Now, two months of trial time, hundreds of exhibits, dozens of witnesses, thousands of miles travelled, too many all-nighters to count, two solid years of work, cash out, nothing in, a second mortgage, everything now funneled to Judge Kraetzer's three-minute reading of the form, down to the last thirty seconds, and the percentages of the remaining defendants.

Judge Kraetzer read the responsibility percentage for the defectively designed gun, which included Bryco Arms, B.L. Jennings, Inc., Bruce Jennings, the distributor, and Willits Pawn: "Collectively, 48%."

Brandon had won the first phase of the trial.

Ruggieri cleared his table, methodically, slowly, going over thoughts about tomorrow. There would be no pause between the finding of liability and the next phase, economic and non-economic damages. In less than twenty-four hours, Ruggieri would be back here giving another, albeit shorter, opening statement. Last week he told the jury that if Jennings was found liable, the next phase, damages, would happen right away. Sue and Clint would take the stand again, as would Brandon for the first time, to testify about Brandon's everyday life and all that entailed.

And Sue would be signing the settlement agreement Ruggieri had finally negotiated with the distributor's insurance company.

As he reached his car to drive home he called the family. Clint answered.

"It's Richard."

"Hey Rich."

"The jury came back with the first phase verdict."

Clint's response was cautious and drawn out. "Yeah?"

"Yeah, it's good news. The jury said the Bryco had a design defect and it contributed to the accident. Jennings and Bryco are going to have to pay."

Clint was quiet for a few moments before he said, "We won?" In the decade since the accident, since his boy had been so close to death it was a miracle Brandon had survived at all, no one had ever called with what could be described as good news about Brandon's life.

"Wow. Damn. Did they, what, um, sorry..."

On his end of the line, standing in the kitchen and only a few feet from Brandon watching TV, Clint's thoughts bumped into each other as the notion of 'winning' sunk in. He hesitated, because it felt weird, and he wasn't sure how to ask, and finally just came out with it. "How much did they say he has to pay?"

"Don't know yet." He reminded Clint that they only needed one-precent to make Jennings responsible for Brandon's medical costs, and the jury would soon deliberate the damages phase, then there would be a third phase, the alter ego part of the trial to determine who would be included in having to pay whatever that 48% amount would be. "So there's still some time, but Brandon won this first part, and that was everything; there wouldn't be a second phase if we hadn't gotten this."

The family would have to be in court the next day, Brandon's first time back since opening statements.

"Great. That's great. Thanks, Rich. See you tomorrow. Thanks." Clint hung up, dialed Perko's restaurant to talk to Sue, and as he waited for an answer he said, "Hey, Brandon, Rich won the first part of the trial."

Brandon looked at Clint. "Excellent. What does that mean, though?"

"Means he's damn good, for one thing. Also means we have to get back to court tomorrow morning." The restaurant manager answered the phone, and when Sue came on some moments later, Clint said, "Hey, Rich won this first part of the trial. He won't know how much for a few more days, I guess, but he said everything's good."

In the restaurant, Sue stayed composed but had the same revelation as Clint, that this was the first call she'd received about her son's accident that wasn't about his health, his medical condition, or something related to the fragility of Brandon's future.

"Damn," she said, "Holy cow."

Ruggieri's next call was to Edith. He left a brief message on her voicemail.

"Hi. We got him."

The damages phase was its own distinct trial. Ruggieri gave his second opening statement.

"We start phase two of the trial this morning, the chance to talk about and for you to get to know Brandon, and talk about his injuries. We're not going to talk about guns anymore..."

He briefly recounted how Brandon had been airlifted to Oakland Children's hospital after the accident, where the family came to know "Dr. Robert Haining, probably one of the best doctors for injuries like this certainly in the state, possibly in the country. He's been responsible for Brandon's care for the last nine years, and he's still responsible for his care.

"Brandon has spent over five-hundred days in the hospital since this accident. He was in the hospital the last time I was here giving the closing argument."

Ruggieri summarized Brandon's medical life, and how whenever Brandon had an urgent medical condition — "eight, ten times" — he had to be airlifted to Oakland because he couldn't be treated in the smaller Willits' hospital, and he described Brandon's multiple operations and ongoing physical challenges — "had a plate in his jaw... had to have his hip disconnected, they had to take apart his hip so he can sit comfortably in the wheelchair... he's got a rod up his back but he's grown since they put it in, and that's causing scoliosis, and there's an issue about whether or not that rod needs to be extended up into the neck, because that will limit the mobility of his head, which right now is the only part of his body that he can move…"

"We'll talk to Sue Stansberry, and ask her to tell us about Brandon's life, his hospital stays, his medical treatment.

"Because this is the damages phase of the trial, where you have to compensate Brandon for his losses, including his medical expenses in the future, his earnings, losses, things like that, I've hired experts so you can evaluate it all… and at the end of this phase you're going to get instructions about the two kinds of damages that Brandon is entitled to, the economic damages, things like medical expenses, past and future, earnings lost, past and future. Dollars and cents. Economic damages, the things that Brandon will need in order to allow him to function on some level for the rest of his life, to keep him going, the medical expenses to keep the engine running.

"The non-economic damages are traditionally referred to as pain and suffering, loss of earning capacity, perhaps, loss of freedom, inability to pursue interests, loneliness, limitation. In Brandon's case isolation, dependence.

"I think this is going to be the hardest job you're going to have in the whole case. You're going to have to try to put a value on all that, things that won't come with a price tag on them. You can't give Brandon back what he really needs, but you have to try to put a dollar value and compensate for it.

"You're going to have to ask yourself, what does that mean to a boy at seven years old when he was shot? What does that mean to a young man at twelve? What does it mean to him now at sixteen?

"All his friends are starting to get driver's licenses, starting to get mobile. What does it mean to him at twenty-five? At thirty, forty-five, fifty-five?

"We're going to also talk with the doctors about the extent to which this accident has caused Brandon to lose years off of his normal life expectancy. What's the value of each year that you might lose off the other end? It's the most important part of Brandon's loss. It's not something that comes with an easy price tag, but you're going to put a value on it as other juries have in the past. It's difficult, but other juries have done it, and you will do it, because it's the only tool that we have.

"I will try to guide you. My role here is not to give you a number and try to make you accept it. My role is to present evidence that you can use to make this evaluation, because you're the only ones who can...

"You are the conscience of the community. Once you've met Brandon, heard about his life, heard the experts on his behalf during these next few days we have, I'm going to get back up here and talk to you again briefly, and ask you at that time not to give Brandon one-cent more than he's entitled to, because he doesn't want it.

"Not one-cent out of sympathy. Not one-cent more than he's entitled to for his injuries.

"I'm also going to ask you not to give him one-cent less."

Newberg and the other attorneys gave their own phase two openings, attempting to convey their understanding of the jury's difficulty in this particular phase.

"...this is going to be probably the toughest part of the trial for you, tough for all of us, a gut wrenching week... We're going to see some photographs that target your heart as people and as parents, see some videotape that will make some of us cry. This is going to be very difficult for all of us.

"Brandon will take the stand, and it's going to be difficult for all of us to listen to, because all of us feel sympathy for him, but it's important that we be aware of that and acknowledge that, but that we set it aside for purposes of this trial, because while sympathy is an important thing for all of us to have, it has no place in this courtroom.

"You are required under the law and you've all given your oath that you will decide the case based on the evidence in this courtroom. And in this phase of the case, what we're talking about are things like the cost of caring for Brandon in the future, the pain and suffering that he's experienced.

"We have experts as well who will come in and talk about some of these issues. And you'll find that there is going to be a wide range of things that both sides agree on…"

Hoffman gave the last of the opening statements, once again focusing on what he believed would ease the jury's approach to what the other attorney's continually described as "very difficult."

"There's nothing at all difficult about what you're about to do. This is the easiest phase of the trial. You've already demonstrated your common wisdom. All you need to do now is rely on your humanity…."

Sue was Ruggieri's first witness. His questions took her back to the hours immediately after Brandon landed at Children's hospital, through the different operations over the first few months and continuing through the years. She described the insertion of feeding tubes, devices in Brandon's throat that allowed him to speak, and fought to keep her emotions in check, which she did until Ruggieri asked her to describe the process of weaning Brandon from the ventilator.

"We would take him off the ventilator for a short period of time. At first he couldn't do it at all. We had to put him right back on. Over time we finally got up to five minutes. Pretty soon it was ten minutes. So we did that for a long — a long time. To go to rehab we had to prove we were going to be stable. We had to be off the ventilator for short periods of time."

It would be hard to argue that every adult, parent or not, wouldn't be moved when Sue described those weeks immediately after the accident.

"They had family housing across the street. I can't remember when it was they finally made me go over and try to get some sleep. I wouldn't leave. I just wouldn't do it. Finally there was this nun from Children's Hospital. She's great. I couldn't have made it through it without her. She finally came over and said, "Hon', there's only so much you can do. Go and get some rest. If you can't get any rest for yourself, you can't take care of that boy."

"That's where I remember thinking, sleep? Who could sleep? My boy was over there fighting for his life, paralyzed. Sleep? No."

Her little boy began wanting her to do things. "The nurses were there, but Brandon had already been through so much, he didn't want any of the people he really didn't know touching him. And so I learned to do Brandon's care at the bedside. There's lots of things you have to do for Brandon. He's got to be cath'd every four hours, got to have a suppository... he has to have his trach ties changed everyday. There's a big ol' routine that I go through with Brandon.

Ruggieri asked, "Are you talking about today or back then?"

"Back then and continued to today. For the rest of our lives."

Sue described the day she, and Brandon, finally, reluctantly accepted that he would never recover from paralysis. Ruggieri handed her a small package of tissues.

"I think today we know reality, but even when we went to Shriners [Hospital] that day to get the electrodes put on, we still had hope that day, because they were saying if we put these electrodes on there, this could happen and that could happen.

"We were all excited. Oh my God! Let's go over and try it. I remember the look on Brandon's face when it didn't move his arm. He was disappointed, and heartbroken. And I tried to be strong, because I see he's already sad and I have to be the strong one. I'm the mom. I have to be strong to take care of him.

"He was crushed. And I think that's probably when reality finally started setting in for us that, you know, this is how it is."

Sue ended her testimony after looking at a series of pictures and describing Brandon's state of mind, his school, and other daily routines.

Brandon's rehabilitation therapist testified as to Brandon's lifelong rehab and medical needs, where those come from, and the related costs for it all. The defense had the unenviable job of arguing how the therapist's costs might be misguided, and introduced their own experts whose costs estimates were significantly less.

Clint was next, describing his daily routine as Brandon's primary attendant.

"I've been there since he was three months old. He's my boy. I taught him how to hold his bottle, changed his diapers. I have three other kids, too. He's as much mine as any of them.

"I wake all the kids up at 6:00 o'clock in the morning. We live up on a hill. We need to get going early. I have to have some of them to the bus. I get Brandon up in the morning, and I cath him, change him, get him dressed, sometimes give him treatments. I feed him, brush his teeth, fix his hair the best I can.

"At 7:00 o'clock the LVN nurse shows up and she comes in, and about five minutes after that the bus shows up, and they both get on the bus and they go to school. And they show up back at the house again about four-thirty. Sometimes he wants to come in and work on the computer for a while, and sometimes he's just tired and he wants to lay down.

"I get him out of his chair, take his shoes off, undress him, maybe put some shorts on or sweatpants. I give him his pills again in the evening and feed him. He likes his music a lot, headphones. I change the TV for him all the time.

"He can't do any of that, anything that he needs and wants and I'm there, I do it for him…

"He usually has way more good days than bad days. If he has a bad day, he doesn't feel good, his head will be hung down, I might have to even go out and help him with his wheelchair and push it into the house. Sometimes he just runs out of energy, or he's just having a bad time and doesn't talk much. Usually I can tell right off. Sometimes he just gets wore out, you know, and he needs to lay down."

Ruggieri was ready to call Brandon, waiting in the corridor in his electric wheelchair, when the defense stepped in with a concern that Ruggieri considered nothing more than another lame, desperate tactic.

The jury was out of the room as Newberg said, "Your

Honor, if Brandon has to wheel up there, has to maneuver around and bumps into things and such, it will unduly prejudice the jury. It shouldn't be allowed, he shouldn't be allowed to do it."

Ruggieri responded. "That's silly, your Honor. He's not going to bump into anything. This is his life, it's how he moves around. Otherwise it will be as if he magically appeared there..."

Judge Kraetzer said, "That's enough. Let's have him ready and mic'd when the jury comes in."

As Brandon was brought in and Ruggieri saw him for the first time that morning, Ruggieri shook his head and smiled. Brandon smiled back, impish, as he rolled into the room. At some point in the months leading up to this day, Ruggieri had deliberately counseled the teen not to dye his hair, because Ruggieri had figured out Brandon liked to have that done, and he didn't want to worry about how the sight of Brandon with bright blue or fire engine red hair would affect the jury. "Telling him explicitly not to do that was probably nothing more than a green light to do just that, though. No pun intended."

Brandon had Sue dye his hair green and blue the the previous day because, in Brandon's simple rationale, "it looked cool."

Ruggieri, knowing that the defense would be hard pressed to make a valid argument against what he planned next, moved in front of the witness chair and right next to the jury box.

"Come on over here, Brandon."

His client would be eye-level and within touching distance of the jurors as he testified.

The jury was brought back into the room and Brandon was sworn in:

Brandon, it's finally your turn to talk.

Okay.

I just want to talk to you for a while and talk about you. Nothing really gory, but just talk about you, about your feelings, and ask you some questions. We heard from your mom and dad the other day about people staring. What's that all about?

It used to bother me a whole lot. Not so much anymore. I mean, now when they stare it's just like I ignore it. Just go on with what I was doing.

How does it make you feel when people stare at you?

Embarrassed most of the time.

You know, I don't have a lot of experience with disabled people — what do you call yourself? Handicapped, disabled?

Anything. It doesn't matter. Disabled, handicapped, physically challenged. Whatever.

As a disabled person, how do you feel going down the street? You're going down the street in your electric wheelchair, what does that feel like?

Most of the time I just completely forget. I've gotten so used to it it's just like I'm a regular person or whatever. People do stare, but I know most people in my town, so it's like most don't stare because they know me.

How about people that glance at you and they look away because they don't want to be looking at you?

I'll ignore it as much as possible.

Does that happen?

Yeah. Every once in a while.

How long have you had this electric wheelchair?

Nine years.

Are you any good with it?

I think so.

Do people ever ask you about the wheelchair?

All the time.

What do they ask you?

How do I run it. That's the most widely-asked question. It's complicated, trust me.

We just come up to you on the street and we've said, my, what a cute multi-colored-headed kid. How do you run that wheelchair? What would you tell us?

Well, this thing right here, the little thing on the side, that changes the gears. The mode, whatever. There's like multi modes in there. There's one where it inclines, one where I change what gear I want to be in. And when I want to drive back, it goes back. Left is left. Right's right. Then I click this again and it goes in reverse.

How do you adjust your speed?

Like I said, changing gears, this is first, second, third and fourth.

You can do all of that with your head?

Yeah.

Before this particular control, you had something I think we heard called a mouth stick?

It was a joystick. Yeah.

Is that better or worse?

Worse, because the way they had it, it was taped with, like, duct tape, and I used to break out in rashes around my face and all of that, so it didn't work too great.

There's been some talk about an operation, doctors may want you to have to extend a rod up your back? As you understand it, what's that all about?

They want to go up further in my neck because I'm overgrown through my back, so they want to go all the way up the column into my neck. I really don't want to do it, because I'll lose mobility in my head so I can't drive my chair.

Do you have mobility anywhere else in your body besides your head and your neck?

Not really. No.

Are you able to move your hands for any significant period?

No.

Can you move your hands at all?

Barely. Wiggling maybe.

Do you have a sense for how you would control the wheelchair if you were to have a rod put up your neck?

No. I have no idea.

...

Do you remember what it was like before the accident?

Yeah.

You were how old when the accident happened?

Seven.

Do you remember being a kid before the accident?

Yeah, some. I have memories.

What kinds of things did you like to do?

I remember lots of rope swings when I was a kid.

Rope swings?

Every house we had at least one rope swing. Chasing lizards. We were doing that a lot.

There must be a lot of lizards up there. I keep hearing about chasing lizards.

It's crazy up there. It's a lizard zoo or something. They're taking over the mountain.

Before the accident, were you active?

Very active.

Did you like any sports?

Baseball.

...

You're sixteen, a sophomore. Do you know if your friends are planning to stay in town when they graduate from high school or not?

They all want to leave. That's what they've told me.

How do you know that?

I know.

Is leaving Willits the topic of some discussion among sixteen-year-olds?

Yes, it is.

Even with all the lizards it has to offer?

Oh, yeah.

Do you know of the kids that you've grown up with, do any of them have plans to go to college?

I do believe my friend Brett does, and my friend Kenny, he's younger than I am, he plans on going to college.

Brandon, I want to ask you about some things that, you know, we normally don't talk about in public. You know, you've probably been poked and prodded and things enough. There's not all that much private level. If we get into something you don't want me to ask you about, just tell me 'I don't want to talk about that.'

Okay.

One of the things I want to know is, first of all, have you ever thought about having kids?

Yeah. I have. It would be pretty cool like to have something to leave behind, you know, when I pass on or whatever. Yeah. You know, to keep the family line going.

You haven't had any kinds of fertility tests or anything yet, have you?

No.

...

When you think about 'Brandon,' do you think, I'm handicapped, or I'm disabled, or physically-challenged?

No.

How do you think about Brandon?

I just think about me, Brandon who lives in Willits, goes to school, has friends, dyes his hair.

We've seen that, I think we can stipulate to that. You said a minute ago sometimes you forget, literally, you really mean that sometimes you forget you're in a wheelchair?

Yes. Completely forget.

And where are you when you forget?

Where am I? Here. I just don't see myself in a wheelchair. I just see what's around me. It's not me.

Are there times when you're out with your friends at a movie or something and you've just completely forgotten about it?

Yeah.

How long did that last?

Until maybe someone will stare at me or something, or I'll remember something. Then I'll be like, oh yeah, I'm in a wheelchair. That's right.

...

You've been off with health problems for a little while?

Yeah, a couple months.

Are you getting some classwork at home so you can keep up?

Yeah.

Are you still planning to graduate on time?

Absolutely.

Your mom talked the other day a little bit about you shutting down. One of the pictures that I showed you sitting in the wheelchair with your eyes shut. She said that's how he does it.

Yeah.

What's that all about?

Oh, that happens once in a while. I mean, not so much anymore, but you have to get me really, really outrageously mad just to shut me down completely. I close my eyes, just imagine somewhere else or remember thoughts or memories, whatever.

What are you trying to do when that happens?

Just get away from whatever situation I'm in.

And where do you go?

I usually don't go anywhere, just think about memories or what I do with my friends, you know. Whatever I want to think about.

But you're still sitting there in the room?

Yeah.

Body's still in the chair?

Yeah.

You just close down your ears and your eyes?

Uh-huh.

And you're shut down?

Yeah. In a way.

...

When you're at school, how do you eat?

My nurse feeds me.

How do you write things down in the classroom?

I communicate with my nurse. I tell her what to write down.

...

We've heard that the friends come over and you guys play Nintendo?

Oh, yeah. That's what we do. It's like a routine.

How does that work for you? How do you play Nintendo?

I watch. I memorize it.

You memorize it?

Yeah.

You tell the other guy what to do?

Yeah. Once in a while. We work as a team in a way.

What's your role on the team?

Thinking.

...

Let me ask you about a couple of medical things. How about this arm thing? Your hand is twisted and your elbow is bent. I understand there's some operation planned for that. What's your reaction to that?

Well, in a way I want to get it done, but I don't like operations. Who does? Some guy has a scalpel on me ripping your arm open. That's not cool.

Well, when you put it that way, I've got to tell you, that looks pretty painful.

I can't feel nothing. It's numb.

No? If I come over and touch your arm, touch you like this, can you feel that?

Yeah.

Do you feel it on the skin or do you feel it down inside?

Down inside.

If you were to close your eyes and I was to tap you on one leg or the other, could you tell?

Yeah.

Really?

Really.

I won't test you. I'll trust you. We heard a car story about some kid in a car screaming call 911.

I didn't say that. I swear.

I promised you I would give you your chance to tell the true story.

Okay.

What's the true story there?

We were driving down the road, my mom started going really fast, and I didn't scream 911. I said, slow down. That's all I said. She over-exaggerated the story, like, really bad.

You understand you're under oath?

I'm under oath. Yeah.

You have to tell the truth under penalty of perjury.

That's the truth.

So help you God?

So help me God.

You told me what you were really concerned about had something to do with your arm.

Oh, I thought it was gone. It was hanging off the side of the seat.

Yeah?

So I didn't see it. In the hospital I had visual contact with my arm and my limbs, and I didn't see it, so I thought it was gone. I screamed my arm was missing, which it was not. That's what that was about.

You verified it was, in fact, still there?

Yes.

Anymore you want to say about the car story?

No. I just wanted to point out my mom was wrong.

{From the front row in the courtroom, smiling like everyone else, Sue said, "Thank you, son."}

...

This is one of those personal issues you don't have to answer. Have you ever thought about suicide?

Once. But, I'm sure everybody's thought about suicide once or twice in their life. But, yeah, I've thought about it once.

I mean, do you ever have times that you feel like what's the point?

Yeah. Once in a while.

Is that frequent or infrequent?

Infrequently. It hardly ever happens.

What do you do when it happens?

Shut down pretty much.

What kinds of things, you know, sort of prompt that? What brings that on?

Well, like, for instance, my grandma Ruby, she has Alzheimer's, so she's not really in touch with reality. So it's like short memory, and she was a big part of my life.

So it's like when I go to see her, she just doesn't know who I am. It's a major heartbreaker.

How about things that your friends are doing? Do you ever get frustrated to the point where they're doing things and you just get disappointed?

No. That doesn't bother me so much.

...

How do you read a book?

Well, people turn the page.

What people?

Well, my nurse usually. I usually read at school.

If you want to read a book, you've got to get somebody to turn the pages?

Yeah.

I was asking your dad earlier when you were in the room listening to music, what if you want the volume turned up or turned down, isn't there something hooked up so you can do that with your head?

No.

...

Okay. Anything you want to say, because I'm out of questions for you?

Not really. I'm exhausted. I only slept three hours last night.

Me too.

I'm tired.

Both sides had called doctors, rehabilitation and educational experts, and economists, each side's witnesses offering divergent conclusions on the projected economies and financials of Brandon's future.

It was time for Ruggieri's second closing argument.

"This part of the trial, what we're calling phase two, this is an audit, if you will, a somewhat gruesome audit that we have to go through, of the damages of what has been taken away from Brandon, of the pain, the loss and the misery, mental and physical both, that Brandon has been through and will go through every minute, every hour, every day, every week of his life until finally he dies.

"And because of this, because of this audit that we have to do today, and because it is by nature somewhat gruesome, I've asked Brandon and his parents not to be here today. It's obviously something very important to them, but I can't talk about this in front of them. And Brandon doesn't need to hear what a tough life he's going to have.

"So what we do hear today is we put a value on life. And today you're not just one in millions voting in an election, you're the conscience of the community. You're acting to value all that has been permanently taken away from Brandon, and to be sure in doing so that the product that caused his problems is correctly priced in the future so that no one else says at $89 this is the best value for your money, and so there are no more hidden costs.

"But this is about compensation. It's not about punishment. I have not made for Brandon any claim for punitive damages, although we certainly could have, but there is no claim like that.

"Defendants came and they took everything that Brandon had and they did it for the money. And now they've been caught, but we're not going to punish them. What we're going to do here today, just like they were bank robbers who came and robbed the bank and took the money and had been caught, what we're going to do today is we're going to count the money that they took.

"We're going to count what they took from Brandon, put a value on it, and we're going to make them give it back. Not one-cent more and not one-cent less. And then we're going to let them go.

"And there isn't a bank robber in the world who would consider that punishment and wouldn't thank his lucky stars to be let off so easy, having taken from a bank or from a person and not to be punished, but just have to give it back.

"And there isn't a bank robber in the world who when being told 'just give us back the money and go' would then try and nickel-and-dime you or argue, well, the bank can get by with less, Brandon could get by with less than full attendant care.

"As if, the bank I took a million dollars from could get by with only getting $900,000 back.

"Even after getting caught, defendants are still trying to get away with something. But you have to remember that they're being held here not for punishment, but for compensation.

"The kind of compensation we're talking about is civilized compensation, not the barbaric compensation that maybe a few hundred years ago or in some other countries they would have had to give an eye for an eye, a life for a life. In our civilization, compensation, not punishment, means money, a judgment for money. And that's all we're here to talk about today.

"I am Brandon's attorney. Brandon does not want sympathy. Brandon does not want punishment. I have to talk to you today on behalf of Brandon.

"If I ask you for too much money for Brandon, you think I'm crazy; if I ask you for too little money for Brandon, you think I'm crazy. All I can do is give you my thoughts. Brandon only wants back what's been taken from him, what he can really never have back and what will never be part of the one life that he has on this earth.

"There's also no issue today about who will pay money, or how much they will pay, or will it be paid, or how it will be paid, or when it will be paid. That's not part of your decision here today.

"Some of those issues will be taken up in phase three, but today you're not here to decide will it be paid or who will pay it, you're here to decide what is the amount — what is the amount of Brandon's damages…

"I warned you the numbers would be huge, and I warned you the only thing you would have, the only crude tool we would be able to give you as a jury to restore for Brandon what they've taken from him would be money.

"Brandon didn't choose that tool. Brandon would like to have his arms and his legs back, but the only tool you've got is money. I warned you about that. And here we are.

"We're here to talk about sums of money that are usually only read about. Most of us don't deal with sums of money like that. I was looking on the internet. A Van Gogh painting sold for $82.5-million. One painting. A Reuben sold for $76-million dollars. These are values that we give to things that hang on the wall.

"What about ball players? A quick look on the internet, there are eighteen players in different sports who are paid over $15-million per year. Per year. They don't 'make' anything. They don't produce anything. This is the value of being able to use the talents that they were born with, a value assigned by society.

"The loss of one airplane in a war, hundreds of millions of dollars. Hundreds of millions of dollars. The losses we read about in disasters, billions of dollars. These are things we only read about.

"This will take courage, because today we're not just reading about it. It will take courage to deal with the enormity of Brandon's loss and the big numbers that we have to deal with, that we can't be timid about, and to try to restore it.

You all assured me if we got to this point in the trial you could do that. It may seem like a daunting task. It may seem that these numbers are so big you just have to run away. Juries do it all the time. And it just takes common sense, and the fairness that you all have...

"And we're going to talk about Brandon's loss, about his damages in terms of economic and non-economic damages. And we talk about that because that's a distinction that's important to the law.

"It's not so important to us in our practical life, but it is a distinction that the law makes, and I'm going to proceed that way. So the law distinguishes between economic and non-economic damages, and Brandon is entitled to both. To both. There's no distinction there.

"The first part of your job is to determine what it takes to take care of Brandon.

"You've been given the figures. We're trying to anticipate everything that Brandon may need.

"Defendants are trying to minimize through their witnesses what Brandon may need. And I'm not going to spend a lot of time on the figures.

"The plaintiff's experts, the people who treated Brandon, the people who met Brandon, the people who went to his house, who met his parents, looked at his medical charts know him best. They're the ones that have his interest at heart.

"The defense experts they put on the stand in one morning, they're hired to litigate, not to evaluate, but to litigate. They're a traveling carnival show of experts, if you will, that take their wagon from case to case. A doctor who never saw the patient; never saw the patient. A life care planner who presents a rebuttal plan that he calls a rebuttal plan, and says in his cover letter, 'I want to be able to assert that the doctor agrees with my rebuttal plan.'

. . .

"And so ultimately, as with any issue, it comes down to trust. It's a question of who do you trust?

"Do you trust Dr. Haining who treated Brandon for nine years? Do you trust [Brandon's rehab therapist]? Or do you distrust them for some reason and trust instead the witnesses that were hired by the gun company to give rebuttal opinions about the life of a young man that they never bothered to meet?

"That's a decision that only you can make; who do you trust? So when we talk about economic damages, one thing we're talking about is medical bills. Brandon to date from the time of this accident until today has had an enormous amount of medical care. He's had over 500 days in the hospital.

"These are his medical records from the hospital, every one of these records, every page filled out by somebody giving him care. Five-hundred days in the hospital. And you can imagine the bills that go with that.

"And the very good news for you is that we're not going to ask you to sift through all those bills and add them all up in the jury room. His Honor has agreed to rule on past medical costs.

. . .

"The main thing I want to talk to you about the intangible losses, what we call the non-economic damages, the main part of what was taken away from Brandon.

"Everything above this maintenance level of existence that we've talked about, everything over and above the cost of the wheelchairs, the diapers, the medicines, the ventilators, attendants, everything that makes life worth living, you know.

"I hope it came through to you when he was here what a remarkable kid Brandon is. And you can see it in his reflection in other people. You can see it in the way that Juanita Joy Riddell [who took care of Brandon's needs through all of his schooling] lights up when she talks about Brandon. He's doing as well as could humanly be expected with a horrendous, horrendous situation that he faces.

"And it gives an inkling of probably what his potential was, because part of why Brandon is such an amazing kid is that, yes, he's risen to the challenge that was presented to him.

"But it's also part of who Brandon is as the person that he was already before this happened. He's one of those people, and always was one of those people, that the more you give them, the more they do with it, the more chance they have, the more opportunities they take, the more they make of it.

"And you've seen the family that he comes from. I guess everybody in the family has a role to play. You know, some kid in the family, he is the troublemaker, some kid is the know-it-all, some kid is the shining star of the family.

"In Brandon's family, that was Brandon. Brandon was the one with the grades. Brandon was the one with the determination. Brandon was the one with the personality. Brandon was the one in that family who was going to go to college. Brandon was the one in that family who was going to accomplish things so that his brother and sister could follow him.

"And Brandon is already outdistancing his parents who are good, honest people that have very limited resources. You know, in America, whoever we are, we feel nothing is more precious than our health and our freedom.

"Even the words of the Declaration of Independence, what do they say? We hold these truths to be self-evident. Life, liberty and the pursuit of happiness. All of those have been affected by defendants here. Brandon didn't lose these, he didn't throw them away, they were taken."

{Here, Ruggieri was briefly overwhelmed with emotion. He turned away and pretended to look for a document on his table, wiping away tears before turning back to the jury.}

"You know, sometimes there's a moment in a trial or in meeting with somebody when you really understand for the first time. It's different for everybody. It was probably different for you.

"For me it was when Clint Stansberry was on the stand and I was asking him about Brandon and how Brandon likes to listen to music. And I don't know what I thought, but Clint said Brandon lies on his bed and puts the headphones on and listens to his CDs. I don't know what I was thinking.

"Well, what does Brandon do when he wants to change the CD or turn-up the volume or is done listening? I guess I imagined he had some kind of a remote control. And what made me really understand just for a second what it must be like is Clint shaking his head like a wet dog and showing how Brandon, when he wants the CD changed, he lies on the bed and shakes his head to try to shake the earphones off so he can call to somebody to ask them to turn it up or turn it down. For me it was that image.

"Something else that I was lucky enough to see, something uplifting, I think. I went to a Wal-Mart with Brandon and his family, maybe a year ago. Wal-Mart is one of those stores, with a greeter. They have this old guy, he must have been 250 years-old. He was wearing one of those vests, and he was inside the door in a little booth.

"It's a great thing, I really like it. We went there, it was Sue and Clint and Brandon in his wheelchair, and me. As we came in, honest to God, this is a true story, this guy said, 'Hello, welcome to Wal-Mart. Hi there, young man. Come over here and let me put a happy face on your hand.' He had happy face stickers. He was nice as anything. Brandon's 15 years-old. He doesn't want a happy face on his hand.

"But, you know, he went along with the program. And he wheeled his wheelchair over there by the guy's booth and the guy had his little happy stickers. 'Here, lift up your hand, let me put it on. Lift up your hand.' His mother said, 'he can't lift up his hand, and you have to put it on.'

"The old guy was embarrassed, very embarrassed. He was a good guy. You can't fault him. 'Oh, I'm sorry. No problem. I'm sorry. Here, let me put that on.' He stuck the happy face on Brandon's hand. 'There you go, young man. Give me a high five.'

"I swear to you, 'Give me a high five.'

"Brandon just smiled and zipped away in his wheelchair and went to look at the CDs. So that for me is the flip side of the coin. On the one hand I've got this image of him in bed trying to shake off his earphones, and on the other hand I have him reacting to the Wal-Mart greeter. Brandon wouldn't fault the greeter. He was doing his best to do a good job.

"That's the kind of thing even under the best of circumstances Brandon's going to face. That's the reality, just a daily part of his life for Brandon. Like the holidays — daily parts of our lives, you know. I'm not going to go through all of this.

"You can think when you're back in the jury room, you can think, what would it be like for Christmas? How would Christmas be different if I was a quadriplegic? How about Thanksgiving, 4th of July? Think about the activities of those days, how it would be different over the next how many dozens of years for somebody who only had head movement.

"Or hobbies. Think of your own hobbies. What do you like to do? Pick the thing — these are just suggestions, because what I'm trying to do is help you get a handle on how to think about this, how to even approach the subject. That's all I can do. Think about hobbies, a favorite thing you like to do, whether it's to curl up in a chair with a good book, maybe it's to work on an engine, needlepoint. Maybe it's to go fishing.

"Think about that from Brandon's point of view. Imagine for one minute doing your favorite hobby as a C2, C3 quadriplegic with head movement, something as simple as reading a book.

"So when we're talking about non-economic damages, we're talking about Brandon always being the odd man out, aren't we?

"It's heartwarming, I guess, when he's a child, when he's young and cute. It's going to be less so when he's an adult. When he's a middle-aged man wheeling around in a wheelchair he's not going to be as cute or charming as he is when he's a 16-year-old kid.

"The worst part is still to come, I'm afraid. I alluded to this earlier. What happens when you turn sixteen? All your friends get a driver's license. All the people you used to entice to come over and play Nintendo for you and you cheer them on, suddenly they have cars. They've got dates. Suddenly they're mobile and independent.

"It's harder to get them to come by. When you're in

Brandon's situation, you're starting a period of loneliness. And it's going to increase when he moves away to college. He'll manage. He'll manage because that's the kind of kid he is. But it's going to get worse.

"It's going to increase when he goes away to college. It's going to be particularly traumatic, more so than for any of us, when his parents die.

"So I think of it in three stages. Three timelines, if you will, of pain and suffering. Maybe this is helpful for you, maybe it isn't. We've had nine years since the accident, nine years of past pain and suffering.

"The doctors, Dr. Haining says with luck he'll live to age fifty-five, mid-fifties he says. I picked fifty-five. That's just a prediction. He's not going to die at age fifty-six because the prediction ran out. That's all we can do is use the best medical prediction we have.

"So age sixteen to age fifty-five. That's going to be a segment of additional years of non-economic loss. And then what about age fifty-five to when his normal life expectancy would have been? If he lives to fifty-five — you'll see in the table you get in the instruction, twenty-one years off of his life, twnety-one years of his life gone. And that's the third time period that Brandon has to be compensated for.

"Which is worse? These are things that you'll be thinking about. Is it the early years, the last nine years, the years where he had hope, where he thought "I might be able to walk, maybe I'll get some movement back." Where he tried to ride that little bicycle, or hung on those little parallel bars. Is it those first nine years with disappointment after disappointment, is that the worst?

"Or is it the later years, now from age sixteen to fifty-five when all of that hope has been abandoned and he's trying to make a life? Even the defense doctor takes the stand and says he's not going to have any neurological improvement.

"The non-economic damages include all of that and much, much, much more. They include the loneliness that he's going to experience, the limitation, the isolation. That's a big one. That's a big one for people in this period.

"Isolation.

"Think of the dependence, what does that mean to a young man? At seven he was used to relying on his parents. Now he's sixteen. What does it mean to be dependent? How about at 21? What does it mean to be totally dependent on others? How about at twenty-five, thirty, thirty-five to be totally dependent on other people? At forty and so on?

"The sense of being a burden every one of those years, of being a charity case, having to rely on others to do the simplest things for you. It includes so much more of non-economic damages. It's such a sterile term. Imagine the horror of waking up for the first time and finding you couldn't move. Imagine learning for the first time that it was going to be permanent, the loss of independence.

"What about solitude? There's another word. Something we all appreciate. Solitude. Can Brandon ever be alone for the rest of his life? He can't live alone. He can't be alone. The best he can hope for is to lie flat on his back on the bed with music blaring in his ears so he can tune out the rest of the world. That's as alone as he can get.

"What about something that maybe he doesn't even recognize at his age, doing things for others. What an important part of our lives that is. Whether it's caring for a sick child or caring for a sick parent, giving somebody first aid, doing public service, trying to improve other people's lives. The loss of the ability to do things for others, and the enjoyment and the pleasure and the meaning that that's gives to life. What about that? I don't know how somebody could go through life without touching.

"What about hugging? What about giving somebody a hug, getting a hug? What about the loss of the family, loss of lineage. If he's lucky enough to have a family, if he's lucky enough, if they allow us to have the fertility testing done in this and he's lucky enough that the fertility testing turns out to be okay, how will he be able to participate with that family? How will he show that family his love? How will Brandon send his children to college?

"So the non-economic damages include all those things. And those are just the tip of the iceberg.

"I just want to emphasize, this is not about sympathy. The defendants are going to get up and tell you don't have sympathy, and that's right. It's not about sympathy.

"Brandon has been thrown into a pit. Sympathy is if you jump into the pit and you hold him and hold him until he dies in the pit. Brandon doesn't want that.

"Empathy is throwing Brandon a rope and letting him climb himself out of the pit. So we're not talking about sympathy. We're talking about helping Brandon to make a life for himself as best he possibly can with what he's got left.

"And the value of that is the struggle that you're going to have. That's the hard part of your job. There's no getting around it. Putting a value on that, what he has to go through, what he can't enjoy, the years he'll suffer, the years he won't have.

"You can look at different things, you can look at how much do we as a society spend to pull a child out of a well. A child falls down a well and we spend millions of dollars digging him out of a well. That's a value in a sense that we put on life.

"I can't give you a figure. I have no particular expertise

in this. They don't teach us this in law school. I can tell you that the financial costs, the economic costs establish only a baseline that keep him alive and functioning. That I know.

"The emotional costs, I know they're much greater. They're priceless. That's where the word comes from. The truly priceless, yet, we have to give them a price. You have to give them a price. There is no legal formula. If there was, I'd give it to you.

"There's no automatic three times economic damages equals your non-economic damages. People hear that. That's not a formula. That's not the law. There's no easy rule of thumb. I look at it, as I told you, in terms of time, in terms of the years of his life.

"We all have only one life. There are no repeats, no 'maybe you'll get to do it better next time.' He's had nine years of suffering. If he lives to fifty-five, he's got thirty-nine years left to make a life for himself, and if he lives to fifty-five, he's got twenty-one years of life taken away.

"Use your wisdom, your judgment, and adjust for the value that you personally place on your life or on a life — or the life of a loved one. Whether it's my million dollars a year or a higher or lower value that you assign to life, and adjust for those three periods of years, the nine-year period, the 39-year period and the 21-year period, adjust whatever the number you pick is. Adjust for your judgment of which is the greater loss, the childhood full of hope and opportunity, the middle years when he would be raising a family and starting memories, struggling — struggling growing up, starting a family, making a life, helping others, being independent. Or is it the final years when you enjoy all that you've made during your life? You enjoy the family, you enjoy the children, the grandchildren, and the loss of those years. Are those more important? Do those have a higher value than the childhood years?

"If you choose to look at the number of years and the three segments of years, and if you choose to start with some kind of a baseline value and put a dollar value on that and adjust it, adjust it for which are the most important, because you're dealing here with crayons, not computers. The tools we're giving you, money to try to solve Brandon's family, these are crayons. They're not computers.

"You're not going to be able to do it exactly. Brandon doesn't want the money. He wants his health. It's not Brandon's fault that we're working with crayons. It's defendants' fault. It's defendants' fault that you're going back into that jury room with something only as accurate as a crayon.

"It's like giving you a crayon to draw a detailed plan of a futuristic skyscraper and sending you back in there and saying you've got to come up with a blueprint for a future skyscraper building, and here are crayons to do it with.

"It's a difficult task, if not impossible. But just like Brandon persevered, just like Brandon sat on that stupid little bicycle and tried to pedal it when we all knew he couldn't, just like Brandon hung on to those bars hoping he could walk, just like Brandon spent two summers trying to train a voice-recognition system so that he could type a little faster, you have to have the courage and you have to do the best with what life is dealing you.

"You have to try and try and try. And sometimes when you go back in that room and you try to draw the plans for this building, this building that's the rest of Brandon's life, sometimes you're going to try to draw those with the crayons, and guess what, you're going to color outside the line. You're going to color outside the line and defendants will complain that's too much.

"They colored outside the line. Sometimes you're going to color inside the line. That's the nature of the crayon. It's not exact. And plaintiff will go without when you color inside the line. But you have to try and keep trying until you've done your best, because Brandon is relying on you.

"Crayons are all that you've got, and Brandon needs that building. You've got to construct Brandon a life, and all you've got are these crayons. And you've just got to do it.

"The building that I'm talking about, this futuristic skyscraper you're going to go back there and draw with this tool of money, this crayon like tool, that building is the rest of Brandon's life. And you've got to construct it now, and you've got to include every room in that — in that building. You've got to include every room he will need projecting out in his life.

"Try to anticipate and imagine as Dr. Haining did, you need to include an elevator. You need to include the phone lines. You need to include the fire alarms, the safety systems, the ventilation, the backup he's going to need for the rest of his life in that building, that metaphor for his life, because Brandon can't come back.

"And this is important. Brandon cannot come back and reopen his case later. If you don't include a procedure that Brandon needs, say, in the year 2015, he doesn't have it. If you forget to compensate Brandon for loss of income for his income in the year 2020, then he won't have any income in the year 2020 when the time comes.

"If you've left something out or if something new come on the market, a magic pill, a bionic arm, anything that wasn't included in the plans that you're going to construct today, Brandon can't come back later and say, 'Mr. Ruggieri, you've got to reopen my case, you've got to call back that jury.' That cannot be done.

"There's only one time to take care of Brandon and that time is now. So you're going to have to take those crayons and take all the time that you need. Brandon's trust, Brandon's hope for the future rests in your hands. And it's up to you to protect it, and I know that it's in good hands."

Newberg began his close by reviewing different approaches to Brandon's ongoing care, a personal assistant vs. a nurse, for instance. He may have lost some of the jurors when he mistakenly called Sue by another name, and ended by reminding jurors they needed to be "fair and reasonable" in determining the amounts, and not swayed by sympathy.

"...There are non-economic damages and we need to talk about those just a little bit. Mr. Ruggieri's right. We can't bring Brandon back to what he was. Brandon will always have his disability.

"However, you cannot put yourself or your children in Brandon's shoes. You cannot do that when you're giving consideration to this matter, and the reason for that is because that would generate your own internal sympathies. And my clients are entitled to your decision based not on sympathy but on what you think is fair and reasonable for the pain and suffering that Brandon has suffered.

"I can't put a figure on that for you, but you have to look at what society is today and what you believe to be fair and reasonable.

"Another thing. Mr. Ruggieri indicated that the defendants are at fault, and that's the defendants here. But we're forgetting one thing, and that is that you also found that Sue and Clint had some responsibility in this matter, and they're not here. They're not defendants in this action.

"So when you look at this, it's no bank robbery.

"None of this was intentional. No one wanted this to happen. This is an accident pure and simple. When your home burns down, you're entitled to get paid the cost of repair, or if you have some valuables and you pay additional insurance or whatever, but you don't just get a hundred thousand dollars simply because you have a hundred-thousand-dollar insurance policy. You only get what's fair. And the insurance company pays what's fair and reasonable.

"And that is what I'm asking you to do today, both in the economic damages that we looked at, there's a reasonable dispute there in the non-economic damages. Thank you."

Hoffman also gave a close, his last opportunity to remind the jury that while his client Jerry Morris bore some responsibility for the accident, Jennings and Bryco had refused to take any responsibility at all.

"...Through their lawyer, Bruce Jennings and the gun defendants' corporations beseeched you to have no sympathy for that child, but I say to you, have no sympathy for Bruce Jennings. He came to this courtroom, was afforded the opportunity to take the stand and tell the truth, or at least just to say 'I'm sorry' to that child, and what did he do? He walked out the door..."

The buzzer sounded on May 6th; the jury was ready.

Once again they filed into the box, sat down, either

looking at Judge Kraetzer or the small notebooks they'd used throughout the trial.

Although he felt calmer about this verdict than in the first phase, Ruggieri concentrated on holding back the wave of exhaustion about to wash over him at any moment. His heartbeat still quickened.

The Judge had already tallied Brandon's past medical bills, to be added to the jury's verdict, as he asked the foreman for the verdict forms. He read the findings out loud.

"What do you find to be the total amount of economic damages to be suffered by plaintiff in the future and caused by the accident involved herein? Answer: $10,400,000.

"What do you find to be the total amount of non-economic damages to be suffered by plaintiff in the future and caused by the accident involved herein? Answer: $35,000,000.

"What do you find to be the total amount of non-economic damages suffered by plaintiff in the past and caused by the accident involved herein? Answer: $5,500,000."

As he had with the reading of the percentages, Ruggieri tallied the amounts on his legal pad. The math was easy, the amounts slightly larger than he had hoped for.

He was relieved even as he was intellectually, physically, and emotionally drained.

But moments later, as Judge Kraetzer polled the jury — asking them directly if what was written on the forms represented exactly what each jury member had decided — Ruggieri heard a response that momentarily placed the entire damages decision in jeopardy.

Two jurors raised their hands as the judge asked, "Is there anyone who does not agree with these amounts?"

Ruggieri hoped the panic he felt wasn't evident on his

face as he waited an interminable few seconds before one of the jurors spoke.

"Yes, your honor, we wanted to award more..."

There was barely a pause between the reading of the damages awards and the judge's description to the jury of how the the alter-ego phase would work, the determination of what individuals and entities would be held accountable for paying the damages. He finished, then gave the jury the next week off. There was a ten-minute break and when the attorneys returned he questioned them about scheduling for the next phase. The jury might be getting the week off, but the work continued for the lawyers. He started with Ruggieri.

"How much time are you going to need to be ready to go? Is a one day break enough?"

"You want an honest answer?"

"I want a reasonable answer."

"My reasonable answer is 'yes'. How many hours in that one-day break, your Honor, about five-hundred?"

Ruggieri was spent, but he needed to complete an extremely important task before he could go home and "drop, just stop. There weren't even fumes in my tank."

He called the family. Clint answered.

"It's Richard. They came back with the amount."

Clint had the same ready-but-leaning-away kind of caution in his voice as he'd had for Ruggieri's call about the liability phase. "Okay..."

"I'll go over the details later, but the important number for now is what Jennings has to pay. Of the total, he and Bryco have to pay half, $24,000,000-and-change. I know you and Sue understand there's still a lot to do, and he's going to appeal and do whatever he can to run from this."

"But, this is a pretty good thing, right?"

"Yeah, it's a *really* good thing. And I've got a bunch of

documents we need to go over, and we have an appointment with an investment counselor to set-up Brandon's medical trust with the insurance settlement. That money is already on its way... "

Clint hung up the phone and fought to keep his thoughts straight. Ruggieri had already explained the insurance settlement to him and Sue, but suddenly it was real, and Clint, to his own surprise, found himself struggling to keep his emotions in balance. He and Sue lived by a few simple rules: don't believe everything you hear, don't count money you don't have, and if you have money, you better use it because "tomorrow ain't promised to no one."

But yet, there *was* money coming for Brandon, money that couldn't, wouldn't ever make Brandon 'right', but would do things for Brandon that family and friends and everyone who had ever helped and done things for him could never have imagined.

Ruggieri had once explained to Sue and Clint that "any money Brandon gets, that money is his arms and legs."

Inside the trailer home, it only took a few steps in any direction, especially by someone Clint's size, to see the family's worldly goods. Forty-some feet from one end of the trailer to the other, ten feet from one side to the other, about an extra twelve-by-twelve feet from Clint's building out a family room, an extra six feet or so of space for Sue and Clint's bedroom, simple furniture, nothing too big, kid-sized beds in Rocky's and Trish's smaller, toy strewn rooms, the hospital bed that takes up most of the space in Brandon's bedroom, the nice TV, an expense that didn't matter because it's where Brandon watches his shows and his friends and brother playing video games.

Clint stepped outside, looked around at the couple of acres, just stood and looked, thinking *this is what we have and we're okay with it, we do fine,* but now their son was about to be given something that could give the boy a future he never, *never* would have had without the jury's award.

Never would have had that future.

Never.

Still hadn't forgiven himself, never would, for his son's condition. *Will always give my life for my boy, nothing's too small to consider, nothing's too big to stop me from doing whatever it takes, whatever he needs.*

So how will all this work?

He had a moment of peace and stillness, unusual for Clint. The next few weeks would be different, really, really different.

He walked to a ladder leaning against the side of the trailer, climbed on the roof to install a new ventilation fan. He had his thoughts and the news all to himself for the moment, and it was time to get back to work.

He finally smiled as he thought about what he'd say to his wife and their son in a few hours.

The Associated Press ran a story after the liability verdict and the next week reported on the jury award, as did the New York Times, the Oakland Tribune, the San Francisco Chronicle and a handful of other newspapers.

New York Times journalist Fox Butterfield wrote about the liability verdict, and was one of the only journalists to include the critical context of the case. He interviewed Ruggieri at length, and Ruggieri put him in contact with Victoria Ni, a staff lawyer with public interest law firm Trial Lawyers for Public Justice, who Ruggieri had shared information with throughout the litigation. Butterfield quoted Ms. Ni explaining that "the crucial issue was that the .380-caliber Bryco semiautomatic was designed in such a way that it could be unloaded only when the safety was turned to the "off" position."

The majority of news articles ran almost identical descriptions of the gun's design defect: *the gun's safety had to be placed in the fire position to unload the gun,* but left out the 'why' of that design change.

Missing was the contextual information that had informed the jury's findings, that Jennings' original flawed design created a gun that didn't operate correctly, and that placing the safety in the 'fire' position had been a design change made by Jennings to hide the flaw, instead of fixing the flaw and leaving the safety fully operational.

As the news hit the wires and word spread among the pro-gun online forums, the verdicts and awards were largely dismissed in forum discussions as wrongheaded, stupid, and the obvious result of an attorney well-financed by anti-gun groups, who had gone after the deep pockets of a corporation rather than hold the babysitter and parents accountable. The views were offered even as the vast majority of gun users opining on the case readily acknowledged that Jennings and Bryco guns were dangerously unreliable and poorly made.

Many of the strongest reactions began, "I don't know anything about the facts of the case, but..." Other similar reactions and comments were simply obscene.

Comment from the N.R.A. remained noticeably absent from articles, discussions or reactions.

For all the press and media exposure during the '90s about the Jennings family, the companies and their Saturday night special crime guns, few people outside the gun industry itself had any notion of Jennings' deplorable business ethics and scheming operations. Even the ATF and the IRS, while generally aware, were in no position to understand the extent of his manipulations.

Through the first two phases, the jury also was unaware.

The jury wasn't allowed to hear about Bryco's lack of insurance, and were only nominally aware by inference of his business and money schemes. Ruggieri had held back those aspects of the case for the third, 'alter ego' phase of the trial. That lack of context and background, and an entrenched obstinacy of many gun-rights advocates, fueled the portrayal of Ruggieri as just another lawyer going after big money.

Newspaper articles also referenced, as the New York Times described, the possibility that "the verdict could be nullified by [pending] legislation in Congress that would protect manufacturers, distributors, dealers, and importers of firearms from such lawsuits."

The jurors looked intently at Judge Kraetzer. The jury had been away for more than a week since the damages award.

"Good morning, ladies and gentlemen. Welcome back. You are entitled to an explanation of what in the world is going on in this case."

He methodically reviewed how phase three, "was going to determine the persons and entities so intertwined with defendants Bryco, B.L. Jennings, and Bruce Jennings that they also should be responsible for the payment of the judgment that you reached." He pointed to Ruggieri's table and several ream-sized stacks of documents. "You see a mountain of paper over there that we were going to review to determine what relevant parts would be shown to you.

"Then, and I don't know that anybody was even contemplating this, we were advised last Thursday morning that those intertwined defendants had all filed for bankruptcy protection in the State of Florida.

"With very few exceptions, once a bankruptcy proceeding is filed, all legal actions against that entity automatically cease. We can no longer proceed with this case at all. There are some exceptions and there was some concern about whether any of those exceptions would apply. Now we know it will be at least another week before the bankruptcy court decides if any of those exceptions apply to this case.

"We have held you in limbo for two weeks, but my decision is to not hold you there any longer, and if it turns out that we're going forward with the remainder of this case, we will impanel a new jury.

"So, you are discharged. The bailiff will escort you out of the courtroom now, and we all thank you for your work."

The jury, visibly stunned, some confused, gathered themselves, filed out of the jury box and out of the courtroom.

In interviews later, the majority of jurors were aligned about Jennings and his absence from the trial: *"... Jennings was really nonchalant, didn't even come back after the first day... Since he didn't come in, the video was all we had to judge his testimony... He sounded incompetent and unsure about a lot of things, and, it hurt him by not being there..."*

But, Jennings had been busy, moving assets, again, and preparing for bankruptcy. Gold bullion, cash, trust assets, and corporate distributions were all in play — others may never have been known.

Jennings' timing was dictated by the progress of Brandon's case. It was his luck that his moves to Florida of money and assets, and his purchase of a million-dollar house — with garage-airplane hangar that led to a runway — occurred before the federal government and Florida tightened bankruptcy laws. Jennings rode the last wave of debtors who were allowed an unlimited homestead exemption from creditors. When Jennings purchased his million-dollar Florida home, he was essentially depositing a million-dollars cash in a place almost untouchable by any legal means.

Ruggieri had never taken a bankruptcy class in law school. "I knew nothing about bankruptcy law, except I had some general awareness that a creditor was better off having a judgment against the bankruptcy filer. I have no idea why I thought that, no idea where that even came from, but it turned out to be a really good thing to do.

"With the judgement we became a judgment creditor, which put us ahead in the line.

"A verdict is a decision, but it's not a judgment. Big difference. The judge gets a verdict from a jury, that's a *decision,* but he has the power to declare that the verdict is wrong, or that something about it needs to altered. He might set the verdict aside, overturn it, so until he enters it as a judgment, things aren't final, notwithstanding an appeal.

"I did know that the bankruptcy filing would stop everything and move the entire case to Florida, and that the defense would appeal the verdict; that's what any attorney in that position would do."

Two days before the actual bankruptcy filing, Newberg had told Ruggieri in the courtroom, in an off-hand, 'just so you know' fashion, that Jennings was "probably" going to file within the next day or two.

"Then Jennings' Florida attorney called Judge Kraetzer and told him the same thing. I did some quick research and that's why I pushed hard to have a judgment entered before that could happen. If I hadn't been able to convince the judge to enter the judgment, then the bankruptcy filing, because it stops the trial, would have left the verdict just hanging, and Brandon would have had a much harder time in the bankruptcy procedings that were to come."

There was one small positive as a result of the bankruptcy. At the very beginning of the trial, Judge Kraetzer had trifurcated the case, liability phase first, then damages, and alter-ego. "I was angry about that, because I wanted to try the liability and damages at the same time, but I was spent by the end of the second phase, completely out of gas. Turned out his decision was a blessing, because although I obviously would have continued, it would have been very, very difficult. I wasn't as ready to go forward as I should have been."

After being dismissed and catching up on the news of the last few months, jurors discovered yet another reason to be upset by the trial's sudden conclusion. *"...We didn't get to finish, and now the whole thing might be overturned anyway by Congress... It's just so, so not right..."*

In April, 2003, the gun industry was poised to receive its greatest gift since its exclusion from oversight or federal recalls by the Consumer Product Safety Commission in 1972.

Barely two weeks before the jury's first phase verdict, the federal House of Representatives voted to pass H.R. 1036, The Protection of Lawful Commerce in Arms Act, best summarized as a bill that would immunize the gun industry against current and future lawsuits.

If the bill became law it could be retroactive to cases being tried even as the bill was initially brought to the House floor. While it may have been luck that Jennings was able to employ his Florida asset protection strategy before the state's liberal homestead exemptions changed, he and his attorneys were almost certainly aware that H.R. 1036 could vacate everything Ruggieri had accomplished.

Newberg had filed a motion immediately after the verdicts, requesting a new trial. Judge Kraetzer denied it, and Newberg then filed an appeal with the California appellate court. The appeal wouldn't be heard for a minimum of several months, following which an application for review could be made to the California Supreme Court, the state's highest court.

If H.R. 1036 became law during that time, it could still potentially negate the original trial's outcome.

When Richard 'Rick' Thames answered his phone one morning in June, 2003, Ruggieri introduced himself and said, "Man, do I have a case for you."

Ruggieri needed a bankruptcy attorney in Florida and it couldn't be just any bankruptcy attorney. It had to be an attorney that, frankly, was as good in his or her practice as Ruggieri was in his. When he had asked an attorney friend for a recommendation, the response had been immediate: "Rick Thames."

Thames is a genial Florida native, an easy talker with the slightest southern accent. He graduated from Florida State University College of Law in 1987, but remains loyal to his undergraduate alma mater. "Proud of them both, but I am a University of Florida Gator."

And he is a very, very good attorney.

Like many law school graduates, Thames took the first position offered right out of law school, a federal clerkship for a bankruptcy judge. It lasted two years and gave him a significant foundation and insight into the bankruptcy process. In 1989 he joined one of Florida's premier law and bankruptcy firms, Smith Hulsey & Busey, working directly with firm partner Steve Busey, described by Thames as "one of the finest lawyers in Florida, a very talented litigator, talented writer, eloquent speaker. Being part of that firm and working directly with Mr. Busey enabled me to learn and experience what it takes to be a great attorney."

Thames formed his own firm six years later, grew it to a five-atorrney firm and quickly established himself as one of the go-to bankruptcy and bankruptcy litigation attorneys in Jacksonville.

Ruggieri gave him an overview of everything that had happened, and Thames initially thought "except for the guns, there really wasn't anything exceptional about the case at first."

"I took about two weeks to familiarize myself with it, and I could sense a few things." Obviously, Jennings had come to Florida to do what others had done, take advantage of Florida's liberal homestead exemption and, it seemed, "to get as far from Ruggieri as he could, because Ruggieri was a bulldog."

Thames brought one of his firm's senior associates into the case, Nina LaFleur, and went to work.

"When I got up to speed and got into the details of the original trial, a couple of things were evident — Jennings had put amazing effort into all these games and misdirection, and Ruggieri had done a tremendous amount of work to take Jennings down. And, regardless of how a person feels about the Second Amendment, and I'm a strong supporter of gun rights, there's no place for Jennings' kind of guns in this world."

As Thames, LaFleur, and Ruggieri burned up the phone, fax, and email lines over the next few months,

Thames realized "I had to reassess my initial thoughts about Richard."

"At first I thought I'd have to manage his expectations, but it became pretty evident, pretty quick, he was more than prepared to stay after Jennings and we were going to spend whatever time and effort we needed to keep going at him and going at him.

"And although it was pretty obvious, Ruggieiri stressed to me that there wasn't anything that Jennings wouldn't do, but I'd seen a lot of similar bankruptcy moves before, where all these guys making quick bucks through all sorts of schemes looked at our area as a haven, bad guys using bankruptcy to try and squirrel away money."

One of the elements of bankruptcy is a determination by the court of whether transfers of cash and assets in the time leading up to the actual filing are direct efforts to shelter assets from an upcoming bankruptcy filing. Payments to certain vendors before others, suspicious large expenditures, and cash or real estate transfers are major actions that raise suspicion.

Jennings' moves could have been lifted right out of a how-to guide on 'hiding your cash.'

"Jennings was sloppy. He did things too fast, and he had an attitude of impunity, of, 'yeah, I did this, so what?' Right after the phase two verdict we found out he went to Europe, came back, transferred $150,000 to a gold bullion broker in Texas, and when we call him on it later he tells the court it was a 'mistake'. He buys a house, for cash, and a half-million-dollar annuity during the litigation, even though he'd never had one before. He should have been more measured."

Bankruptcy provides temporary relief to people or entities that have amassed more debt than can be repaid.

It's available to anyone or any organization, from a person, to a business, to a city.

It is not a free pass, however, on spending above one's means. Its effects on the filer will last years, but when it works as intended, as it did for General Motors after filing Chapter 11 in 2009, a company or business can use the shield of bankruptcy to reorganize and emerge from a negative position better able to grow a profit, saving jobs and contributing to the economy.

Other drastic situations, where a company waits until its debt-to-assets ratio is insurmountable before it files, or there is fraud, or a massive financial judgment, often lead to the company going out of business. If a large corporation files bankruptcy, media coverage may include the phrase 'pennies on the dollar', with whatever assets exist — cash, real estate, building, manufacturing equipment, cars and the like — to be sold at a bankruptcy auction and provide some benefit to creditors.

Despite his ethically bereft strategy of keeping Bryco and B.L. Jennings 'judgment proof' — virtually cashless and mired in apparent debt — bankruptcy was a legal, available option for Jennings, just as for any other person or business. Different kinds of filings — Chapter 7, Chapter 11, Chapter 13 — are based upon the status of the filers and whether the filers seek reorganization or liquidation. Chapter 7 is the scorched earth of bankruptcy: crushing debt, minimal or no assets, no ability to repay; everything that isn't nailed down is sold at a bankruptcy auction, including intellectual property, customer lists, brand names and the like. The remaining debt is forgiven, 'discharged', and everyone moves on.

The total number of Jennings-related bankruptcies was eleven. All were filed as Chapter 11. The court later converted to Chapter 7 the cases of Bruce Jennings, Janice Jennings, Bryco Arms, and B.L. Jennings, Inc.

Jennings was now positioned to do exactly what he had described in the BusinessWeek magazine article years before.

As subpoenas and motions uncovered Jennings' network of manipulations, Ruggieri and Thames methodically chipped away at the figurative walls behind which Jennings had hidden his and his companies' real worth.

Jennings' Florida attorneys opposed every motion filed by Ruggieri and Thames. Through summer and into the winter of 2003, Ruggieri and Thames uncovered Jennings' asset manipulations — the houses, the planes, cars, the annuity, cash, and on, and on — and fought to bring everything into the bankruptcy and under control of court appointed trustees.

And with each opposition, Jennings' attorneys invoiced the 'estate' (the Bryco/Jennings assets under control of the trustees) that would be used eventually to pay the bankruptcies' largest creditor, Brandon. Essentially, the fiercer the defendants' opposition, the more 'work' generated, the more the attorneys would bill for the services, reducing the asset pie which would eventually be divided between the creditors.

All eleven bankruptcies had been assigned to Hon. Jerry Funk, a Georgia native who passed the bar in the late-'70s, operated a Florida law firm with a partner for seventeen years, and was appointed to the Federal bankruptcy court in 1993.

Thames' had a long relationship with Judge Funk. "He was the presiding judge for the first Chapter 11 case I had in that courtroom. He and I weren't absolute beginners, but we were both still learning. He learned to be a judge while I was learning to be a lawyer. And he's a very good judge."

"Bankruptcy court exists to find a fair and balanced plan for everyone. Judge Funk was appropriately blind to any hype from either side." In many business-related bankruptcies, employees face significant financial hardships if they lose their jobs, "so keeping the business going in some fashion is often a priority, because that's the golden goose."

That frustrated Ruggieri at times, knowing that bankruptcy was just a check mark on Jennings' list to avoid responsibility at any cost. In the early stages, based on what was before him, Judge Funk rightly treated this as he would any 'normal' bankruptcy. "The case is a pendulum, and in the beginning the petitioner gets all the breaks, usually." Ruggieri's pursuit of Jennings into bankruptcy court, making appearances and filing objections, "was atypical for this area."

"But, over the course of this case — and I have been around talented people all my life — I was occasionally dumbfounded by Ruggieri's diligence, his memory, his ability to know every document and where it was. His style was a lot different than anything I'd ever experienced. He's one of the most talented attorneys I've ever come in contact with in twenty-seven years of practice."

For Sue, the months after the end of the trial "were nuts, it was crazy, and stressful, but it really changed Brandon's life."

The insurance settlement established a medical trust and also reimbursed most of Brandon's California Medi-Cal payments for his emergency transportation and care since the accident.

After the payment, he still owed California's Medi-Cal system just over one-million dollars.

Brandon's medical trust, overseen by an independent trustee, gave Brandon financial assistance with a daily spectrum of medical, quality of life, and home health care issues. While the recovery was substantially below the estimated level of medical and health-related costs Brandon would incur over the rest of his life, its life-changing effects were immediate. The first approved expenses were a new van and a house, purchased by Brandon (*"Hey Rich, I'll bet I'm the only seventeen year-old you know who owns a house!"*), that he and the family moved into two months after the end of the trial.

The house, a large bi-level, was toward the top of a curving road at the north end of town, less than a two-minute drive from the high school. There was space for everyone, for Brandon's medical equipment and hospital bed, and the location was high enough to have views above the tree tops, looking out over rolling hills and land extending several miles to the west.

Sue would spend many more days over the summer and fall signing dozens of documents, conferring with Dr. Haining and the trustee to create Brandon's long term care plan. Clint built out Brandon's spacious room, installing systems that would ease and enhance Brandon's life, and make it easier for Clint to take care of his boy.

Ruggieri expected, and had told the family, that the bankruptcy would last at least several years. In December, Thames called with news that, unforeseeably, was the first in a series of events that would culminate under the intense focus of every major news and media agency around the world.

Chapter 9

"IT IS ORDERED..."

The moment Ruggieri finished reading the letter Thames had just forwarded to him, he thought, *this is bullshit.*

The mid-December 2003 letter from Jennings' Florida attorneys described a dire situation, a proposed resolution claiming to be best for everyone involved, and requested an "immediate response." The letter stated explicitly that this was an attempt to agree on a resolution to the bankruptcy without involving the time and expense of the court, and that the letter and its content would be confidential, not part of the court record.

According to Jennings' attorneys, Bryco was paying six-hundred-dollars a day rent at the recently sold Bryco plant, a significant, continuing drawdown of the bankrupt company's assets currently worth, at best, "$100,000" according to several auction companies' estimates obtained by Jennings' law firm. Bryco was two days past when it should have vacated the premises, and the new landlord could evict the company at any time.

These factors had reportedly motivated Jennings and his lawyers to find a potential 'inside' buyer who would purchase Bryco's assets for $150,000, which they asserted was the optimal amount the estate could ever hope to receive.

Thames immediately recognized "a manufactured crisis," especially since the 'rent' was actually being funneled to Jennings' RKB Investments via an agreement with the new landlord, and the estimated value of the company's assets had dropped since Bryco first filed bankruptcy.

Thames called Ruggieri and conferenced in Jennings' attorneys. The conversation was direct and short.

"Who's the buyer?"

"Mr. Jimenez, Bryco's plant manager."

"Our immediate response, as you have requested, is 'no.' Nothing in this proposal, especially the purchaser, is acceptable. Nothing."

It was Jennings' first attempt since the Maxfield verdict to use his decades-old strategy: find someone to sit in the 'owner' chair while Jennings continues to control the company.

In February, 2004, Jennings' attorneys submitted a two-page motion to the court, possibly the shortest document ever filed in the case's long legal history, a mere seed that would soon grow into an epic series of events.

Jennings' attorneys asked the court to approve their proposed private sale despite Brandon's objections. Citing the impracticality of moving the assets across the country, the filing described how selling the assets "in place" (the current California location) and eliminating rent payments would "bring funds into the estate [and] significantly reduce the estate's expenses." And, since Bryco would "shortly cease manufacturing operations," the sale property wouldn't be needed by the estate.

Ruggieri's and Thames' objections to the sale rebutted Bryco's valuation of the assets; asserted that Bryco had not only already ceased operations, it had already terminated all employees; and noted the proposed sale's lack of details as to what would actually be sold.

Their documentation also included a concise history of Jennings' and the Ring of Fire's use of bankruptcy to avoid responsibility; noted that the plant foreman's annual $30,000 salary precluded his ability to access $150,000 cash without outside funding, which would likely come from Jennings in some fashion; and detailed how Jennings was already siphoning and sheltering the cash from Bryco's sale. They also outlined the steps of how Jennings would eventually, through financing the 'new' Bryco, regain control of the company.

Jennings' attorneys called the objections "unsupported innuendo… Maxfield and his counsel's ranting illustrates once again why Bryco chose to file bankruptcy… Bryco and the other debtors in these related bankruptcies are faced with ideological opponents who think nothing of filing unsupported, diatribe-laced briefs deliberately designed to run-up estate expenses and to cause as much harm to the debtors as possible…"

One point in Jennings' attorneys' tit-for-tat revealed that "contrary to Ruggieri's assertions" as to the uncertainty of what would be sold, not only had Bryco already provided a list, Ruggieri had previously toured the Bryco plant, "so [he is] familiar with the sale property."

Indeed, Ruggieri had toured the plant. Nothing was being manufactured in the expansive, unassuming one-story building on the day of Ruggieri's visit, but a few people, including Jimenez — keeping their distance from Ruggieri at all times — were doing odd jobs, moving a box here, sweeping there.

Jennings escorted Ruggieri and a videographer through the building, occasionally making small talk and answering questions about the building's various areas.

Several rows of idle tools and equipment stretched across the manufacturing floor, open cartons of gun frames and various gun components between the machines. Shell casings littered the floor of a test firing room (where an employee had once been wounded), a space barely twelve feet wide but at least fifty feet long, stacks of tattered paper targets on the floor at the far end. Palettes stacked with cartons of guns ready for distribution filled a shipping area.

At one point Jennings walked away to take a phone call. Ruggieri continued with the camera operator, rounded a corner at the rear of the building, and discovered a dozen stacked file boxes, a trove of documents from the only case prior to Maxfield's that had pierced Jennings' asset sheltering wall. These were the financial documents that Jennings' and his ex-wife, under oath in depositions in 2003, had testified they destroyed in a "house cleaning" in 2000.

As the year came to a close and Ruggieri began his battle in court to stop what he knew in his gut was a sham sale, Bryco's plant manager, Paul Jimenez, had already filed a new business name for his soon-to-be gun company: Jimenez Arms. Ruggieri wouldn't discover the filing for months, although it had been made two weeks before the mid-December 'inside' buyer letter from Jennings' attorneys.

As if there wasn't enough for Ruggieri to work on and keep track of, the federal bill introduced the year before that would give blanket immunity to the gun industry was coming up for a vote and being hotly debated on the Senate floor.

He couldn't afford to ignore it. Passage of the bill in its present form could negate almost everything he'd achieved for his young client.

Ruggieri had previously sent a letter to California Senator Dianne Feinstein, a staunch and successful advocate of gun regulation, detailing the toll Brandon's accident took not just on the family but the community, the state, and "ultimately, the judicial system."

The Maxfield case, he wrote, "has a much more powerful message than just that of a pistol that was designed so that a user has to move the safety to "fire" before unloading. The critical issue is "why?" The answer is — Bryco's actions show EXACTLY how a gun company acts when it has immunity.

"It provides a clear look into our future if a firearm immunity bill is passed. Bryco thought that it already had the immunity that this bill would formalize — it thought that it had a practical immunity because, until this jury evaluated Bryco's pistol according to the same standards that we expect of any other product, no gun manufacturer had been held responsible."

He went on to describe the choices and decisions Bryco made to hide the gun's design flaw. "THIS is the kind of decision that a manufacturer makes when it believes it is immune (either practically or legally) from liability for its actions."

He closed with, "My client's case is currently on appeal. Clearly hoping that congress will take action to let them off the hook for the $24-million judgments, Bryco Arms, B.L. Jennings, Inc., and Bruce Jennings have already requested and received multiple extensions of time to file their opening appellate brief — thus ensuring that Brandon's case will remain "pending" and subject to dismissal for purposes of the immunity legislation.

"Please do not let Bryco, or any gun company, or anyone, callously make victims of their customers and our limited social resources and get away with it."

When he hadn't received a response, he emailed the senator's office the day before the scheduled floor debate. David Hantman, then chief counsel for Feinstein, quickly responded. "Is this all true? It's unbelievable. With your permission I may have [the Senator] give a separate statement based solely on your comments."

On February 25, 2004, Senator Feinstein brought Brandon's story into the debate as she stepped to the microphone on the Senate floor:

"...One of the cases that could be affected by this legislation, though this would ultimately be decided by a judge, is that of Brandon Maxfield, a seven-year-old from my state...

[the senator described the events and trial]

"...The bottom line, is that Brandon's case was not frivolous. The jury did not think it was. Without the threat of lawsuits, companies like the one that made the gun in this case will have little incentive to change the design, but this legislation would remove the threat of that suit, depriving Brandon of compensation but, even worse, depriving the public of this key avenue to improving the habits of gun manufacturers...

"In doing so, the bill effectively rewrites traditional principles of liability law, which generally hold that persons and companies may be liable for their negligence even if others are liable as well. This bill would essentially give the gun industry blanket immunity from civil liability cases, an immunity no other industry in America has today...

"The bill does allow certain cases to move forward, as its supporters have pointed out, but these cases can proceed only on very narrow circumstances. Countless experts have now said this bill would stop virtually all of the suits against gun dealers and manufacturers filed to date, many of which are vital to changing industry practice and compensating victims who have been horribly injured through the clear negligence or even borderline criminal conduct of some gun dealers and manufacturers…

"The exemptions in the bill, even the new bill, set a very high burden of proof of negligence for plaintiffs, allow for a very slight number of cases against gun manufacturers to be filed, and only protect a limited class of cases against sellers…"

In late June, 2004, the bankruptcy court approved the proposed private sale of Bryco's assets.

Without hard evidence of Jennings' active involvement behind the scenes, despite Jennings' documented history of financial manipulations, and, notwithstanding Jennings' prior statements about using bankruptcy to evade legal responsibility and reinvent his company, the court had no compelling legal reason to stop the sale.

For Ruggieri, the sale was such an obvious ploy that upon receiving the court's order, anger and frustration momentarily consumed him. It would be many months before his instincts about Jennings and the sale were proved to be entirely accurate.

He, more than anyone on the planet, knew how resilient, how successfully evasive Jennings could be, and he had long since accepted how much work lay ahead to recover Jennings' hidden assets. But the relatively swift approval of the sale, at least for this court, put Ruggieri in a position for which he hadn't been fully prepared. Now, instead of focusing on the bankruptcy, he was forced to concentrate on stopping the sale, playing catch-up instead of moving ahead.

Under normal circumstances, a sale of assets outside

of bankruptcy court could be beneficial to all the parties and cost-effective for the judicial system. Ruggieri saw it instead as an impending disaster, and vowed not to let it happen, even if he didn't yet know how.

If the sale went through, Jennings would emerge from bankruptcy financially bruised but with everything in place to pick up where he left off. Not only could he continue to make guns and remain in charge without being directly connected to the company, no federal or state law, no regulation, not even the jury's verdict in Brandon's case could force Jennings to stop selling or making the Bryco Model 38 or any other gun based on that flawed design. With an inventory of at least 60,000 gun components ready for assembly, Bryco could be selling newly assembled guns within weeks of the sale.

Not that the company would have to wait that long — Jennings was already sitting on 20,000 guns he could sell right now. While the court had only just approved the sale of Bryco's machinery, gun-making components and gun frames, Jennings had orchestrated a gun victory months before, right under the court's figurative nose.

Jennings petitioned to allow a loan of cash from B.L. Jennings, Inc. to Bryco, so that Bryco could assemble guns and deliver them to B.L. Jennings, which would then sell the guns to bring in cash for the company, and the estate. B.L. Jennings now had the completed guns, and by the time Bryco's private sale was approved, all Jennings needed was the court's approval to sell them.

Now Ruggieri was fighting two battles: stop the bargain basement sale of Bryco's assets to Jennings' handpicked buyer, and prevent 20,000 defective guns from slipping out of the court system and onto the streets.

A mistake by the court provided Ruggieri some breathing room. Brandon's case was not the only litigation suspended when Jennings filed bankruptcy. There had been several pending lawsuits against Jennings. Those plaintiffs were now also creditors, and Ruggieri kept in regular contact with them.

Shortly after the court's approval Ruggieri heard that several other creditors had not received notice of the sale, and had no opportunity to object to it.

When Thames pointed this out, the court rescheduled the sale date, allowing objections by creditors other than Brandon Maxfield.

It would take anywhere from days to weeks for the court to find a new date, and while it could be assumed that it might add at least another month to the schedule, Ruggieri felt mounting pressure to devise some kind of strategy, something outside of the court system. An eventual sale of assets was a certainty, either to an individual or through an auction, because that's part of the bankruptcy process. If another potential buyer offered the court more than the $150,000 for the proposed private sale, Jennings, in some fashion, would certainly object, perhaps be forced to offer more, and that would then — still only possibly — move the court to hold a public auction.

A public auction would allow anyone with funds to purchase the assets, though that 'anyone' could include still Bryco's manager or someone else in Jennings' pocket. Still, an open auction would be better than an insider sale, and would ensure a fair market price.

Ruggieri's options were few, with only one solution that could prevent Jennings from using a version of the 'new' Bryco Arms to resume business as usual.

Someone who understood what was at stake needed to buy the assets and put them to a different use.

It couldn't be Brandon, because any funds he recovered were for his medical trust. Ruggieri seriously considered making an offer himself. It wouldn't be easy, considering the debt load he had carried and continued to amass, but, objectively, he might be able to pull it off.... up to a point. With everything he knew and understood about Jennings, he couldn't even manage an educated guess as to what Jennings would do to maintain control of Bryco.

The court put all his considerations to rest by denying Ruggieri's latest objection to the sale and prohibiting, for now, any submission from Maxfield or Ruggieri to buy the assets. Judge Funk also added something unusual for most of the country's court systems, but which had become a required element in all Florida-based litigation. He *ordered* both sides to mediation.

Judges often suggest mediation, sometimes *strongly*. It is a meeting between all sides, facilitated by a professional mediator, with the intention of resolving issues before or during litigation. Ruggieri knew many highly effective Bay Area mediators, but he also knew that mediation was doomed unless both sides wanted to participate and had faith in the mediator.

The court ordered the mediation, to be held in the San Francisco area, and selected a mediator picked by Jennings' Florida attorneys.

Ruggieri had never heard of him.

He steamed about it as he drove to the meeting in San Francisco. As he parked and walked to a small office building, he mulled over the only settlement he was willing to discuss: no less than three-million dollars, and turn over any remaining Bryco guns now under the control of B.L Jennings, Inc.

Jennings had refused that demand previously, and Ruggieri he hadn't given it much thought since.

When the mediator arrived, slightly late, he gruffly introduced himself, plopped his briefcase next to the table, looked at Ruggieri and said, "I haven't had an opportunity to look through the documents yet, but let's start by getting you to drop this three-million dollar number. You've got to come off that, let that go."

Ruggieri was stunned. He thought, *I've got a $24,000,000 judgment, a gunmaker who has run across the country to avoid it, and a mediator who admits not reading anything about the case, who crashes in here and tells me my three-million settlement demand is too high.*

Ruggieri responded aloud, and out of reflex. "Are you fucking with me?"

He walked back to his car less than twenty minutes later, the mediation "a disaster," neither side moving on the amount, neither side moving on the 20,000 guns.

Still, there hadn't been settlement talks or offers of any kind until this. It was time for a conference with Brandon.

It was too important to do over the phone, and he hadn't seen the new house yet, so he made the almost three-hour drive to Willits.

He turned off a main road and up a steep, paved driveway that wound through trees for a few hundred feet until it leveled off at the front door of the house. Two thick Rottweilers ambled up and waited next to the driver's-side door as Ruggieri stepped out and gave them both a quick pat.

Clint opened the front door. "What do you think?"

"Looks great."

"C'mon in. Wait to you see the inside and the view."

Brandon and Sue said a quick hello from the roomy kitchen as Ruggieri walked in. He almost chuckled out loud, remembering the family's narrow, confining single-wide as Clint led him to the living room. Clint opened the sliding glass doors to the deck and they stepped outside to see the view of tree tops, hills, and blue sky.

He walked back to the kitchen, returned a shouted "Hi!" from Rocky, somewhere in a downstairs bedroom, and "Hi Rich!" from Trish, somewhere down a hall off the living room.

This would be one of the most important conversations Ruggieri had ever had with any client. Brandon could, as always, talk over things with his parents, talk to whomever he wanted to, but only he had the authority to tell Ruggieri what to do.

They sat around an oval table in a corner of the kitchen, Ruggieri facing Brandon in his wheelchair between Sue and Clint.

Ruggieri told them about the court's approval of the private sale and its subsequent postponement. He spoke with his usual directness that had endeared him to the family — "We're getting screwed, but I'm still working on how to stop this from happening..." — and then it was time to talk about "settlement money and guns."

"Brandon, I can't tell you what to decide, I can only tell you what could happen from the decision you make. I work for you, and for something like this you have to tell me what you want me to do."

"Okay."

"I told Jennings $3-million is an amount you will consider but you won't accept a settlement that doesn't include Bryco's guns. They said, we'll talk about money but we keep the guns. So now, I have to know what you want to do and what you're willing to accept."

"Okay."

"If they give you $3-million, we release all of them from the bankruptcy. If they give you the guns too, you know we wouldn't actually have them delivered to your garage or anything…"

Brandon laughed. "That would be so awesome. But, if we got them, could we do something else with them? We could crush them or make them into a statue."

"Sure. But, if they keep them, they are going to sell them to fund the settlement, the $3-million they will pay you."

"Huh. What kind of guns?"

Ruggieri knew he would always remember this moment. It would rip him up to let Jennings put 20,000 more of the these guns on the street, but it had to be Brandon's decision, as it was Brandon's loss, and the money was Brandon's compensation. Ruggieri believed most people would take the money.

But this was no ordinary teen, obviously. Brandon quickly focused on the guns, not the money.

"Semi-autos, with the same design flaw."

"How many?"

"Twenty-thousand."

"What would he get to do with them?"

"If he has them he can do whatever he wants, but most likely he'd sell them to replace the money that goes to you."

Brandon fixed his eyes on Ruggieri. "He'd be able to sell twenty-thousand guns that are the same kind of gun that shot me?"

Clint's stoic expression didn't change. Sue looked away.

"Yes."

"And no one could stop him, not us, not anyone."

"That's right."

"That's just wrong."

"Brandon, you have to look out for yourself. You can't

change the world and you don't owe anyone anything. No one will ever fault you for putting yourself first, because if you don't no one else will."

"What if I say no?"

"Then we continue trying to make him pay the judgment, and we think of some way to keep the guns off the street. We can figure that out later, but right now I need to know — can you give up the guns?"

For a few quiet seconds, Brandon moved his eyes to the side, as contemplative as Ruggieri had ever seen him, a Buddha-like introspection for a teenager. Ruggieri, prouder of Brandon than he'd ever been, thought that no one so young should be placed in this situation.

He finally turned back to look at Ruggieri. "No. If there's no guns we don't do it. I don't care about me, I'm not going to let him put one more kid in a wheelchair."

None of the bankruptcy's other creditors had anything close to Brandon's claim, but they all had the same rights in the process. Linda Bullard was one of those creditors. In 2000 she had sued Bryco, Jennings, and the trusts for the death of her teenage son, inadvertently shot by a Bryco pistol that had jammed and later fired when it fell onto a table.

Joel Grist, an affable Georgia native, was Bullard's attorney. Ruggieri and Grist knew each other from the earliest days of Brandon's case, with lawsuits against Jennings as the connection. They had previously met through an introduction by TLPJ attorney Vicki Ni at a round table event held by the Association of Trial Lawyers of America (now known as American Association of Justice).

The attorneys liked and respected each other. Ruggieri's tenacity on behalf of the other creditors provided

Grist with a special insight into Ruggieri's character. Like Brandon's case, the Bullard case had been stopped and brought into the bankruptcy, "and Ruggieri negotiated and talked with us all about the value of our client's claims, and he could have crushed our interests like an eight-hundred pound gorilla, just pushed us aside, when you compare all of our claims to Maxfield's. He could have ignored us or left us to fend for ourselves, but he never did that. He worked to carve out a $2.2 million pool for creditors that wouldn't have existed if not for his relentlessness."

So when Ruggieri called Grist about fighting the private sale and said, "I've got an idea that might help us all…" Grist already knew he'd do whatever he could.

It took him less than a week.

Grist submitted a motion on behalf of his client, objecting to the sale and making a counter-offer. Grist and Ruggieri had managed, with remarkable speed and a willing network of contacts, to provide $175,000 that Grist could offer in his client's name as a counteroffer to the private sale. It was $25,000 higher than what Jennings' attorneys had described as the "best the estate could hope for." The court had specified that Jimenez, the inside buyer, would have to present a cashier's check to the court within fifteen days of the order approving the sale. Grist's motion informed the court that while it was still waiting for some kind of proof that Jimenez had the money, Grist could deliver his client's check immediately.

Ruggieri believed this was the move that could push the court to approve a public sale.

The court had the ability to deny the motion outright, but this would give Ruggieri and the other creditors the basis to appeal. A denial was unlikely.

The court could also accept the higher bidder's money,

a buyer with money in hand, which would be a better deal for the pool of assets destined for Brandon. But that would almost certainly be hotly contested by Jennings' attorneys, and, odds were, followed by a higher bid.

An escalating offer/counteroffer between two private buyers would be an auction. If the move worked, Ruggieri would have accomplished part of what he'd fought for, to stop the 'private' sale, which to him was nothing more than the next step in Jennings' plan.

Ruggieri mulled over the likely vs. the unlikely: Grist's motion unlikely to be dismissed; unlikely the court will accept the higher amount and ignore that at least one bidder believed Bryco's assets were worth more; likely the court will order an auction of the assets.

If that happened, the high bid would take the assets, no matter the bidder.

Ruggieri had followed his call to Grist with a quick email to Vicki Ni — *Working with Joel on an idea, but thinking seriously that we need a "white knight" who can step in and help if there's an opportunity to bid for the assets...*

She responded quickly: *I'll go through my contacts, but here's someone who can get the word out — Eric Hauser.*

Eric Hauser was a twenty-year public relations pro in 2004, an energetic and effective advocate of progressive, grassroots, public interest causes. His career included work for Senator Bill Bradley in the mid-'90s, and as Bradley's press secretary for the Senator's 2000 campaign for President. He was well known around Washington D.C. and had a deeply personal commitment to his one-hundred and growing list of clients and causes he'd taken on since founding his firm in 1996. "We serve only progressive and public interest clients, because we believe as they believe, that what we do day-to-day is not about profit, it's about justice."

Ruggieri sent Hauser an introductory email with an overview of the case and the impending sale. Hauser called him "as soon as I finished reading the email. Everything about it resonated with me."

They talked at length, exploring Ruggieri's white knight idea. When Hauser hung-up he immediately called a meeting with his firm's senior vice president, Tracey Zimmerman, and senior associate Jason Dring.

Zimmerman had been the firm's first employee, had worked on a range of campaigns that included Planned Parenthood and the ACLU, and had managed the Hauser Group's daily operations for the year that Hauser had served as Bradley's press secretary. Dring, with the firm since 2001, had a special ability and the experience to take hard-to-publicize efforts and get them mainstream media exposure.

Zimmerman took the lead and put together a media plan to blanket the country with awareness of Brandon's story and the Jennings-manipulated sale. Still not knowing if or when the private sale would be scheduled, the plan's timeline was ambitious relative to its urgency and national in scope. It was "a two-track media approach, focusing on the human interest stories with Brandon at the center and investigative report pieces."

She listed a dozen nationally recognized media and news outlets, and how they would be pitched about Brandon's story. She also suggested the need for a website that would include the background of the lawsuit, bios on Brandon and Ruggieri, and, astutely, as it would turnout, a donations page.

Ruggieri shared his idea with Thames — find someone to make a counteroffer for Bryco's assets, and making some kind of public appeal. Thames initially didn't give it much of a chance, given the shortening timetable and the fight they'd get from Jennings' attorneys.

When Ruggieri shared some of the ideas from Zimmerman, Thames thought, *this is the craziest thing in the world. Who's going to do that?* "I just didn't think someone would actually contribute to something like this, but Richard assured me there were people out there who would. I was skeptical, certainly."

As Hauser and his group pulled together media packets and drafted Brandon's and Ruggieri's stories, Ruggieri realized that if a public auction was approved, and someone stepped up in to buy the assets, then… what? If everything went Brandon's way, either Brandon or some white knight would be the owner of a gun company. Brandon had already agreed he wanted to get the assets if he could, but he certainly didn't want nor was he licensed to be in the gun business.

And what about the possibility of multiple people who might all want to be white knights, or a bunch of entities coming in as white knights but changing into black knights once they had a gun company?

For it all to work, whether it was one or one-hundred white knights, the return on any money donated for a successful bid would have to be the the destruction of any guns and the assured end of the company known as Bryco Arms.

Ruggieri thought through the best possible solution: a nonprofit could buy the assets with the express intent of destroying or repurposing them in some fashion, and donors could get a tax benefit.

After a hurried call in which Ruggieri proposed that Brandon could form a nonprofit to fight for the assets, and a quick "Yeah!" of agreement from the teen, Ruggieri sent an email to Hauser and began to file the necessary papers. The only one thing he didn't have was a name.

He had conversations with a few creative friends and confidants, listing dozens of potential names, but none had that special something. When the right name came to him, it came about because he'd had to stop thinking about it.

He was drafting a motion, typing the words 'Bryco Arms' for the thousandth time and the more recent 'Jimenez Arms' for the hundredth time. His mind wandered. He thought of the last time he saw Brandon, how the teen used head movements to control his wheelchair, arms clutched to his chest in permanent, nonworking spasm.

"I knew it immediately, and when I typed it, it was just so right. I called a designer I had used before, told him the name, and he had a stunning logo ready for us in just a few days."

The designer sent a digital version of it by email. Ruggieri looked at it, then immediately forwarded it to Brandon and Eric Hauser.

It was a chrome-like, sculptural circle, inside the circle two muscular arms in a Yin-Yang fashion, holding a gun between two hands, the gun's barrel twisted into a knot.

The name Brandon's Arms circled the design.

The first media story appeared in late May. "Campaign Seeks to Halt Gun Makers' Bankruptcy Ploy," an online feature story written by Dick Dahl for Join Together, a national nonprofit organization focused on gun violence and substance abuse issues. Dahl had interviewed Ruggieri by phone for almost an hour, and the resulting 1,800-word piece provided an extensive overview of the case and Jennings' history. Ruggieri also shared several recent, disturbing developments with the journalist.

Entities and individuals filing bankruptcy must reveal their assets to the court. Ruggieri discovered that Jennings' second ex-wife, Janice, had failed to disclose that she owned Shining Star Investments, a limited liability company (LLC), in Texas. After Ruggieri brought it to the court's attention, Janice stated she wasn't hiding it, she had "forgotten" to report it because "it does no business and has no assets." But she also had to admit that she had recently obtained a Federal Firearms License for the company and that she had business discussions with Jimenez.

As Dahl explained in the article, "according to Ruggieri, the separate entity that actually owned and distributed [Bryco's] gun inventory, B.L. Jennings, Inc., would likely spring back to life under Shining Star Investments… Ruggieri believes that Jennings' next step would be to ask the court to transfer the assets of B.L. Jennings, which includes an inventory of some 22,000 handguns, to Shining Star."

The article also included the link to Brandon's Arms' website, with Ruggieri explaining, "We're making an appeal for a 'white knight' to come forward and say, 'I don't want to see millions of these junk guns put back on the street, so here's some money, then sell off the machinery and maybe recover half of the money, take a tax deduction for the rest."

The media floodgates opened on June 30th.

New York Times reporter Fox Butterfield, who had interviewed Ruggieri immediately after the first trial, interviewed Ruggieri, Brandon, and Jennings' Florida attorney, and wrote a half-page story that appeared above-the-fold on page one of the Times' National News section.

The story — "Paralyzed by a Gun, Boy Now Seeks to Buy Maker" — accompanied by photos of Brandon, Ruggieri, and the Bryco Model 38, began with another revelation:

"The California attorney general's office has intervened in a federal bankruptcy trial in a way that could help a teenager buy out and shut down the manufacturer of a semiautomatic handgun with a design flaw that has left the boy paralyzed from the neck down since the age of 7.

In a highly unusual action, Randy Rossi, director of the firearms division of the California Department of Justice, wrote to a federal bankruptcy judge in Florida yesterday that Paul Jimenez, the man the judge tentatively approved to buy the manufacturer, was ineligible to make guns because he lacked federal and California firearms licenses.

Therefore, Mr. Rossi wrote to the judge, he was "submitting this written objection to the sale" on behalf of the California attorney general, Bill Lockyer."

The article expanded on Brandon's story, the sequence of events that led to the Florida bankruptcy, Ruggieri's attempt to stop the private sale, and the scheming that still seemed to pervade everything about the bankruptcy's real purpose:

"Mr. Ruggieri has objected to Judge Funk's decision to allow the proceeds of the sale to Mr. Jimenez to be deposited in the bank account of [Mr. Jennings'] law firm, rather than a neutral party.

"Here's the attorney who advised Jennings on how to hide his assets now being in charge of holding the money to pay the creditors," he said.

The federal bankruptcy trustee in Jacksonville filed a motion with Judge Funk supporting Mr. Ruggieri's complaint."

The article ended with a quote from Brandon, who, as Ruggieri and the country would soon find out, handled his rising prominence in the media spotlight with a level of class beyond his years: "...Last week Brandon was in Children's Hospital in Oakland, Calif., for what he said in a telephone interview was a very minor operation, a skin graft to relieve a pressure sore. Brandon said he harbored no personal grudge but wonders of Mr. Jennings, "How can he look at himself in the morning, knowing some kid is going to be injured by one of his guns?"

Hauser and his crew worked their contacts relentlessly, pitching a story that quickly became the story no one wanted to miss. Over the following two weeks, every national news organization interviewed Sue, Brandon, and Ruggieri. An Associated Press (AP) article appeared in two-hundred newspapers. People magazine gave Brandon and Sue a full page, with photo. The BBC interviewed Brandon over the phone. Newspapers in nine countries reported the story.

In mid-July, CNN and CBS News came to Oakland Children's Hospital to do on-camera interviews of Brandon, where he was still being treated. The teen was personable and sincere, at one point earnestly saying to CBS reporter John Blackstone, "I've got a job to do, I'm determined to do it, and I'm gonna do it. If I bought [Bryco], I'd melt down all the guns and keep kids from getting hurt. Maybe God dealt me a card to get these guns off the street."

Sue agreed to be in the CBS interview, handled the first few questions well, and stayed composed until asked to describe what Brandon was like before the accident.

She managed to say, "Before the accident, Brandon used to ride bikes, run with his brothers..." before she sobbed and turned away from the camera.

When the CBS report aired in the early evening of July 12th, it included file video of Jennings, the voiceover offering a few quick sentences about Jennings' history, and that Jennings had declined to be interviewed for the report. The segment then cut to Jennings in 1998 saying, "The basic right of firearm ownership has been in this country forever."

Dan Bennett wasn't much of a television watcher, but that night it was on in his comfortable living room as he sat next to his girlfriend, Colette, and stretched out his long legs. He was reading the newspaper as Brandon's piece aired.

Colette nudged him and said, "Listen to this."

He put the newspaper aside and watched, and was close to fuming before the report finished. "This guy takes no responsibility, spits in the face of his own customers. It's insulting that Jennings makes these crap guns and doesn't give a damn that people are hurt by something *he* made and sold."

Colette looked at him as he went off, and said, "So do something about it."

Bennet was financially well established, and he'd worked his butt off for thirty years to get there.

His parents were from New York, and he'd lived there as a young child, but he'd grown up in San Antonio and considered it his home. He'd been entrepreneurial early on, "never had many real jobs," starting a T-shirt company in college "until the business got so big so fast I couldn't finish school."

His San Antonio-based company grew successfully

and he stayed with it for almost thirty years, but in 2001 "I began to get out, primarily because my kids weren't going to take over, and I had no family to bring in. I didn't want to sell it to someone who would leverage it up, so I took some time to think about what I'd do; about ten years, actually."

He was splitting his time between San Antonio and an apartment in New York City, and flew "hundreds of thousands of miles every year, for business mostly." He began selling off the company in pieces over the next five years and took more time for himself, did more personal travel, including a month spent in Tibet. He trekked the Himalayas, "and thought about things. You spend a lot of time looking down at your feet as you're moving up and down and through these majestic mountains and places, and when you look around, your own smallness becomes really, really apparent to you. It shifts how you think, about things, about yourself, and what you're doing"

Only a few days back from that trip, "I'm sitting in my office and asking myself, why am I doing this? I don't want to die at my desk, y'know?" He noticed "a pimple on my elbow, a boil or something, and I came home and and my arm starts hurting." When the pain continued for the next week he went to his doctor, who immediately sent him to the hospital. He had MRSA, a treatment resistant, life threatening staph infection most likely picked-up during his trip.

"I spent eight days in the hospital, a lot of time to think and come to the realization that I wanted out of the business, to go do whatever else I felt I should do, so I decided to finally just sell the company."

Which was where his life was when he saw the CBS News story.

He wrote down a few notes and in the morning called

his longtime executive assistant, Christine, told her "track down this California attorney, call him and tell him I want to talk to him about helping Brandon Maxfield."

Donations to the Brandon's Arms website picked up as public awareness of his story spread. The nonprofit's website included photos of Brandon, described the case, the upcoming sale, and a provided a growing list of links to news stories.

A small, independent documentary crew was now following the story, gathering footage of the family, news clips, and interviews. A few days after publication of the AP and People magazine stories, the crew recorded Ruggieri in his office. Emails to Brandon's Arms now had surpassed several hundred.

He paused as he read one, shaking his head and saying, "and we're really getting a lot of obnoxious emails rolling in now… Not going to read that one out loud…won't read that one… here's one, 'Leave guns alone and just live your life'… I'm sure Brandon would appreciate that little bit of wisdom, y'know…"

The country was weighing in. For every message of hope and encouragement, like the note with the international money order air-mailed from a young man in Germany, or the eleven year-old girl who donated money she'd been saving for a new bike, there were at least as many berating Ruggieri for being a greedy attorney financed by anti-gun groups, and attacking Brandon personally with disparaging messages, including many that were downright vile, like, '*…fuck you, if I ever see your crippled ass on the street I'll shoot you myself…*'

Ruggieri, usually as unflappable as an astronaut, was caught a bit off guard and more than a little dismayed.

He pushed away from the computer screen and looked directly into the documentary camera.

"There is a definite lack of critical thinking going on in this country, in a number of subjects. We ought to teach a class in in critical thinking, how to think about subjects and not be buffaloed by baloney little platitudes, whether they're political platitudes or whether they're platitudes about guns — guns don't kill people, people kill people — teach people how to think about issues. That would be really worthwhile.

"Also a lot of the people who don't like this and are very upset and very angry, when I read their emails they're not really upset about Brandon's case, they're upset because they don't understand the laws in this country. They wave the flag as being great Americans and defenders of the Second Amendment, but they completely scoff at the whole jury system, they completely scoff at the division of the three branches of government. They don't seem to understand that we have negligence laws in this country, and that products manufacturers by American law are responsible for the safety of users and have been in California since 1963.

"They think this whole gun control thing is between the guy using the gun and the gun industry, but it's not. What about the bystanders?

"You get some guy over here who likes guns and he wants to have a gun and the gun industry wants to give him a gun, and that's fine, but what about the bystanders who get hurt, like Brandon? Brandon had nothing to do with that gun. What if while you're pulling a gun out to shoot someone it goes off because it doesn't have a safety on it or it's defectively designed, or it blows up in your hand and a fragment of it hits me in the eye.

"They say 'the gun wasn't at fault, the user of the gun

was at fault.' Well, yeah, of course the user of the gun was at fault but so was the gun, and the law in every one of the fifty states provides for comparative fault, provides that each person bears their liability according to their percentage of the fault. That's American law, if you don't like that go change it but don't yell at Brandon, he didn't make the law.

"So on the one hand they say that they're great Americans and what we're doing is un-American, but it seems that when you read what they're saying, they don't have a clue what American law is. It's amazing."

On July 15th, two days after the CBS News report aired and as the documentary crew recorded in Ruggieri's office, the computer made the *dink* sound of a new incoming email. Ruggieri read the email, quickly logged on to the bankruptcy court's website and read it aloud for the crew.

"I just got notice, what the court has done in response to these bids; it has ordered an auction of Bryco's assets on August 12th, 2004, at 1:30 p.m. in Jacksonville, Florida. The auction is open to all parties. Minimum bid is $175,000."

"This is exactly what we wanted from day one, the opportunity to have a fair and open bid for these assets. This gives Brandon's Arms additional time to raise more money and compete with any other bids."

"Finally, after all these months, we've got what we asked for."

But it now also meant yet more work for Ruggieri. He had gone nonstop on Brandon's case for five years, and he knew the bankruptcy would take at least several more.

He had managed to stay relatively healthy and sane so far, partly attributable to a mix of thirty years experience, a precise, mission focus approach to the work, and the unwavering support of his wife Edith, who, as an attorney herself, understood the stresses and machinations of litigation. It was through a personal interest of Edith's, outside of legal work, that Richard found a counterbalance to the intensity of his professional life.

Each weekend for two years, Edith, and for the last several months now Ruggieri, drove a few minutes from their house to a block long, high-roofed, cavernous building. Skates in hand they'd enter Berkeley Iceland, a sixty year-old ice arena favored in its prime by recreational skaters and, during the '70s and early '80s, many Bay Area-based international competitive skaters.

Edith had been taking figure skating lessons for several years, and Ruggieri now joined her for his own basic lessons. The ice, one of the largest rinks in California, was a favorite of families and teens, and for Richard it was enjoyable time far from the physical and intellectual environment of an attorney.

The weekend after notice of the August auction, Edith practiced her spins, watched by her coach at one end of the ice, and Ruggieri practiced on his own nearby. His skate blade caught a patch of rough ice and he went down, not particularly hard, but he put out his left hand as he fell. Pain shot through his wrist.

He thought he'd shake it off, but Edith's coach encouraged him to take a break. Ruggieri sat in the bleachers for a few minutes, "and I realized I was suddenly very warm, a bit woozy, and I hurt like hell."

He'd broken his wrist.

Whether it was destiny or happenstance, there was an upside in that it had happened in this period just before the auction, when so much of the relentless typing of motions, letters, and filings necessary for the case thus far was already completed.

The court had ordered Jimenez to disclose the source of his funds, money which had already been forwarded to Jennings' Florida attorneys. The Bryco building's new landlord had deferred the initial rent and loaned Jimenez, the new tenant, $150,000 in exchange for a security interest in the assets, despite Jimenez not yet actually owning the assets.

As Ruggieri prepped for the trip to Florida, where he would bid as Brandon's Arms' representative, Grist and the other creditors had agreed to pull out of the auction so Brandon's Arms would be the only additional bidder. Donations still came in but had leveled off, and Ruggieri could see that without some kind of bump in awareness or the appearance of that long hoped for white knight, Brandon's Arms would be able to make an opening bid, but not much more.

His office phone was rarely quiet for more than an hour, but one afternoon, with only a week before the auction, he chose to answer instead of letting it roll into voicemail.

"Hi Mr. Ruggieri, my name is Christine and I'm the executive assistant for Mr. Dan Bennett. He's a business owner and saw a news report about you and Brandon. He'd like to help with your efforts."

"That's great. We have a website for donations, just go to..."

"Mr. Ruggieri, sorry to interrupt, but he'd like to help you with the auction itself."

"Great. In what way?"

"We understand the auction is in Florida, so he thought that if you could meet him in Texas he would then fly you to the auction, and assist you financially."

"He flies? He's a pilot?"

"No sir, he's not a pilot, he has jets. He'd fly with you on his jet."

"Really. He has jets?"

"Yes. He's the real thing, I assure you."

Christine explained that Bennett had recently sold his business, heard Brandon's story, and suggested if Ruggieri would take a commercial flight to Houston he could then be picked up by Dan's jet, fly to Florida together and work out details about the auction. "Give me your flight information and I'll take care of the rest."

He hung up and sat for a few moments before hitting the Internet and looking for information about Bennet and his company. There wasn't much, other than the company was a major apparel manufacturer and distributor. He didn't find anything of note about Bennett.

He had a white knight, maybe, or, because of the story's awareness around the country and the vehement, occasionally threatening email messages directed at him and Brandon, maybe Mr. Bennett was something else. Ruggieri had to consider the possibility that this was an odd set-up of some kind.

During an hour-long conference call the next day, Hauser, his team, and Ruggieri discussed the logistics for the auction, and Hauser shared a major 'get' — Good Morning America would broadcast a live interview by Diane Sawyer of Brandon and Sue in California the morning of the auction.

Jason Dring would be with Ruggieri and a documentary crew in Florida on auction day. Brandon and Sue would wait in Ruggieri's office, with another documentary crew, where several reporters would interview them after the auction.

Ruggieri shared his story about the call from Bennett's office, concluding with "if he's real, we might actually have a chance at this thing. If he's not real, I might be calling you from the middle of nowhere…"

Chapter 10

THE AUCTION

As Ruggeri walked into baggage claim at Houston's airport, he spotted a young man holding a sign with Ruggieri's name on it.

"That's me."

"Welcome to Houston, Mr. Ruggieri. I'll assist you with your bag and drive you to the private flight area."

Ten minutes later the car passed through a special gate and onto the tarmac, stopping alongside a waiting Falcon 10 business jet. Ruggieri walked up the steps and inside the stylish, leather and walnut trimmed jet's interior. A moment later a different, slightly older man followed Ruggieri inside.

"Hello, Mr. Ruggieri, hope your flight was okay."

"Hi. Dan?"

"No, actually, I'm your pilot. We're going to pick up Mr. Bennett in San Antonio. It will be just over ten minutes, then we'll continue on to Florida. Would you like something to drink?"

They lifted off a few minutes later, Ruggieri still concerned this could be some kind of set-up or misdirection. They touched down in San Antonio, taxied to a stop, and the engines idled as the pilot opened the door. A moment later Bennett ducked his head as he stepped through the jet's doorway, smiled and held out his hand to Ruggieri.

"Hi Richard, I'm Dan."

"Good to finally meet you. Thanks for the ride."

They were a couple of guys in a private jet at 40,000 feet, heading to Florida at over 500-knots. After some small talk, they chuckled as Ruggieri shared his early concerns about possibly being kidnapped and discussed the schedule for the next day.

"A guy named Jason from the PR firm will be with us, and so will a camera crew. Hope that's okay with you, but really, if you were hoping for anonymity you're screwed because the press will be there when we come out."

"That's fine, long as you don't mind me just pointing to you and saying 'that's the guy you want to talk to.'

"No problem. You'll be left on your own for a bit, though, when I step away to talk to Brandon when it's over."

The jet made a brief stop for fuel, and as they waited Ruggieri's cell phone alerted that he had a voicemail from Thames. He tried several times to hear the message, but the signal was intermittent and he couldn't connect before they resumed the flight.

Ruggieri stepped out of the hotel elevator and crossed the lobby to the restaurant, his thoughts jumbled from everything that had happened in the hour between their arrival in Jacksonville and now. He'd finally accessed the voicemail from Rick, and it wasn't anything Ruggieri would have predicted. *"Richard, it's Rick. He's offered to settle."*

Before he unpacked he was on the phone to Thames' office.

"I just got your message. How much?"

"Three-million; they want to go over details with us tomorrow before it goes to Judge Funk."

"The guns? They know Brandon won't accept anything without the guns."

"They said they're fine with the guns."

"So the auction's off."

"No, Bruce wants the auction to go on."

"That can't be right. He's going to give us three-mil' *and* still have the auction?" Why on earth would Jennings pay three-million-dollars and then spend more money in the auction, money which would also go to Brandon and to the other creditors.

"I agree, it makes no sense to me either."

"They've just made my dinner awkward..."

Bennett looked up as Ruggieri entered the restaurant, and although they'd only spent a few hours together, Bennett sensed something wasn't right.

"Everything okay?"

"We might have a settlement."

Bennet glanced at his watch. "Just now?"

"Happened while we were in the air, actually. There was a voicemail that I tried to pick-up when we we were refueling, only got it just a few minutes ago. This is Jennings, though, and there are some things about it that aren't clear. If it's real, there probably won't be an auction."

"Damn."

"But, supposedly, Jennings wants to have the auction anyway, that's why I'm not sure about the settlement offer. We're going in prepared for the auction."

Back in California, Sue, Brandon, and Sue's mother Kandace had checked in to a hotel near the Oakland airport. The GMA interview would happen at five the next morning in one of the hotel's meeting rooms. Arrangements were made to do the remote from the Oakland hotel, an alternative to the local affiliate's studio because the ABC news crew could still easily set-up and uplink to the satellite, and Sue wouldn't have to worry about negotiating San Francisco's traffic or its hills.

Despite the emotions that had welled up during the CBS News interview at the hospital, Sue had agreed to this interview as soon as she was asked. "They told me this would be different, I'd be sitting next to Brandon and we'd be talking about the auction and the lawsuit, and I can talk about that because it makes me more angry than anything else."

"This is all for Brandon, so I won't ever say no to anything like this, even if it's hard for me. And, heck, it's Diane Sawyer! It's a little scary, kinda, but Brandon's always ready to go."

"I think the toughest part was being up and ready by four-thirty."

Clint and the kids would watch from home, then he'd take them to school.

No matter the outcome, by the end of the day tomorrow everything would have moved forward. News organizations around the world would be watching, but as the night of the 11th turned into the morning of the 12th, a couple of attorneys in Florida, and one white knight from Texas, wondered if the auction would happen at all.

Sue and Brandon entered a spacious room filled with equipment. Four men methodically worked amidst several large lights on tripods, stepping around open equipment cases and over dozens of cables on the floor. One of the men introduced himself as the producer and guided Sue and Brandon to a corner of the room so brightly lit it looked bathed in sunlight, at its center a chair ready for Sue.

One crew member attached tiny microphones to the lapel of Sue's suit and to Brandon's shirt. Never being denied a teen's fashion of the day, Brandon had chosen to wear a white knit cap with black stripes that matched well with his Hawaiian-style, black and white print shirt. He also wore his lip ring.

The producer handed two small ear pieces to Sue, one for her and one for Brandon. "You'll hear the director in New York tell you that the segment is starting, and that's when they'll begin Dianne's intro, and about a minute later you'll hear Dianne talking to you and Brandon." He pointed to the camera on a tripod ten feet-away. "We can't set it up so you can see her, but when you talk to her just look right at the camera and know she's there looking right back at you. It'll be about five more minutes. Brandon, you ready?"

"Yes I am. You ready mom?"

"I am honey."

The camera operator focused and locked down the shot, then shut down one of the lights so it wouldn't be so warm as they waited for the cue from the other side of the country.

A voice in their ear pieces said '*Here we go...*', and millions of viewers across the country watched as Diane Sawyer looked into the camera and said, "Today, a bankruptcy court is going to be auctioning off a gunmaker specializing in handguns. Why is this something worth watching? Well, there's a teenager who's waging an Internet campaign to buy the company and melt the guns down to destroy it. Why? Because of what happened to him."

As Sue and Brandon waited for their cue, viewers saw photos of Brandon before the accident and heard Sawyer's voiceover describe how a bright, fun little boy was accidentally shot and paralyzed. A photo showed seven-year-old Brandon in the ICU, and a recent clip of Brandon in Children's Hospital, describing how before the accident, "I wanted to be a baseball player..." As Sawyer briefly described the lawsuit, video showed the inside of the Bryco factory, then cut to a clip from Jennings' deposition as he answered "no" several times to Ruggieri's "Did you have any engineers evaluate the gun's design… any safety evaluations…".

It was back to the live feed, Sawyer on one side of a split screen, welcoming Sue and Brandon on the other half of the screen, then asking Sue, "of the $24-million that the jury said you should be awarded, how much has Bryco paid you?"

Sue answered, "Not one cent."

"Do you expect them to pay you?"

"We pray that they'll pay us."

A bit more Q and A, and as Sawyer talked about the Web campaign, video rolled showing graphics from the website, and Sawyer talked about how donations had come from all over the world.

The interview lasted a few more minutes, Sawyer and Sue exchanged pleasant goodbyes, and it was over.

Later they loaded up and headed to Ruggieri's office to wait for the early afternoon call that would tell Brandon whether or not his nonprofit was the owner of a gun company.

After watching the GMA interview, Ruggieri and Bennett walked the few blocks from their hotel to Thames' office. Bennett wore khakis and and a dress shirt, Ruggieri was in his attorney uniform — navy blue suit, shirt and tie — both men enveloped by the smothering, summer Florida humidity. The normally thick, moist air was even more so that morning due to an advancing hurricane expected to make landfall on Florida's Gulf side within forty-eight hours.

The documentary camera operator and his audio tech were already setting up in Thames' conference room as Ruggieri and Bennett arrived. With several hours to go before the auction, Nina LaFleur joined them, Jason Dring from the Hauser Group arriving a few minutes later. The camera operator recorded the group making small talk about the approaching hurricane and possible travel delays, and about the GMA interview that morning, which Ruggieri had watched and said "was as good as it gets."

The crew left to set-up outside, as the legal team discussed several other aspects of the case that would be dealt with regardless of the auction's results, even though they wouldn't know if there was going to be an auction until they went to the courthouse.

Jennings and Jimenez were already in the courtroom, seated next to each other in the first row, as Ruggieri, Thames, Bennett and Dring walked in, and Judge Funk, seated at the bench, called the attorneys over to the jury room for discussions about the potential settlement.

Bennett took a seat in the front row behind Ruggieri's table, and glanced up to catch the first of many hard stares he'd get from Jennings over the next hour.

In the jury room, to Ruggieri's surprise, Jennings' attorneys agreed to the $3 million settlement, and still wanted the auction to proceed, which, to Ruggieri, "made no sense to me, but, okay, let's do this."

Back in the courtroom, Ruggieri sat at his table in front of the railing, called 'the bar', that separates the attorneys, jury box, and judge's bench area from the spectator seating, which was almost full. The courtroom was twice the size of Department 16 back in Oakland, where this long road had begun. It was sleeker, more ornate and marbled, a higher ceiling and with more space in front of the fence.

Bennett stayed in the front row directly behind Ruggieri, joined by Thames, LaFleur, and Dring.

Jimenez moved to the table on the other side of the room from Ruggieri. Jennings, his attorneys beside him, remained in the front row behind and slightly to the right of Jimenez.

Ruggieri realized "Dan and I hadn't talked about how we would work the auction, because at first it seemed there wasn't going to be an auction, and now here we were." Bidding would start in a few minutes. Ruggieri simply turned and asked Bennett, "how much do we have?"

"$100,000."

"I know now is not the time to be a jerk about it, but I am a lawyer, so can I have something to that effect in writing?"

Bennett smiled. "And I am a businessman, so, yes, of course." He pointed to a legal pad Ruggieri had on the table. Ruggieri grabbed it and handed it to him with a pen. Bennett quickly wrote, *Brandon's Arms has $100,000,* scribbled his signature and handed Ruggieri the pad.

As Ruggieri turned back, Bennett remembered something from many years before that he had never shared with anyone and hadn't thought about since. After his company had grown and become more successful than he'd dreamed, Bennet read about a neighborhood benefit being held for a San Antonio boy with cancer. He couldn't say for certain why news of the event caught his eye or what it was about it that stuck with him, but the morning of the benefit he drove to the working class neighborhood, parked, and watched as the street became crowded with families. Many people arrived in barely working cars and trucks, laborers and migrant workers bringing food and drinks, kids playing games, and people putting dollars into donation jars. He watched for twenty, maybe thirty minutes before he got out of his car, walked through the crowd and placed a check for $50,000 in one of the jars. As he drove away a few minutes later, he smiled and briefly wished he could be there when they looked at the check.

Judge Funk asked, "Are the bidders ready? Identify yourselves and let's begin."

"Richard Ruggieri for Brandon's Arms, your honor."

"Paul Jimenez, Jimenez Arms, your honor."

"Alright, an opening bid of $175,000 is required."

"Brandon's Arms bids $175,000."

"Jimenez Arms, $180,000."

They continued in five-thousand dollar increments and quickly hit $200,000. Ruggieri paused, turned in his seat and whispered to Bennett.

"I want them to think I'm hesitant, so let's talk a bit."

But Bennett was slightly confused. "Why are you bidding so low?" He played along with Ruggieri's idea, clenching his fist and gesturing, but he was concerned. "Let's put some real money out there and scare their ass." He glanced at Jennings' team — to a man they glared at him. He grinned. "They are going nuts trying to figure out who the hell I am." He pointed to the legal pad, Ruggieri handed it to him and Bennett quickly put a line through his previous note and wrote, *you have $200,000.*

Bidding hit $275,000 and continued, Ruggieri waiting longer and longer between his bids. At $300,000, he picked up the legal pad, left the table, sat in the first row and conferred quietly with Bennett.

"This is going to go on." Ruggieri had been bidding

small increments in hope of bluffing Jennings into thinking Brandon's Arms had reached its limit, because at some point, "I thought they would reach their own limit and we could put some real money up and blow them away. And if they were going to win, I wanted to make them really, really pay. But I could tell it was aggravating Dan."

Bennett wrote *plus $50,000.*

With each bid, Bennett watched Jimenez glance at Jennings before turning back and upping the amount. "It was so obvious, so corrupt. It started to get under my skin." He reached for the pad, circled the previous amount and wrote *plus $50,000.*

Bidding rose to $400,000… $450,000… $495,000… $500,000.

Ruggieri turned to Bennett and said, softly, "I'm going to say five-hundred-five, that alright?"

Bennet waited a few seconds before he said, "Yes."

"Your honor, $505,000."

Jimenez peeked at Jennings, sitting stone faced and staring straight ahead. He turned back and looked at the judge. "Jimenez Arms bids $510,000."

Ruggieri and Bennet, without saying a word to each other, knew at that moment there was no amount Jennings wouldn't spend to keep Bryco.

All eyes were on Ruggieri, including Judge Funk's.

"No further bid from Brandon's Arms, your honor." Ruggieri's emotions were mixed. "I thought, well, at least we got the price up there, and it's all going to Brandon and the creditors, and there was the $3-million settlement, plus Brandon's share of whatever was in the bankruptcy estate.

"Over the space of a minute or so I'd go from being satisfied we'd gotten such a better amount, to feeling deflated, wondering if we'd settled too cheap, and I still couldn't understand why the auction had even happened after we had talked about the settlement."

Dan wasn't happy about the result even though he knew "this was still, from a practical perspective, a win for Brandon. But I had gone way over what I'd expected to contribute. I thought it would be a couple of hundred-thousand. I was shocked."

Everyone packed up and walked out of the courtroom as Judge Funk instructed the attorneys to stay and go over the details of the settlement. As people slowed near the door, Bennett walked right up to Jennings, looked him in the eye and said, "Congratulations on getting your company back."

Jennings stammered, unsure how to respond before Bennett walked out of the room.

"I knew what had just happened, and I wanted him to know I knew it."

With the courtroom empty of spectators, Judge Funk scanned the papers before him.

"Mr. Jimenez, you have already deposited $150,000 toward the assets, the court must receive your balance of $360,000 by August 19th. Please step out now." Jimenez left the room. "We have a settlement between defendant Bryco and plaintiff Brandon Maxfield, is this correct?"

Ruggieri spoke quickly. "Your honor, we require detailed specifics before we formally agree to the settlement, and Mr. Maxfield requests that Mr. Jimenez provide documentation about the source of the over half-million dollars he just guaranteed to the estate. Our basis for this request is the history in prior and in these proceedings of fraudulent practices by the defendants, including false statements made under oath, and Mr. Jimenez's connection to the defendants. I'll also point out to the court that according to the records of California's

Department of Justice, Mr. Jimenez does not yet have a license to manufacture guns."

"You'll submit motions to the court if you want to compel discovery regarding the source of the funds?"

"Yes your honor."

"Let's move to the settlement then."

"Mr. Maxfield is prepared to accept defendant's offer of $3-million and the 20,000 guns that currently are..."

Jennings' attorney interrupted. "There are no guns as part of the settlement offer."

"That's not our understanding. I made Mr. Maxfield's requirements very clear, that he would not accept any settlement that did not include the existing guns."

"That's not what we said at all. We did not include the guns because B.L. Jennings, which has the guns now, intends to sell them so those proceeds can fund the settlement."

"Your honor, this is so wrong. My client, paralyzed for life by one of 'those' guns, would never agree to that. Never."

Judge Funk looked back and forth between the attorneys. "Sounds to me like there's no settlement here."

Ruggieri was angry, but controlled. "Respectfully, your honor, not only is there no settlement, I request an immediate order preventing the sale or transfer of any Bryco guns, wherever they may be physically located now, until they can either be destroyed, or transferred to either California's Department of Justice or the ATF for destruction."

"Your honor, Mr. Jennings believes selling the guns would bring great financial benefit to the..."

Judge Funk stopped him mid-sentence. "As the guns were not part of this auction, and they are not suitable for just anyone to obtain, we'll hold another auction at a date to be determined, but the sale will be for destruction only, under the control of the appropriate regulatory agency. The purchaser may do whatever with the remains, but they will be destroyed. If there are no bidders the guns will be destroyed anyway."

"That works for Mr. Maxfield your honor."

The attorneys left the courtroom and milled around the corridor for a minute before everyone walked outside.

The documentary crew was set up and already recording as Jennings and Jimenez came out of the building together and walked away, Jimenez casting a quick glance at the camera just as he walked around a corner and out of sight.

A half-dozen reporters gathered, speaking first with Jennings' attorney, then asking Ruggieri for comments, but he asked for a moment "to make a confidential call to my client."

Sue, Brandon, and Kandace had yet to arrive at Ruggieri's office, and his calls to Sue's cell phone went unanswered. He phoned one of the documentary crew waiting in his office, who informed him that the family had called and was still on their way. Ruggieri, frustrated and sweating in the humid Florida heat, had wanted to talk to Brandon first and be able to tell the press Brandon's reaction, but decided he should talk to them now.

Thames had already been interviewed, explaining that while Brandon's Arms hadn't succeeded today, "There are many hearings to go in this case, and there will be other opportunities for Brandon to have an impact. He is committed to this and we want to thank everyone who contributed to this cause."

Ruggieri joined the press scrum and told them he was still trying to reach Brandon. He fielded several questions before he was asked if Brandon had been prepared to not win.

"I think Brandon believed, and still believes until I've had a chance to speak to him, that there wasn't a chance of *not* winning. He's a seventeen-year-old, so, like any teenager he has no sense of 'losing', he doesn't have a notion of not winning. And because he's been handicapped since the age of seven, and he's had to overcome so many things in life, and has overcome them all, he doesn't know about losing, doesn't know about failing, and, I think..."

For the briefest of moments, as had happened only once before as Brandon's attorney — during his final argument at the first trial — Ruggieri struggled to maintain his composure, taking a quick breath before continuing. "...I think Brandon's going to be very upset."

He answered questions for another minute before his phone rang with the call from his office.

As he stepped away he answered and spoke to Sue.

"I'm afraid I have to tell you that we lost."

In his office, Sue's face registered her disappointment, as she listened to Ruggieri say "the bad news is we lost," and then surprise as he said "...the good news is we made him pay a half-million dollars." Brandon, reclined in his wheelchair next to Sue, sensed what was being said. Ruggieri described how a "large donor" had come in at the last minute and kept putting in money "until we got to $505,000, and when Jimenez bid $510,000 we simply didn't have any more.

"We did the best that we could with help of people all over the world, and none of us have to feel that we didn't do everything we could."

Tears began to well in Sue's eyes as she said, "That's right, we did the best that we could. And you, you did the best job that you could have ever done and we appreciate that."

Brandon was surprisingly sanguine, almost grinning, even though he knew the effort had failed. Sue handed the phone to Kandace to hold up to Brandon's ear as Ruggieri had to again say, "we lost," but that it had cost Jennings over a half-million dollars.

Then Ruggieri said, "I'm sorry."

Brandon replied, "No, we did the best we could."

They talked for another minute before Ruggieri hung up, the attorney and his young client affirming that they would still focus on ways to publicize the danger of Jimenez's and Jennings' guns.

In Ruggieri's office, Sue, wiping away tears, said, "That's a lot of money. It's amazing that someone can file bankruptcy and still come up with that amount of money."

Brandon was obviously disappointed, but his young, never dimmed spirit brightened the mood just before the reporters, still waiting in the hall, were allowed in. He smiled as he said, "This is like being on Who Wants to be a Millionaire and getting all the way to the last question, and you screw up."

Ruggieri walked back to the waiting reporters.

"Brandon is upset, but his message to you was that he's not giving up. Also, it's not over for Brandon. This sale of these assets was only one part of the ongoing bankruptcy proceedings where Brandon is fighting to collect his $24 million judgement."

He answered questions for another twenty minutes.

Bennett waited nearby, away from the reporters, but he agreed to answer a few questions for the documentary crew. Several reporters noticed and wandered over as he was asked why he'd gotten involved.

"I was motivated, as a donor, because I think it would be better for us to not have these Saturday Night Specials all over the country. I'm from Texas, we all have guns, that's not the issue."

He was asked if he agreed that if not for his involvement the bidding wouldn't have gone to triple the original approved sale amount.

He looked down, shifted on his feet, as if physically trying to distance himself from the question. "I don't know if that's quite right; I tried to help but it didn't work. I was trying to get the gun company away from the man."

Several news programs that night had brief segments on the "Teenager's dashed dreams." There were clips of Sue and Brandon, Brandon handling his interview admirably. The Bay Area's NBC affiliate began with a close-up of him. He had added dark sunglasses to his shirt and knit cap ensemble. "Well, I regret to inform everyone that we have lost, unfortunately. We were going to melt the guns down, but now, that ain't gonna happen." The news segment ended with Brandon saying, "I know he won't fix the gun's problem, he wants money. I just hope that when he looks in the mirror he sees the kid who bankrupted his company."

The next morning Ruggieri accepted Dan's offer of a return flight to the West Coast and was in Oakland for a hearing on Brandon's case that afternoon.

Morning newspaper editions carried the update about the auction. Forty-eight hours later, Brandon Maxfield's story was out of the national news cycle and fading from the public's consciousness.

A month later, however, the New York Times and several other newspapers revisited the case with the results of Ruggieri's investigation into the source of Jimenez's funding for the auction. Subpoenaed bank records and other documents revealed that on the morning of the auction a Jimenez Arms bank account's balance was a few dollars. By the end of the day $430,000 had been wired into the account for an order placed by Shining Star Investments, the business that Janice Jennings claimed she had forgotten to disclose to the bankruptcy court because, a month prior to the auction, it had no assets and wasn't doing any business.

Since that testimony she had also received a Federal Firearms License.

And the half-million-dollar order was placed even before Jimenez Arms received approval to manufacture firearms.

During this period Jennings' attorneys and Ruggieri continued settlement discussions, but until it could be confirmed that the sale transaction was legitimately funded, settlement was impossible.

The saga continued through fall and early winter. Jimenez began operations in the former Southern California Bryco plant, the bankruptcy continued in Florida, and Ruggieri obtained Brandon's permission to begin a new campaign aimed at Jimenez Arms' guns. He started with a letter in September from Brandon's Arms to Jimenez, which included "complete transcripts of the trial and experts depositions…to be certain that you are on notice of the safety defects in the Bryco line of pistols."

The letter also asked "if the defects found by the jury" were going to be fixed before offering guns for sale, a legitimate question given that the tens of thousands of parts Jimenez acquired through the auction were destined to create guns with the same flawed design as Bryco's.

Brandon's Arms then sent a flyer to every licensed firearms dealer in the country, warning that the new line of Jimenez Arms guns coming on the market were essentially the same gun that had led to a $24-million judgment against the previous manufacturer and the sellers.

In late September 2004, Jimemez Arms submitted three 9mm models described as "prototype 1" to a Certified Handgun Testing Laboratory for California madated handgun testing. Of the five testing labs then certified by the Department of Justice, this was the only one actually located in California.

A California manufacturer of handguns is required to submit three exemplar guns for testing and approval before the guns can be "sold, transferred, manufactured, etc." Each exemplar had to pass three tests: fire the first twenty rounds without a malfunction; fire six-hundred rounds with no more than six malfunctions and without any crack or breakage of an operating part that increased the risk of injury to the user; and pass a drop test, in which the gun should not discharge after being dropped six times from a height of one meter onto a concrete slab, in a different orientation each time (barrel down, upside-down, etc.).

The Southern California-based laboratory declared that all three guns passed, and Jimenez Arms submitted the declaration to the attorney general's office for approval.

From the earliest days of the case, Ruggieri had established relationships with the ATF and the Californian Department of Justice. While never disclosing anything to Ruggieri about Jennings-related investigations, both agencies readily accepted information Ruggieri uncovered in his research, and, in response to Ruggieri's Freedom of Information requests, provided him with non-confidential information in return.

Ruggieri's own investigation alerted him that Jimenez

was on the cusp of distributing the first Jimenez Arms guns.

In December, Ruggieri retained three of the other certified labs to independently obtain and test the same Jimenez Arms model, which the labs purchased directly from Shining Star, Janice Jennings' Texas company, which now advertised as the exclusive distributor of Jimenez Arms guns. Ruggieri instructed each lab to obtain and test the guns. Ruggieri would not directly purchase, see, or have any knowledge of the guns before being sent the test results.

The three labs each independently acquired and tested three exemplars. All nine guns failed. None passed the 600 rounds test, and several experienced trigger failures, cracks, and magazines falling out during firing. In early January, 2005, Ruggieri, on behalf of Brandon's Arms, sent a letter with the test results to the California DOJ Firearms Division requesting decertification of the Jimemez Arms Model JA-9.

The DOJ's reaction was swift. A January 13th letter from the office of the California Attorney General to Jimenez, "confirms our conversation January 13, 2005, informing you that effective this date you are to cease manufacturing the Jimenez Arms JA-9 and JA-9 (Black) handguns. These handguns have been removed from the California Roster of Handguns Certified for Sale based on substantiated information that the JA-9 failed subsequent testing conducted by a certified laboratory..."

The attorney general's office would have the guns retested, reinstated if they passed, and if they didn't Jimenez had the right to request reinstatement through proper channels.

Jimenez chose, for whatever reason, not to request reinstatement. He chose to leave.

On February 16th, Las Vegas Sun reporter Kevin Rademacher's story broke the news that Jimenez Arms was moving to Nevada. Ruggieri had known that some kind of move was coming, based on reports to him of activity at the former Bryco plant.

Quotes and statements attributed to Jimenez in the story said he had planned the Nevada expansion before California officials ruled the company's guns were unsafe. "All I have to say is that my move, it was planned for months and months." He also disputed the ruling, saying that officials did not follow protocol in accepting third-party test results. "That's what I believe," he stated, that Ruggieri had "purchased and purchased and purchased until they found one that failed."

Included in the article was a statement from the Nevada Attorney General's office. "There's nothing preventing a business from moving into Nevada and setting up shop. Whatever legal problems they have in California are in California."

Two weeks later the Los Angeles Times also reported on the move, quoting one of the lab owners as saying, "I've tested a lot of guns, and this one, by far, had the most significant number of failures of any gun I've ever tested."

In a follow-up message to the Las Vegas Sun, Ruggieri pointed out that Jimenez's claim of the Nevada move being "planned for months and months" was at odds with Jimenez having signed a five year lease on the former Bryco plant only six months before.

A local television station in Northern California and the region's newspaper of record, the Press Democrat, carried several stories about Jimenez's move out of state. The local TV news program described the DOJ's decertification of Jimenez Arms' gun, and included a clip of Ruggieri saying, "What Brandon's case says to manufacturers who turn a blind eye to safety features, whether it's with guns or anything else, is that you will be held accountable."

But it was the news anchor's introduction of the segment that provided a more philosophical interpretation of Jimenez's departure from California.

"Seventeen year-old Brandon Maxfield of Willits has scored another victory..."

***

EPILOGUE

Ruggieri had assumed, as any informed attorney would, that the bankruptcy would take several years to complete. The legal fights revolved around assets that Jennings' attorneys tried to exclude from the estate and Ruggieri fought to keep in. The largest were a $3-million house that had been fraudulently transferred, several-million-dollars in trusts, and a half-million-dollar annuity.

Brandon graduated from high school in 2005 with a 4.0 GPA and that same month was honored with the Distinguished Leadership Award by the San Francisco-based Legal Community Against Violence (LCAV), a public interest law center dedicated to preventing gun violence. At a dinner event in his honor, he was photographed with then San Francisco mayor Gavin Newsom and California Attorney General Bill Lockyer, and gave a moving speech that concluded with, "I look forward to a time when we can work on other important issues, a time when we won't have to talk about dangerous guns anymore." He received a standing ovation from the crowd of more than seven-hundred.

Ruggieri was also honored that summer with the 2005 Steven J. Sharp Public Service Award by the American Trial Lawyers Association (ATLA), an award given each year to the ATLA member whose case "most exemplifies the power of the American civil justice system."

Years went by as Ruggieri and Thames continued to

work on the bankruptcy. Each major ruling in Brandon's favor was appealed by Jennings' attorneys, six months to a year passing before each appeal was decided. Among the rulings in Ruggieri's favor were the disqualification of Jennings' attorneys, and the rejection of their claimed fees of $1.5-million.

The 20,000 guns that had been fought over in settlement talks were eventually purchased by Jimenez for destruction and reuse of component parts.

The Senate bill to give immunity from lawsuits to gun makers was amended to allow, within the narrowest of parameters, product defect lawsuits like Brandon's.

From the auction in 2004 to 2012, Jennings' attorneys filed multiple, unsuccessful appeals attempting to reverse the bankruptcy court's findings or orders in Brandon's favor.

By autumn of 2012, most of Jennings' known assets had been recovered. The tally, though nowhere near the full $24-million owed to his now twenty-five year-old client, was significant: the settlement with other parties involved in the California trial, the auction proceeds, and several million dollars more over the course of the eight-year bankruptcy.

Jennings' Florida house remained exempt from creditors, who would have to wait until the property was sold or converted to 'non-homestead' purposes before collecting.

It had been an incredible journey for everyone involved.

There was one last, karmic twist to come.

Orlando's WFTV News broke the story first, reporting that over the weekend of September 14th, 2012, Federal agents had "served a search warrant on Bruce Lee Jennings' million-dollar Port Orange home in the Spruce

Creek fly-in community." Jennings was arrested, charged, and pled guilty to federal charges of possessing and distributing child pornography.

He was sentenced to ten years and one month in federal prison, followed by ten years supervised probation, and required to register as a sex offender. The government instituted forfeiture proceedings on his house as an instrument of his crimes. As reported by the Daytona Beach News-Journal, "nearly 1,500 images and over 3,000 videos of children being sexually abused or exploited" had been discovered on Jennings' computers.

As his homesteading asset became vulnerable once more, Jennings used the moves he'd relied on for much of his business life. He had married again, retaining sole title to the house. Within a month of his arrest, however, he deeded the property jointly to himself and new wife, who then filed objections to the forfeiture, claiming she was a "victim" and "innocent third party."

In May of 2013, without notice to Brandon, the federal government agreed to a deal with Jennings: the property would be sold, Jennings would forfeit $500,000 of the proceeds, and the remaining $700,000 of the sale price would be considered the legitimate protected homestead property of his wife, and, therefore, exempt from claims by Brandon or any other creditors.

Brandon's only option was a petition for remission of some or all of the forfeited amount to himself and two other victim-creditors. As of September 2015, his petition was denied, he appealed, and he awaits that decision.

As of 2015:

Sue, Clint, Brandon, and Rocky live in Brandon's Willits home. His sister Trish is raising a family. Brandon's nonprofit is no longer active, but, "I still may bring it back when I'm ready." His health is stable, much better than many in his situation, and he has spent his years traveling, including a cross-country trip in his motorhome from California to New York, to Florida, and back again. His occasional trips to "Las Vegas and its clubs are my favorite destinations."

Jerry Morris reached a confidential settlement with Brandon (approved by Judge Kraetzer); his whereabouts are unknown.

Attorney Joe Hoffman still practices law in the Bay Area.

Paul Jimenez is still the owner of Jimenez Arms, still operating in Nevada. Between 2005 and 2007, ten Jimenez Arms gun models were banned from sale in California.

Janice Jennings still owns and operates Texas-based Shining Star as a distributor for Jimenez Arms.

Attorney Joel Grist still practices law in Georgia, and his client was finally awarded $7 million in her lawsuit against Jennings, the trusts, and other parties.

Eric Hauser closed his PR firm and accepted an executive position with the AFL-CIO as director of communications.

Attorney Richard Thames continues to practice law in Jacksonville, Florida, and is one of the most respected bankruptcy attorneys in the country.

Dan Bennett lives in New York, travels with his wife Colette and their family, and remains involved in philanthropic causes.

Richard Ruggieri is retired, his wife Edith is a senior attorney with the California Supreme Court, and they both still skate. They live in their East Bay home of over thirty years.

Attorney Thames says, "Ruggieri is one of the most

talented attorneys I've ever come in contact with in twenty-seven years of practice."

Hoffman described Ruggieri's work as "brilliant."

Brandon, along with his family ever grateful for Ruggieri's work on their behalf, says, "Rich? He's a great guy. And he's funny as hell."

And of Brandon, Ruggieri says, "Brandon Maxfield is a true warrior and a friend — representing him has been the highest honor of my professional life."

*****

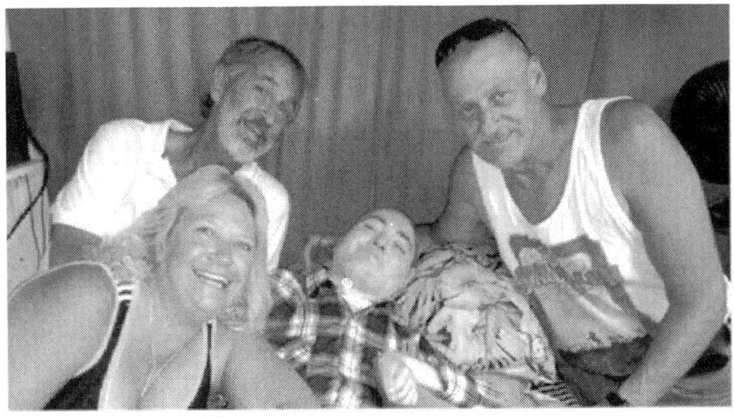

Left to right, Sue Stansberry, Richard Ruggieri, Brandon Maxfield, and Clint Stansberry.
2015

AUTHOR'S NOTE -- A PERSONAL PERSPECTIVE

America's gun problem will not be solved until everyone accepts that there is a problem. Parroted, agenda-driven platitudes, steadfast refusals to accept facts and data, and the paranoid pronouncements — from either side of the gun issue — of a country going to hell in a handbasket, all stop any movement toward a future safe from the misuse and proliferation of guns.

It will take the acceptance of regulation to create that future.

Regulation is the reason we thrive and succeed in this country. Anyone who thinks otherwise needs to realize that every moment we live, work, and succeed in this country is due to BOTH our constitutional rights and the regulation of those rights in a free society.

You can yell "Fire!" in your own home, but you can't do it in a theatre. You can say "I'm going to kill you," out loud, but if you say it out loud to another person, you can be arrested. You can purchase a powerful rifle, but you can't purchase a missile.

Your freedom is guaranteed, but your life in America is not a free-for-all. If you want to do anything you can think of, purchase an island and have at it. If you want to the opportunity to be healthy, wealthy, and wise in America, you have to accept being part of a society that understands how best to take care of itself fairly and safely.

I know the notion of regulation really prickles many people. So, take note of how the components upon which we rely to enjoy our modern lives — transportation, workplace, homes, recreation — are, in general, regulated for our benefit:

You are not poisoned by the food you eat or the water you drink, your house doesn't burn down when you turn on a light, you're not driven off the side of the road or T-boned at an intersection, not electrocuted when you grab a microphone, not choked by the air you breathe, not killed or sickened by the effects of asbestos, lead, cyanide or thousands of other harmful chemicals, not horribly injured in car accidents that might have killed or maimed you in a similar accident twenty years ago, not unlawfully eavesdropped upon, not arrested for your personal views, and not harmed in hundreds of other ways because of regulation.

There is no perfect society, but there are great societies and we are one of them. America is the only country with the values, rights, freedoms, and opportunity that every other country wants to emulate.

Everyone wants to be us, but no one wants our gun problem.

An industry that answers to no one, that has immunity no other industry has, is dangerous. We see the impact of it every day. We will remain the only nation that spills its own blood this way, on its own soil, until we overcome the ignorance, greed, and misguided, stubborn beliefs that prevent everyone — including the gun industry — from coming together to create a safer future.

ACKNOWLEDGMENTS & THANKS

Richard Ruggieri opened the doors of this story for me. He gave me access to voluminous file material, he gave me his time, his thoughts, and, although it might not have been his intention, he also gave me an opportunity to observe what it means to be a great attorney and a man of unquestionable integrity. He never allowed me to be anything but accurate and succinct as I wrote this story, and never refused an information request, even when it meant going into the database of the case, trial, and bankruptcy two, three, five, or eight years later. He's also a relentless, accurate editor.

When Richard told Brandon, Sue, and Clint that a guy wanted to write their story, they had no idea that guy would hang around for years or that it would take a decade to get the promised story into the hands of readers. But, they never kicked me out, they trusted me, and they, like Richard, are now my good friends. They shared details and thoughts that were as poignant and brutally honest as the questions were intrusive, but they never faulted, never refused. Thank you for your trust and your friendship. Special thanks to Terry Johnston for being the communication bridge, and for wearing your loyalty on your arm.

It might seem, to those of us outside the legal industry,

that Joe Hoffman had an unenviable task for his part of the story, yet he also never refused an interview request, was always gracious and forthcoming, and I could sense how important it is to him that people everywhere have an understanding of how something that seems readily apparent can have complex undercurrents of causation. While many of us will never need Joe's services, society is healthier with him in the mix. Truly.

Dan Bennett shared his personal history, details of his early years, and of how and why — philosophically and practically — he came to help Brandon. Until I contacted him several years after the auction, he had never really shared with anyone why he called Richard and said, "I want to help Brandon." Dan Bennett is one of those good guys, is why.

Richard Thames is a major player, a successful, well-regarded attorney, and a gentleman. His respect for the legal mentors in his career shapes him to this day, certainly came across in our conversations, and is obvious in his professional success and status in his legal community.

Juanita Joy gave me poignant, professional, and personal views on Brandon's return to school after the accident, through to his successful graduation a decade later. Her knowledge, observations, and insights were invaluable.

These people and organizations gave me their stories, opinions, permissions, and provided details on everything from law, to trauma protocols, to jury selection: Edith Lavin, Vicki Ni of Public Justice, Eric Hauser, Joel Grist, Vivian Robertson, Mark Robertson, Alvin Tripp, Toni Holder, Dr. Robert Haining and Oakland Children's Hospital, Dr. Michelle Gitler, Willits' Howard Memorial Hospital, Jennifer Hardcastle and Redwood Empire Air

Care Helicopter (REACH), John McCollugh, the Mendocino County Sheriff's department, Carter Lord, and Michael Thourot. Thanks to Garrett McDonough of the Law Center to Prevent Gun Violence, and Greg Habiby, for the photo.

My screenwriting partner Lorraine Evanoff continues to champion this story in L.A. Special thanks to my sister, Moe, for thinking of me as her brother who's a writer, and for being in the same class as Lorraine.

I cannot overstate the importance of my family's and close friends' support over the eleven years it took to finish this project (and it's not 'all' done yet…). Bill Lee's support at the beginning of this project directly enabled me to write the first third of this book. John DeGroot's loyalty helped me finish it. Linda Lee has been cheering for me since day one. Kristina Holmes' and Beverly West's guidance on a different project made this one better.

Special thanks, respect, and gratitude go out to my friend and documentary partner Barry Schienberg, one of the finest videographers I've ever met, and member of the "nicest guy in the world" club. Dude, we're going to make this happen, but first…bagels.

To my good friends and fellow writers Bob Spryszak, Mark Osmun, and Karen D'Or, thanks for sharing ideas, listening, and, as writers, leading by example. Thanks also to those writers whose great work continues to influence me every day: Jon Hassler (man, I wish I'd mailed you my fan letter before you passed), Richard Russo, Susan Power, Scott Turow, John Casey, Anne Lamott, Barry Lopez, Peter Matthiessen, and Jon Krakauer.

To my Indiegogo supporters, my lasting thanks for trying: Lawrence Bai, Jill Biagi, Alice Boylan, Percy Brandon, Sharon Cooper, Karen D'Or, Tim Duncan, Camie Foust, Rodney Feak, Brian Fies, Dan Finn, Linda Lee, Jim

Love, Tim Miller, Benita Mattioli, Julie Nichols, Theresa Norton, Libby Rouan, Gloria Schwartz, Bob Spryszak, Cathy Steinberg, Jill Thomas, Maria Williams.

Elizabeth, Elizabeth, Elizabeth... I'd need another book just to list everything you continue to do for me, everything you continue to be to me. You are everything.

ABOUT THE AUTHOR

Michael W. Harkins writes, and also consults on communications and media projects, from his home in Northern California. His previous book, The Way to Communicate, a guide for developing enhanced personal communication skills, was released in 2010. His forty-year creative career has included work for and with a wide variety of clients, including Jackson Family Wines / Kendall-Jackson, Gatorade, USC Keck Medical Center, the American Red Cross, Thrice Fiction magazine, and NorthBay Biz magazine. His commentary has been featured on NPR's All Things Considered, and his early concert industry work included tours with Journey, Bruce Springsteen, and Michael Jackson.

He is a long-time volunteer hawkwatcher with the Golden Gate Raptor Observatory, he volunteers with the Wild Horse Sanctuary of Shingletown, California, and the American Red Cross, and is a former adult literacy tutor for Sonoma County.

Made in the USA
Middletown, DE
24 March 2016